90-0974

Margaret J. M

November 17, 1975

CRIME AND JUSTICE IN AMERICA

A Paradox of Conscience

The probability that the criminal justice system will suffer a complete breakdown before the year 2000 should not be discounted. If law and social control systems are to accommodate change in their environment at the necessary rate, a new philosophy, as well as quite different operating procedures, must be worked out. . . . If we wish for a better kind of future for criminal justice, we must start to invent it now.—Leslie T. Wilkins.*

---

* "Crime and Criminal Justice at the Turn of the Century," *The Annals of the American Academy of Political and Social Science*, Vol. 408 (July 1973), p. 13.

CRIME AND JUSTICE IN AMERICA

A PARADOX OF CONSCIENCE

by L. Harold DeWolf

HARPER & ROW, PUBLISHERS

NEW YORK
EVANSTON
SAN FRANCISCO
LONDON

1817

FIRST EDITION

Designed by Sidney Feinberg

Library of Congress Cataloging in Publication Data

De Wolf, Lotan Harold, 1905 –
    Crime and justice in America.
    Includes bibliographical references and indexes.
    1. Criminal justice, Administration of—United
States.   I. Title.
KF9223.D48   364   75-9335
ISBN 0-06-061911-2

75 76 77 10 9 8 7 6 5 4 3 2 1

To the revered memory of
my student and cherished friend
Martin Luther King, Jr.,
who stirred many Americans
to seek justice with new urgency

Contents

Preface   *ix*

PART **I**

American Democratic Society Besieged by Crime

1. *Present Crisis of Freedom Under Law*   *3*
2. *Influences on Crime Outside the Criminal Justice System*   *10*

PART **II**

Criminal Justice in Trouble

3. *Public Disrepute of Criminal Justice*   *17*
4. *Injustice in Criminal Laws and Agencies of Enforcement*   *23*
5. *Injustice in the Courts*   *31*
6. *The Waste of Corrections*   *37*
7. *Confusion and Conflict of Purpose*   *47*
8. *Rehabilitation in Many Modes*   *58*

PART **III**

Formation of the American Conscience

9. *Puritanism: a Paradoxical Heritage*   *71*
10. *The Great Awakening and Jeffersonion Humanism*   *79*
11. *The Rush for Riches: Its Social Cost*   *88*
12. *Race, National Origin and Violence*   *98*
13. *Minority Religions*   *109*

14. *Time and Space in American Culture*   *116*
15. *Two Americas*   *122*

PART **IV**

An Ethical Philosophy of Criminal Justice

16. *An Emerging Ethical Consensus*   *133*
17. *A Basic Philosophy of Criminal Justice*   *156*

PART **V**

Social Defense and Restoration in Practice

18. *Fortifying the Community*   *177*
19. *The Victim: Forgotten Person of American Criminal Justice* *184*
20. *Criminal Law: Its Scope and Penalties*   *195*
21. *The Police*   *205*
22. *The Courts*   *209*
23. *Corrections*   *216*
24. *Citizen Responsibilities in Criminal Justice*   *227*

Notes   *235*
Index of Topics   *263*
Index of Personal Names   *267*

Preface

Studies leading to this book began in 1925 when, as a student in theology at Boston University, I attended a lecture at Harvard Law School by Dean Roscoe E. Pound. In that lecture America's premier philosopher of law described the inefficiency and injustice into which the criminal law and procedures of this country were increasingly entangled. He challenged the moral leaders and especially the religious leaders of America to provide new grounding in basic ideals of justice and to give fresh impetus to reform.

Later, as a Professor of Systematic Theology and teacher of ethics, I formulated a plan for extended systematic work on this subject and shared it with Dean Pound. In 1954 he wrote, "I welcome Dr. DeWolf's project and am glad heartily to endorse it. An interdisciplinary research, directed to the religious foundations of morals and morality—the background of the legal order, making the resort to force, which is its ultimate reliance unnecessary in a majority of cases, and making the ultimate resort to force tolerable when it becomes necessary—has real promise of a beginning of better things." There is much more, but this suffices to show the generosity of his encouragement.

At that very time I was teaching a seminar on criminal justice, with assistance from Albert Morris, criminologist, and Albert Beisel, Professor of Law. Miss Dean Hosken wrote a searching Ph.D. dissertation under our interdisciplinary direction, entitled *Prolegomena to a Christian Philosophy of Penal Justice* (Boston University Graduate School, 1957).

In January 1972 the National Endowment for the Humanities granted assistance with expenses for my project and since retirement from the offices of dean and professor at Wesley Theological Seminary in June of that year I have been able gratefully to devote full time to this work. It will be observed that the ethical foundations with which I am here concerned are philosophical and traditional as well as interreligious.

Besides the persons already mentioned, I am indebted for assistance in the older days to Paul W. Tappan, Miriam Van Waters, and Chief Justice Stanley E. Qua of the Massachusetts Supreme Judicial Court.

My principal consultants in the work leading directly to publication of this book have been Samuel Dash (before his service with the Senate "Watergate" Committee), Gerhard O. W. Mueller, and Julius Stone. In the historical study of American culture Clarence C. Goen has been especially helpful. Other American scholars who have been generous in consultation and other assistance have included Lloyd E. Ohlin, Marvin E. Wolfgang, Harold J. Berman, Nicholas N. Kittrie, Albert Morris, Leslie T. Wilkins, M. Robert Montilla, Paul K. Deats, Peter A. Bertocci, and Robert B. Coates. Among public officials, present or retired, who have been especially generous with the giving of their time and thought are the late Chief Justice Earl Warren, Judge Luther E. Youngdahl, Judge Philip M. Fairbanks, James V. Bennett, Norman A. Carlson, Robert L. Smith, Jerome G. Miller, Kenneth Guza, Winston E. Moore, John O. Boone, Virginia W. McLaughlin, Richard A. McGee, Kenneth McDaniel, Robert Gribben, Lloyd McGeehee, Donald Bordenkircher, Kyle D. Grasty, Robert F. Perkins, Nelson P. Kempsky, Edward Combs, and Larry J. Moss. I am indebted also, for encouragement and help of various kinds, to Louis W. Norris, Charles E. Curran, Roger L. Shinn, Walter G. Muelder, Major Jones, J. Philip Wogaman, Laurence M. Hyde, Jr., James E. Johnson, John R. Warner, Robert W. Moon, Larry E. Adams, and Robert L. Dutton. Edward J. Black and Sherrie Black served as assistants in an early stage of the project.

In gaining perspective and examining alternative responses to crime, I was privileged to consult with scholars and visit agencies of criminal justice in Mexico and four European countries. It is impossible to mention all the people abroad who were generous and helpful. Yet I must speak of some who opened doors and contributed thought of especially memorable importance. They include Antonio Sánchez Galindo and John L. Groves of Mexico; Igor Andrejew, Jerzy Jasiński, Stanislaw Walczak, Jan Skupiński, Arnold Gubiński, and Mr. and Mrs. Z. Antoni Mezyński of Poland; J. Arthur Hoyles, Graham Ballinger, Leslie Lloyd Rees, and William J. Gray in England; Johannes Andenaes and Ragnar Horn in Norway. For the fruitful visit in the Netherlands I am especially indebted to J. van der Grient, L. H. C. Hulsman, W. van Halm, F. E. Frenkel, S. Slagter, Gillis van der Linden, and Paul Verberne.

In addition, both here and abroad I have been assisted by many people unnamed, including judges, teachers, correctional officers, students, prison chaplains, policemen, inmates of prisons, and ex-offenders.

Again I am indebted to my wife Madeleine, who has typed two drafts of this, another book, done proofreading, cared for much correspondence, and made important suggestions along the way.

In using the notes at the back, the reader should observe that full bibliographical data regularly appear at the first citation of a book and after that only a shortened title, usually accompanied by the author's surname. Index references to notes give the page in the text where the reference to the note occurs.

Of course none of my many consultants and advisers should be thought responsible for the opinions I have supported. The data, findings, and conclusions do not necessarily represent the views of the National Endowment for the Humanities.

Washington, D.C.   L. HAROLD DEWOLF

PART **I**

AMERICAN DEMOCRATIC SOCIETY

BESIEGED BY CRIME

Present Crisis of Freedom Under Law

A. A Troubled Nation

A paradox of conscience has bedeviled the American people, particularly our legal order—and disorder—ever since the colonial years. The reader will find documented a curious and tragic contradiction between two ethical traditions which have been deliberately cultivated throughout our history. In our handling of crime we still try persistently to follow both, with disastrous results.

We are beginning the third century of our independence, with its proud dedication to "the proposition that all men are created equal." We are engaged again in a life-and-death conflict "testing whether that nation, or any nation so conceived and so dedicated, can long endure."[1] This conflict is raging in our city streets, homes, banks, gasoline stations, and department stores. It is fought every day and night in our parks and on our highways. The warfare between the lawful democratic order and crime is fought even within the government itself. It pours out unpredictably across the countryside. The enemy cannot be recognized by uniform and no battlefronts are marked on the map. The struggle is deadly for all that and the outcome is uncertain.

Our present conflict with crime is a struggle for the very existence of our democratic republic. Every crime is both a symptom and a further aggravation of an insidious infection eating at the vitals of our national life. Crimes have many victims; but one victim is always the health and strength of American freedom. There is no guarantee that this freedom will survive.

There are many signs of moral and political strength in the United States. They are to be seen in open elections which still, in spite of massive corruption and deception, produce many surprises for the manipulators; numerous staunchly independent and ably edited newspapers and media commentaries; the exposure and prosecution of criminal abuses of power in a national administration; some beginnings of long-overdue Congressional reform; genuine efforts for public good by many churches and other free associations of citizens; and the studious concern of countless individuals for true justice, freedom, and peace.

Nevertheless, the facts about crime should sound a clear alarm in every heart which cares for freedom in the United States and in all the world which needs an example of robust democracy here. Let us look at some of the alarming realities.

B. The Disturbing Volume of Crime

Statistics on crime are so variable in rigor that precise figures on most crimes are unobtainable. But a crime of one kind nearly always appears in the reports of this and other industrialized countries, namely criminal homicide. In that, how does the United States compare with other developed countries? Per 100,000 population, in 1968, white males in the United States committed three times as many criminal homicides as males of all races in Canada, seven times those in France, eight times those in the United Kingdom or in Japan, and ten times as many as by the males in Scandinavia and the Netherlands. Nonwhite American males per 100,000 committed ten times as many as white males, doubling the total American male average.[2]

The statistics add plausibility to the less reliable comparisons of other crimes which show the United States as having rates per 100,000 people of from two to ten times as many forcible rapes, robberies, and aggravated assaults[3] as Canada, England and Wales, or Denmark.[4]

There are less developed countries which have worse criminal records than ours. In 1965, for example, the Philippines had 8,750 murders or 27 per 100,000 people, as compared with 9,850 in the United States or 5.1 per 100,000 population.[5] This is small ground for American self-assurance, when it is observed that in 1965 the Philippines were drifting steadily toward anarchy and would soon lose most traditional democratic freedoms to pass under a dictatorship in 1972.

Before we go further we must be clear as to what we are discussing. In common speech we often use the word "crime" to describe any conduct which we deeply dislike or which we regard as gravely immoral. Of course on this basis everyone could make his own list of "crimes" and objective statements of quantity would be impossible.

Strictly speaking, a crime is a violation of criminal law. The question of the scope which ought to be covered by criminal law is a debated issue which will be discussed in Chapter 20. However, the truth will stand that only acts contrary to criminal law are literally and correctly called crimes.

Even that is too broad a definition for some purposes. We feel uncomfortable about designating as crimes some violations of the criminal code, such as driving an automobile at 40 miles per hour in open country near a small town, in a zone where the posted limit is 30 miles per hour, or betting on a professional football game, or dropping a candy wrapper on the sidewalk. We may heartily disapprove some or even all of these acts, but we do not usually mean to include such minor legal offenses when we worry about the crime problem.

To see the magnitude of our failure to control crime, let us begin by looking at the seven kinds of serious ("Index") crime on which the Federal Bureau of Investigation receives and reports records from all jurisdictions in the country. These types are (1) murder and nonnegligent manslaughter, (2) forcible rape, (3) robbery, (4) aggravated assault, (5) burglary, (6) larceny-theft (before 1973 larceny of more than $50 value), and (7) automobile theft.

Reported Index crimes in 1973 were 8,638,400. Of these, 7,768,900 or 90% were crimes against property, while the remaining 10% were violent crimes against persons, or, in the case of robbery (4% or 382,680), against both persons and property.[6]

What these figures mean in wasted lives of the offenders may be imagined by anyone who has become acquainted with even a few of the people going in and out of our prisons. What about the victims? In 1973, 19,510 murders and nonnegligent manslaughters were reported.[7] Drunken driving is a non-Index crime. But it kills far more people. It is estimated by the Safety Council that about 25,000 persons are killed by drunken driving each year. In addition, 416,270 were victims of aggravated assault, and 51,000 were forcibly raped.[8]

In economic terms, the President's Commission on Law Enforcement and Administration of Justice reported that the Index crimes cost, in 1963, about $1.4 billion. According to the same Commission, white collar crime —fraud, embezzlement, "forgery and other," and unreported commercial theft—cost more than twice as much, over $3 billion.[9] The FBI reports that in fiscal year 1974 robberies and other thefts took $27.1 million from banks and other federally insured financial institutions, while embezzlement and fraud, which are not counted as Index crimes, took from them $151.1 million or more than five and one-half times as much![10] The figures given do not include the great cost of *fighting* crime, currently more than $4 billion per year.

The published statistics of crime are gross understatements of the reality, not only because numbers cannot adequately represent human values, but also because the actual numbers of crimes are far greater than the number of arrests or even of crimes officially reported. The President's Commission on Law Enforcement and Administration of Justice examined results of several surveys of households in comparison with official records. The result? "These surveys show that the actual amount of crime in the United States is several times that reported in the UCR (Uniform Crime Reports to the FBI)."[11]

In large part the great excess of Index crimes beyond those reported results from the failure of victims to call the police. The people say they did not call because they thought the police could not help or would not want to be bothered, or they wanted the matter to remain private, they did not want the offender to be punished, they feared reprisal, or they had other reasons.

Even among Index crimes reported to the police many are not included in the Uniform Crime Reports. The FBI system requires the reporting of all citizen complaints of Index crime. However, independent studies show that the practice does not conform to the rule. When city officials want to create alarm to get larger budgets for fighting crime they press for complete reporting. When they want to present a favorable image of improving conditions there is little insistence on faithful recording. Without strong pressure for complete reports, police officers avoid paper work by under-reporting.

For example, the police of Washington, D.C. have been under heavy pressure from the White House (which, through the Attorney General, appointed the D.C. Chief of Police) to reduce crime, and in the political campaign of 1972 President Nixon and his supporters made much use of reported crime figures in Washington to prove that he had been fulfilling his pledge to reduce crime sharply. The Bureau of Social Science Research in September 1972 found that the Washington police, over a period of a year, had been filing no reports in about 40% of the cases which they investigated. In fact, between June 1971 and June 1972 the percentage of complaints not included in the UCR went up from 36.6% to 41.2%. The police did not make their earlier records available. Hence, although crime was probably reduced, it is impossible to determine how much of the claimed reduction of crime between 1968 and 1972 was only a reduction of reports.[12] Other cities have shown similar changes in the rigor of reporting in various periods.

Surveys by the Census Bureau for the Law Enforcement Assistance Administration in 1972 show that in thirteen selected cities, actual crimes outnumbered those reported to the FBI by ratios ranging from 1.4 to 1 in Newark to 5.1 to 1 in Philadelphia.[13]

To sum up, then, we see that serious and especially violent crime in this country is four to six times as high as in other Western industrialized countries which seek to maintain basic democratic freedom. Reported Index crimes here are shockingly high. If we include the greater number of crimes not reported to the police, the smaller but significant number reported to the police but not appearing in the Uniform Crime Reports of the FBI, and add the non-Index crimes which take even more life and property, then we see a yet more alarming picture.

While the rate of crime is fearfully high, over a period of years it has been moving rapidly higher. Between 1960 and 1973, the FBI reports, violent crimes recorded (criminal homicides, forcible rapes, robberies, and aggravated assaults) increased by 203.8%. This means that for every 100 such crimes reported in 1960 there were over 300 in 1973. Reported Index crimes against property only (burglary, larceny-theft, and automobile theft) increased 153.3%, or about 253 such crimes in 1973 to every 100 in 1960.[14] For the first six months of 1974 the FBI reported a further increase in every category of Index crime.[15]

C. Increasing Favor Toward a Police State

The most conspicuous public response to the high and increasing rate of crime is the sounding of such slogans as "tough law and order" and "cracking down on crime," while there are placed in legislative hoppers many proposals for more severe punishment and for limiting traditional freedoms. Yet, as we will observe later, such measures often have the actual effect of increasing crime, leading to angry calls for still more of the futile severity.

One of the more disturbing trends is the effort to stifle the independence of journalism and of commentaries on television. There has always been frequent complaint from politicians that certain journalists were being unfair or irresponsible in their presentation of news or in editorial comment. But the concerted attacks by the executive branch between 1968 and 1973 went far beyond that level. Former Vice President Spiro Agnew's constant attacks on the press and on national television commentators over a two-year period had the effect of leading many people to suppose that reliable information on national affairs could be gained only from the government itself. We can discount Mr. Agnew's feelings, in view of his subsequent downfall. The more disturbing fact is that so many people applauded his attacks and believed blindly the official bulletins. In a time of much division, high crime, and hence general anxiety, it is easiest to believe that the head of state knows best and to leave it to him. This is the mood which led to dictatorships in Germany and Italy in the 1930s and the Philippines in 1972.

But the verbal attacks on the press prepared also for illegal wiretaps on newsmen and their sources and repeated efforts of the Justice Department to compel newsmen to produce their unpublished notes, with names and addresses of their tipsters. Only the Constitution as interpreted by the courts has prevented these tactics from reducing television, radio, and the newspapers to subservient organs of the government in power. The White House announced also that it would be submitting legislation to require local television stations to assume more responsibility for news and news commentary, depending less on the nationwide broadcasting systems and their well-known commentators. As was quickly seen by many defenders of the free media, this was an effort to reduce the influence of strong, independent voices which had gained and were in a position to hold wide public confidence. If, through the executive department's licensing power, which would be used in such legislation, the influence of these independent voices could be reduced, it would be easier to gain unquestioning acceptance of the official propaganda.

While these attacks have probably had considerable effect in promoting caution or timid subservience in the news media, many news people have continued on their independent course with courage. So long as Congress is not stampeded into repressive legislation and the courts continue to rebuke the Justice Department and defend the independence of press and citizenry, we continue to be blessed with much freedom of information. But the pressures against it are strong.

Fearful of crime and disorder, many citizens tend to view dissent with suspicion and support efforts to bring conformity. In short, their thinking is moving toward the welcoming of tyranny in the name of American patriotism, analogous to flag-waving dictatorships in other lands.

Similar in mood and portent is the understandable popular impatience with the "constitutional niceties" of various court decisions in criminal cases, which have had the immediate effect of releasing strongly suspected defendants because of abuses by the police or public prosecutors.

When a poor Mexican-American named Ernest Miranda was questioned by police and confessed that he had committed a rape, he had not been told that he could call a friend, could have a lawyer, and could refuse to answer questions if he wished. As a result the Supreme Court reversed the conviction. Ever since that time the Miranda decision has been a favorite object of attack by people who think the way to reduce crime is simply to "get tough" with all suspects. True, the FBI had adopted the practices required by the Miranda decision twenty years earlier and educated people of means had usually known or acted as if they knew all along that the police had no right to make them bear witness against themselves. But quite naturally repelled and frightened by the many crimes of violence, the popular reaction to the Miranda decision assuring the same protection to the poor and uneducated being questioned by local or state police was an outcry of protest.

In view of that response it is not strange that there are innumerable cases handled by local police and rural courts in which these rights are not observed. To observe them would probably let some guilty people go free.

It might also have protected some innocent people against the imprisonment in which they now find themselves. Even with all the legal protections in force, many innocent people tell the police what they think they want to hear and sign what the police ask them to sign. For a poor and ignorant person, to be in the hands of the police can be an awesome experience. If he has no friend or counsel to advise him and give him confidence he is all too likely to do anything he can to try to please the police.

Those who would reverse the Miranda decision by constitutional amendment or otherwise would move us another step down the road toward a police state, where people are ruled by the leaders and the police, not by laws.

The Justice Department, supported by the White House, repeatedly declared, between 1968 and 1973, that it had a right to apply wiretaps without court order when such procedure was declared necessary to protect the national security. Moreover, the national security has been interpreted broadly enough to include efforts to get evidence against organized crime. Fortunately, the Supreme Court has rejected this extended interpretation and the courts have repeatedly refused to admit evidence gained by such unauthorized wiretaps.

The spying of a government on its own citizens in the presumed privacy of their homes is characteristic of police states and abhorrent to believers in democratic freedom, excepting in cases where evidence can be given a court that there are specific criminal activities afoot and that the listening devices are needed to obtain clinching evidence. Instances warranting such invasion of privacy are rare and precedents are dangerous. It is bad enough to live in fear of private criminals. Invasions of our personal lives by the police are much more dangerous still.

Yet so long as crime continues to grow, the emotional, ill-considered calls for overriding all such citizens' rights for the sake of order will probably continue. As have many other peoples, we could learn too late that tyranny legalizes what we have feared as crime and then there are no police to call for protection since in such a state the police and rulers are the criminals.

D. Severe Testing of Our Democratic Republic

Rampant crime and ineffective responses to it are testing the constitutional liberties of the United States to the very depths. What then? Should we not fight the crime by a little relinquishment of constitutional liberties? May not some small doses of police state strategies save our democratic republic from collapse?

The trouble is that repressive tactics are addictive. Repression always falls disproportionately on certain classes of people who already feel themselves excluded from the best opportunities and privileges of the society. This increases their hostility and then more repression is required to hold down the lid. The repression must be increasingly forceful and severe, adding to the destructive trust in solving problems by force and violence. That vicious circle leads to further increased disorders and the consequent losses of liberty we fear.

Are there better ways? Indeed there are. They are not simple, but they are clearly marked out for us by our finest American traditions and various recent studies.

2

Influences on Crime Outside the Criminal Justice System

Whenever we start to discuss causes of crime someone objects, "Criminals are the cause." It is obviously true that people who commit crime commit crime but this remark is not very helpful. I am not a determinist who believes that individuals are mere robotlike creatures of heredity and environment, with no genuine freedom of choice and so with no moral responsibility. Far from it! But our choices are made in various social settings. No matter what metaphysical explanation we give, it will remain true that when people live and make their choices in some social environments several times more of the people will choose to kill or rape or rob than when they are in other environments.

If we are serious about wanting to reduce crime we must attack several of these crime-nurturing conditions. Anger against criminals is understandable. But what we do with offenders after their crimes are committed is important chiefly because of influence our action may have on the future behavior of our citizens. Other conditions have more effect on that than do the processes of criminal justice. We are not very intelligent when we keep our attention focused on past crimes and the people who have committed them, while neglecting to change the seedbeds of crime which lie before us in plain sight.

What are the conditions especially conducive to crime? Here we must limit ourselves to two with some of their ramifications.

A. Crowded, Poverty-Stricken Inner Cities

1. Concentration of Index crimes there.

Ramsey Clark writes, "In every major city in the United States you will find that two-thirds of the arrests take place among only about two per cent of the population. Where is that area in every city? Well, it's in the same place where infant mortality is four times higher than in the city as a whole; where the death rate is 25 per cent higher; where life expectancy is ten years shorter; where common communicable diseases with the potential of physical and mental damage are six and eight and ten times more frequent. . . ."[1]

When large numbers of youth are undereducated and unemployed,[2] when many feel that their whole neighborhood has been shut out from the opportunities which others have used to gain wealth and power, juvenile delinquency and crime flourish.

2. Combating such conditions.

To reduce significantly the crime of the inner city we must make a concerted attack on unemployment, bad housing, inadequate prenatal and medical care, and the ethnic prejudice which is usually one destructive force in the situation. Nearly 94% of all arrests for Index crimes are for crimes against property (including robbery which is against persons also), so economic motivation is critically important. But when a community is exploited, demoralized, and alienated, that condition is conducive to all kinds of crime and all forces which produce it must be thoughtfully and persistently combated.[3]

The more we have of economic, political, and social justice, the less alienation and crime we shall have and hence the less we must depend on the processes of criminal law enforcement. Unless most citizens voluntarily obey the laws because they regard themselves as having a stake or a responsibility in the government and community, we ask the impossible in expecting our law enforcement agencies to maintain a law-abiding social order.

B. Excessive Individualism in the Affluent Community

1. The excessive competitive drive for riches and power.

In the first chapter we observed that white collar crimes take an even heavier toll of life and property than do the highly publicized Index crimes. Moreover, when affluent people who are obviously inside the economic and political power structure embezzle funds, defraud each other, cheat the government, and exploit the poor, and when they abuse their offices of trust to enrich themselves and enhance their power, they create a climate of disrespect for law and morality.

Edwin H. Sutherland found that about 60% of the largest American corporations had been convicted in the courts of criminal violations.[4] The seven executives in the notorious 1960 case of dishonest conspiracy of electrical companies who actually served time in prison received more sympathy and support than condemnation from the business community.[5] Corruption of public officials and their violations of law are common, from police patrolmen up the ladder all the way to the White House.

When President Richard M. Nixon was driven from office under charges of crime and when Vice President Spiro Agnew and many other high officials were convicted and sentenced for a variety of crimes, a frequent comment on the street was that all politicians were crooked. This is not true, but it is obvious that many are so. It is evident also that the business community is full of tax evasions, padded expense accounts, and dishonest conniving of wide variety.

2. Weakening of the family.

The same hard-driving individualism which corrupts government and contaminates business also weakens family life, breaks up marriages, and leaves children without the security and guidance needed to develop citizens of integrity and loyalty to community interests. In too many homes each member follows individual inclinations for profit and pleasure, with inadequate regard for others in and outside the home. While such homes are especially frequent in urban areas of pervasive poverty, they are numerous also in affluent suburbs.

Some youthful offenders come from stable, public-spirited families, with parents who have given much loving guidance. Most do not. Most juvenile delinquents and later serious criminals come from broken homes or homes with one or both parents alcoholic or lacking in apparent sense of responsibility to home or to the larger community.[6] It is often difficult or impossible to determine how to compare the importance of the home and the neighborhood in causation of delinquency and crime.[7] But it is hard to argue with the findings of Sheldon and Eleanor Glueck in this matter.

The Gluecks compared "500 persistent delinquents with 500 true nondelinquents," carefully matched "not only in respect to general intelligence, ethnico-racial derivation and age but also with regard to residence in culturally and economically underprivileged areas." They found that three of the five statistically most significant factors differentiating the delinquents from the nondelinquents were *"affection of mother for boy, supervision of boy by mother* and *family cohesiveness."* The crime-producing factors were also very significantly accentuated by the mothers' working outside the home.[8] In other instances, however, not selected for any of these criminogenic factors, the mothers' working outside the home, while statistically significant, was not so to a major degree. Most mothers from depressed areas who work outside the home do so because of urgent economic need. The responsibility for this condition is widely shared.

3. Changes needed to counteract these forces.

If we are to reduce these causes of crime among the affluent as well as in other segments of our society we must reduce the vast chasm of opportunity between the wealthy and powerful, on the one hand, and the despairing poor, on the other. It is a scandal that this wealthiest of nations ranks fifteenth in the battle against infant mortality and that both medical and dental services are almost nonexistent for millions of our citizens.[9] The myth of materialistic individualism as a special virtue must be refuted. The strength of the family must be renewed. The ties of mutual responsibility and concern in neighborhood and community must be cultivated. We must remove the aura of special privilege which enables persons of wealth and power to think of themselves as above the law and beyond the requirements of elemental virtue.

C. Criminal Justice Now Ill-Suited for Its Essential Part in Needed Changes

Efforts to bring about such reductions in crime-producing conditions as we have enumerated would not relieve us of the necessity for freshly examining and revising our system of criminal justice. Crime is here and we must deal with it. Besides, every one of the social changes needed, if taken seriously, would require new legislation. But legislation is no more than advice unless put into effect with some provisions for enforcement. It is true that enforcement may be through licensing, taxation, or other devices. But even these provisions must at some point be enforceable by criminal sanctions. Hence, while it is true that the reduction of crime requires much more than the direct dealing with it by the police, prosecutors, courts, and correctional systems, most of the measures required soon direct our attention back to these components of criminal justice.

If we are in earnest about example-setting by community leaders then we must treat white collar crime as seriously as the crimes of the poor and powerless. The family as first line of social defense must be strengthened by the criminal justice system, rather than being undermined or destroyed, as it commonly is now. To eliminate racial discrimination we must protect civil rights by law as well as teach universal brotherhood and sisterhood. As health care is extended, the public must protect itself against those practitioners who would dishonestly exploit the system. We cannot require the affluent to bear their much heavier rightful share of the tax burden without depending on criminal law to support administrative penalties when necessary.*

Unfortunately, the system of criminal justice in the United States is not performing its present work very effectively. Without reducing some of its present load and making other major changes in the system itself it cannot be expected to perform dependably the new or expanded tasks which we need to assign to it.

The aim of these first chapters has been to provide a background for our main task to which we now turn. We must examine present deficiencies *within the criminal justice system* itself and evaluate the ethical ideas implicit in it. Then we will assess the traditional ethical resources which American culture can bring to the task of correcting its system of criminal justice, and finally delineate with some concreteness the main tasks of reforming that system for more effective and just handling of crime.

---

* Specific proposals on several of these matters will be presented in Part Five.

PART **II**

CRIMINAL JUSTICE IN TROUBLE

3

Public Disrepute of Criminal Justice

Everyone knows that our system of criminal justice is not satisfactorily limiting or reducing crime. The system is not alone in the blame for this sad state of affairs. Urbanization, mobility, racial discrimination and strife, economic deprivation, and other social conditions together have major roles in developing our scandalously high and rising rate of crime.

Yet a heavy responsibility does rest upon the system of criminal justice which daily aggravates some causes of crime. There is much evidence indicating that it is in need of drastic change.

The public view of the law and the system of enforcement is critically important. Respect for law throughout all levels of society is more effective in maintaining order than any amount of enforcement can possibly be. Our hope of reducing crime must rest heavily on increasing that large number of people who obey the law because they believe in it. They think the acts forbidden by the law ought to be forbidden and they think the personnel and processes of enforcement are fair. When large numbers of people do not hold such views, but regard the law and its enforcement as arbitrary and prejudiced or inept and corrupt, the rate of crime will be high, whatever sentences are given the small fraction of offenders who are arrested and charged.*

Most Americans do refrain from crime out of respect for law or because most of it concurs with their own moral judgments regarding acceptable conduct. But the high rate of crime indicates that an appallingly large number do not share these sentiments.

There are yet wider circles of people for whom the moral force exerted by the system of criminal justice is so weak that they do not cooperate in its procedures even while themselves refraining from crime. This gap between criminal law and its procedures, on the one hand, and the moral convictions held by large numbers of citizens, on the other, is dangerous and must be narrowed.

---

* *How* small a fraction will be indicated below, B, 1.

A. Widespread Lack of Cooperation with the Police

The most evident presence of criminal law in the sight of most citizens is the police officer. Public attitudes toward the police are therefore an especially significant barometer of attitudes toward the system of criminal justice. In the segments of the population most critically important for law enforcement the barometric reading is disturbingly low.

Those parts of the population including the most offenders involved in Index crime are the nonwhite people of the inner city and the young people. Their attitudes toward the police are therefore especially important.

According to the FBI, nearly half (44.7%) of all arrests for Index crimes in 1973 were of youth seventeen or younger. Violent crimes hit their peak at age eighteen and property crimes at age sixteen.[1] To say that the police are not well liked by large segments of the young is a gross understatement. Authority figures generally are widely resented by present teenagers and young people through the college years. The police cannot escape that general attitude of rebellion. But in the late 1960s and earliest 1970s, great additional hostility came to be focused on the police.

Police efforts to control and to disperse political demonstrations against the Vietnam War, the overreaction of police at the 1968 Democratic Convention in Chicago, and the deadly police shooting of students at Kent State and Jackson State Universities brought the relationship to a high pitch of hostility and suspicion. Since early 1972 I have not seen on any university campus the formerly frequent extreme scribbled slogan, "Kill the cops," or the more common and more insulting equivalent, "Off the pigs," but there continues a strong undercurrent of resentment. A police raid on a student rooming house in search of drugs, or even the appearance of city police on campus, may still be enough to touch off a student protest. The suspicions are mutual. The result is a kind of cold war between police and college students in many university communities.

Young people of similar age who are not in college have not equally organized and publicly expressed their negative feelings toward the police, but resentful attitudes are prevalent among them. It is common to hear the male youth, especially, say that the police pull them off the road and give them speeding tickets when older drivers are going by at higher speeds, treat them with contempt or hostility on the streets at night, and otherwise discriminate against them.

The police tell a different story about youth, a story of harassment, drug traffic, vandalism, dangerous driving, and public disorder. They have the figures of automobile insurance companies to support their reports, at least of the dangerous driving.

The President's Commission on Law Enforcement and Administration of Justice found "significant differences based on age" in attitudes toward the police and concluded, "Tension . . . exists between the police and youth generally."[2] A survey among junior high school students in Cincinnati showed that "only 44 per cent of white boys disagreed with the statement that 'the police accuse you of things you didn't do'; only 54 per cent disagreed that the 'police try to act big shot' and that the 'police try to get smart with you when you ask a question.' "[3] This would indicate that the suspicion and hostility begin early. It should be remembered that it is also at junior high age that the most arrests for serious first offenses occur.

The disproportionate number of arrests for Index crime among the nonwhite population has already been noted. It is not mere coincidence that among nonwhite people and especially nonwhite boys, the group from which the proportionately largest number of Index criminals come, there are especially large numbers who think the police unfair and brutal.

In the Cincinnati survey of junior high students "only 41 per cent of the Negro boys . . . disagreed with the statement that 'the police are mean,' " while their answers to other questions about the police were even more unfavorable. A study in the inner city of Washington, D.C., by in-depth interviews with 50 boys "concluded that, as a result of real or perceived excessive force, humiliation, and other police practices, they regarded the police as 'the enemy.' "[4]

Surveys of opinion have shown that most people acknowledge that police are important in controlling crime. On this point there is little difference between racial groups. Indeed, "The staff report of the U.S. Civil Rights Commission on 'Police-Community Relations, Cleveland, Ohio,' concluded that the 'most frequent complaint [of Negroes] is that of permissive law enforcement and that policemen fail to provide adequate protection and services in areas occupied by Negroes.' "[5] Black people in all parts of the country made this one of their two most frequent complaints about the police.

At two crucial points the belief that the police provide inadequate protection may have as bad practical results as the belief that they are prejudiced or brutal. Obviously, if boys see that many crimes are being committed without any arrest resulting, the atmosphere will be more conducive to their attempting to share in the illegal profits others are making. The same observation makes victims and observers disinclined to report crimes to the police.

If actual crimes or suspicious movements are not reported the police can seldom do anything to prevent an incipient crime or to apprehend the criminal when the offense has been committed. The President's Commission notes that "citizen assistance is crucial to law enforcement agencies if the police are to solve an appreciable portion of the crimes that are committed," then quotes from a report of the Houston Mayor's Law Enforcement Committee: "To most Negroes, policemen constitute an outgroup whose members are antagonists toward them. Consequently, they will do nothing to help the police. . . . They are afraid they will be treated as roughly as the criminal."[6]

When it is remembered that even the very victims of crime report to the police in fewer than half the cases, and it is observed how many people see crime being committed without reporting, it is to be expected that only a small proportion of crimes will result in any arrest and that many arrested will have to be released for lack of witnesses and hence of evidence. Such lack of initiative and cooperation is very widespread in all sectors of the national population, but the negative attitudes and noncooperation are much more pervasive among the youth and the nonwhite citizens than elsewhere.

B. Loss of Confidence in Law and the Courts

There can be little doubt that much of the indifference and hostility shown toward the police is actually due to lack of confidence in the whole system of criminal justice which the policeman represents on the street.

1. Charges of corruption and ineptness.

Even though the public does not generally know what a very small proportion of actual offenders the system brings to trial or to pleas of guilty, there is wide perception that most of them escape arrest or are released without effective prosecution.

What proportion of felonies reported to police do result in arrest, conviction, and commitment of the offenders? In a study released by the National Institute of Mental Health Center for Studies of Crime, Clarence Schrag has found that in one year (1965) 2,780,000 felonies were reported to the police. These felonies resulted in arrests in just over one-fourth of the cases or 727,000. Of persons arrested 280,000 were assigned to juvenile courts; 177,000 were charged with felonies. Finally, 160,000 were found guilty by court verdict or guilty plea[7] (mostly from plea bargaining). Thus from the felonies reported nearly 10% resulted in juvenile court jurisdiction, 6.39% in charges of felonies, and 5.8% in convictions of felonies. Of those convicted a total of 98,000 were committed either to prison or to jail, constituting $3\frac{1}{2}$% of felony commitments resulting from the Index crimes reported to police in that year. As already noted, only about half the crimes committed are reported to police.

Especially do the ringleaders in lucrative crime seem to lead a charmed life. Their names may become familiar even to casual readers of the daily press; yet no charges are brought against them. The suspicion grows that they and their friends are paying public officials for looking the other way. Scores of little people are picked up, put through the short cut of plea bargaining, and variously sentenced. Their bosses live like kings at the pleasure resorts or establish their homes in the respectable neighborhoods of affluent suburbs. If the officials running the system are not corrupted then they must be hopelessly inept, it is said. In either case there is not much to be gained by trying to cooperate with them.

Indeed, many people have had experiences like mine in a small western town. I tipped the county sheriff to the fact that a local entertainment center was a cover for a variety of criminal activities. Two weeks later the sheriff appeared at the obviously forewarned center, casually looked around, and made a public speech in praise of the proprietor, with his "clean" place of business. The sheriff's corruption became the more obvious when I sent similar information to a federal enforcement agency and observed that in less than a month a raid netted several men who were soon serving sentences while the center was closed forever. Usually there is no such second power to which to appeal and citizens interested in fighting crime give up in disillusioned frustration.

2. Charges of softness.

Among middle-class suburbanites there are few conversations about crime, without some talk about "soft-headed" or "permissive" judges who allegedly let dangerous criminals off with light sentences or with none. The public outcry after the 1972 United States Supreme Court decision against capital punishment as currently practiced expressed a popular demand for harsher, not easier penalties.

3. Complaints that the system is irrationally vengeful and barbaric.

Over against the people calling for sterner punishment are others who, like Karl Menninger, complain about the "crime of punishment"[8] as currently practiced in our criminal laws and prisons. None of them are indifferent to crime and few would say that the criminals bear no responsibility for their deeds. Many would, like Menninger, want to change the dominant motif of the system from punishment to reformation. Many would take note of the unusually severe penalties provided in American criminal law as compared with provisions and practices in Western Europe.

Some critics of our prison system feel so deeply its fruitless inhumanity that they do not report criminal offenses observed or crimes against themselves, lest they become responsible for the further degradation and ruin of fellow human beings.

C. Grounds of Such Public Disrepute

1. Scapegoating.

When there is anything wrong with our society it is natural that people look for a scapegoat. The high and rising rate of serious crime is deeply disturbing. Who is to be blamed?

The basic causes of crime lie mostly outside the system of criminal justice. But those causes, such as high mobility, urbanization, poverty in the midst of affluence, racism, and the national tradition of individualistic aggressiveness, are too general and psychologically too discomfiting objects of blame. It is easier to blame "those people" whose business it is to control crime: police, prosecutors, legislators, courts, and corrections officials.

2. Actual corruption and incompetence.

When all the exaggerations which the desire to find a scapegoat produces have been taken into account there remain grounds aplenty for extreme dissatisfaction with the system of criminal justice as it now exists. There is real corruption, a small part of which is exposed occasionally to public view. The rackets which require publicity to sell their wares—like illegal gambling, prostitution, and drug peddling—could not exist on the present large scale without paying off many police and other officials.

That there is also wide incompetence among the police, in the offices of public prosecutors and defenders, on the bench, and in our corrections departments is obvious to anyone who looks. Considering some current methods of selection and generally low levels of training for most places in all these segments of the system, this is no cause for wonder.

3. Flagrant injustice.

Anyone who follows such matters fairly closely has encountered plain cases of rank injustice meted out in the name of criminal justice. Some are peculiar individual cases which could be ascribed to the random failures of human beings. Others follow widely pervasive patterns endemic in the existing system.

If a system of justice is to be respected it must be worthy of respect. That is, it must be *just*. We must therefore give especially serious attention to pervasive patterns of gross injustice. As we examine some types of injustice we shall encounter certain basic and unresolved questions about our handling of crime in the United States.

4

Injustice in Criminal Laws and Agencies of Enforcement

A. Unjust Laws

Even without a careful definition of justice it is evident that some laws, in combination, are unjust. When laws prescribe severe penalties for small offenses and lighter penalties for intentionally more injurious ones, or when certain conduct is subject to a harsh penalty in one place while the same conduct is not forbidden at all by the criminal law of a similar jurisdiction, injustice is obvious.

Forty-seven states were reported in 1971 to have criminal laws forbidding sodomy or any kind of "unnatural" sexual relations. In 45 of these states the laws made no exception of relations between husband and wife. On the other hand, it was reported, "Connecticut, Kansas, and Minnesota do not punish sodomy."[1] That the disparity is real, not merely nominal, is attested by the fact that between 1963 and July 1969, in the city of Dallas, Texas, alone, there were 451 arrests for sodomy, a nonoffense in Kansas.[2]

Penalties against forcible rape are generally severe and it is rightly regarded as a serious crime. Likewise, when a man takes advantage of a young girl's immaturity to have a sexual relation with her, even with her consent, this is properly treated as a serious offense by the criminal laws of all states, under the name of statutory rape or carnal knowledge. But how young must a girl be to be protected thus by the law?

If she is *ten* years old, she is on her own responsibility in Florida, South Dakota, and New Mexico. (Note the wide geographical distribution.) On the other hand, woe to the young man who falls for the allurements of a young woman *twenty* years of age in Tennessee! For even if she not only consents, but actively seeks sexual intercourse under the age of twenty-one in that state the man who unites with her commits statutory rape. The decisive age is eighteen in New York and many other states and there are further variations.[3]

Similarly, "A consensual homosexual act which is legal in Illinois is a misdemeanor in New York and can be punished as a felony by life imprisonment in some states."[4]

Writing in the *American Bar Association Journal*, Gerald Stern says, "Possession of small amounts of marijuana in some jurisdictions may not result in any official sanction—not even arrest—while in other jurisdictions the same offense may result in a prison term usually given to a convicted rapist or mugger."[5]

An example of the latter is in California where simple possession of marijuana on second offense is declared by law to be a felony punishable by a sentence of two to twenty years. On the other hand, the maximum punishment in California for voluntary manslaughter or for grand theft is ten years.[6]

Many states draw no distinction in criminal law between the experimental one-time user of marijuana and the commercial pusher of hard narcotics like heroin and cocaine. By the law of Alabama, a juvenile caught in possession of marijuana for the first time may be sentenced to five to twenty years in prison. For any repetition of the offense the penalty is raised to ten to forty years. For the commercial exploiter the penalties are no greater.[7]

According to the Texas Penal Code of 1961, even a first possession of marijuana was subject to "confinement in the state penitentiary for not less than two (2) years nor more than life." For a second offense the *minimum* penalty was ten years. A committee of the Texas Senate reported that according to a survey conducted in the spring of 1971, 46% of the students in the University of Texas at Austin, or more than 18,000 students on that one campus alone, had tried marijuana. According to the law, any one of them, if caught, could have been sentenced to life imprisonment as if he or she had committed first degree murder.[8] Actually, in 1972, the Report stated, "In sum there are six first offenders serving sentences of thirty years or more for marijuana possession in Texas, three of whom have been sentenced to life."[9]

On the other hand, the use of beverage alcohol, demonstrated to be much more addictive, dangerous, and criminogenic than marijuana, is not only legal but socially acceptable. After making this observation, Gerald Stern asks, "How do we continue to implore people to respect law which is so outrageously inconsistent?"[10] The Texas Senate Drug Committee reporting with such fervor the injustice of the situation in 1972 led to corrective legislation in 1973. However, the same irrational and vindictive spirit which produced the "outrageously inconsistent" legislation of 1961 is still at work in the writing of bills before Congress and many state legislatures.

In Nebraska a woman can incur for prostitution a penalty of not less than one year nor more than ten. On the other hand, a person either pimping or operating a house of prostitution, if charged, faces a minimum penalty of a $200 fine or three months and a maximum of $1,000 or six months. Compare ten years for a prostitute with six months for the boss running the business!

On the other hand, under the Hawaii Penal Code of 1972 prostitution is a petty misdemeanor (Sec. 1200) with a maximum penalty of 30 days (Sec. 663); while the operator of a house of prostitution, involving no coercion and employing no women under fourteen, commits a Class C felony (Sec. 1203) that carries a maximum of ten years imprisonment (Sec. 661). In the perspective of Hawaii law, and of truth, the Nebraska statute concerning prostitution is a flagrant case of male chauvinism!

Another type of criminal law in which wide disparities occur is the setting of mandatory sentences for repeating offenders. The possibility and general desirability of longer sentences to recidivists, whether on probation or in confinement, for rehabilitation or punishment, is virtually universal. But there the uniformity ends.

Many states specify mandatory (not maximum) terms for convictions of repeated offenses. But how many offenses and what kind will require such sentences, and how long will the special sentences be? Life imprisonment is required on a fourth conviction in Colorado, Nevada, New Mexico, Ohio, South Carolina, Vermont, and Wyoming, and on a third conviction in Indiana, Kentucky, Tennessee, Texas, Washington, and West Virginia. In Tennessee the judge is required by law to sentence the three-time offender for life with no parole ever. In none of these laws is the type of offense specified and some include misdemeanors in the count. In 1963 and 1965, under Texas law on recidivism, two burglars were sentenced on second offense to 99 years each. In one of the cases the two offenses had been five years apart.[11] It should be recalled that burglary, by definition, does not involve violence or threat of violence to anyone, else it would become robbery and perhaps other offenses in addition.

Such mandatory sentencing laws, by ignoring the type of offense and all the circumstances, produce some quite irrationally cruel results. "A life sentence for petty larceny reflects a loss of proportion which the Advisory Committee [of the American Bar Association] would suggest is intolerable."[12]

Other evils follow. When heavy mandatory sentences are prescribed by law, a few people are disproportionately punished, but most prosecuted offenders falling within the category altogether escape conviction under the mandating law. When mandatory prescriptions seem unrealistic juries may simply find people innocent. More common is the kind of result which is reported from West Virginia. There a study in 1956 disclosed that the discretion of prosecutors brought it about that "only 79 of 904 eligible [were] actually prosecuted as recidivists."[13] The other 825 offenders escaped any prosecution as repeaters.

In other words, the prescribing of mandatory heavy sentences by law forces prosecutors and courts into an all-or-nothing policy in each case, resulting in overpunishment of some and no punishment of others under the relevant statutes. Often the path to justice is thus blocked by law. Moreover, the deterrent effect is sure to be small when very few violators suffer the prescribed penalties.

B. Unjust Procedures

Injustice in the operation of criminal law results not only from inherently unjust laws, but also from procedures all along the way of enforcement. Gross differences in the treatment of offenders violating the same laws frequently result from decisions of police to arrest or not, and of prosecutors to file charges or not.[14] Extreme disparities commonly result from ability of arrested persons to secure effective legal counsel and pretrial release by bail or otherwise. Ninety percent of convicted persons are convicted without trial by pleading guilty, usually through private procedures of plea bargaining.[15] In this process there are almost unlimited opportunities for injustice. If a case goes to trial, here again there are great inequities in evidence.

Actually there is no one system of criminal justice. The phrase is a euphemism for a collection of organizations and procedures which are but loosely coordinated, and of official participants who often view other agencies in the "system" with resentment, suspicion, and ill-concealed or open hostility. The police, especially, often feel that they are left alone to keep order in the community while being undercut by the lawyers, the courts, and the parole boards. Partly because of this very alienation the police sometimes use procedures which result in flagrant injustice.

The feeling of the police is readily understandable. They must confront criminals face-to-face. After they have made arrests, often at some peril to themselves, they frequently see the suspects freed for lack of sufficient evidence to prosecute or released by the court on what appears to the police as a minor technicality. While he awaits trial the suspect may be granted pre-trial release and commit a new crime. If a conviction is assured the offender may still be sentenced to probation, with little supervision available, or after a short term in prison he may be let out on parole. In such cases the police are often convinced that he will very soon commit more crimes and the police will have to take the trouble and risk of arresting him again. Often police work seems not only lonely and ill supported, but frustrating and futile. It is bad enough to have to outwit the clever crooks; but often the neighborhood the patrolman is trying to protect and even the judge, lawyers, and parole board, supposed allies of his, all seem to be aligned against him in his war against crime.[16]

The Staff Report to the National Commission on the Causes and Prevention of Violence declares, "There is no 'system of criminal justice' operating. There is only a non-system of discontent and rivalry between the segments of the system who often feel that their own special mission is being undercut by the cross-purpose or malfunctioning of the others."[17]

Frequently defendants who have means to obtain bail, experience to know the tricks of the trade, and lawyers able and willing to play their game escape trial and conviction by the strategy of delay. Since the courts are chronically overcrowded considerable delay can be won simply by failing to demand speedy trial. Then additional time is gained by the lawyer's protestation of conflicting engagements, lack of opportunity to prepare, unavailability of a key defense witness, illness of the defendant, and the like. Eventually, witnesses for the prosecution become unavailable or forget details and become unconvincing. The prosecutor drops the case or the judge throws it out of court.

Even defendants eager for speedy trials which they must await in jail often wait for a year or more. Presumed innocent until proved guilty they are locked up in overcrowded jails waiting their turns. Why? Look at the case load in our biggest city. Leonard Downie, Jr., writes, "The volume of criminal cases in New York City's court system has more than doubled in a decade, and each judge must face as many as 200 serious criminal cases each day. Despite the haste . . . there are, on any given day, more than 7,000 criminal defendants in jail awaiting their turn in New York City courts."[18]

Defendants are not the only people who experience injustice in the procedures of the system. If the law is to be enforced it is essential that victims and bystanders report crimes and that both be available to serve as witnesses. For many law-abiding citizens such experiences are very disillusioning contacts with American criminal justice. Often they are required to go to court for many days on the chance that the cases to which their testimony is related may be called. They may at last testify, but much more often the cases are settled by plea bargaining or otherwise. Meanwhile they have spent countless hours standing in corridors or sitting in courtrooms where unrelated processes were taking place. They may be losing heavily by absence from work and receiving absurdly inadequate compensation, sometimes less than a dollar a day. So far from being treated with appreciation for their voluntary services as citizens they are commonly shown so little consideration that they vow never again to admit having observed a crime.

Policemen are often important witnesses. In many jurisdictions their court appearances are on their own time—an especially burdensome imposition. On the other hand, if they are luckily in jurisdictions where they can appear in court on paid police time, this means that the hours wasted while waiting for cases vaguely scheduled and often postponed are taken away from critically needed police work.[19]

C. Unjust Police Action

The task of the policeman, especially in a large urban department, is both difficult and confusing. He finds himself in a conflict of roles and it is hard for him to know what is expected of him.

Most of a policeman's time on patrol is spent in order-maintaining and service functions: helping to find a lost child, reporting a traffic accident, making sure that shop doors are locked after hours, warning children against disturbing or dangerous activities, assisting people immobilized on the street by illness or accident, quieting domestic quarrels, and other important and useful activities other than law enforcement. Citizens generally appreciate these services but are likely to take them for granted excepting possibly the rare occasions when they themselves face emergency needs.

On the other hand, the dominant understanding among urban policemen is that if an officer is to impress his superiors and get frequent promotions, he needs to get a reputation as an "aggressive cop" who makes a large number of arrests. To accomplish this he stops people on slight grounds of suspicion or for petty infractions ordinarily overlooked, questions them, and hopes that among the many he stops some will prove to be subject to arrest for serious offenses. Indeed, his very aggressiveness may frequently provoke hostility and then actions which themselves provide ground for arrest. The patrolman who prefers to give warning but friendly counsel to the youth on the street corner, rather than building an arrest record, may turn many a youth away from a career of delinquency and crime, but usually he does not get much credit for it from his superiors. On the other hand, if a policeman is rough and discourteous toward the wrong people—especially businessmen and the politically more influential people on his beat—this may get him into trouble with his superiors and counteract all the good image he can develop by his aggressively achieved arrest record.[20]

In these circumstances the ambitious policeman is all too likely to be the helping gentleman to the more settled or affluent citizens, and to appear in a suspicious and aggressive role to the less stable, youthful, rootless, and poor people. Especially likely to be regarded as fair game for harassment by ambitious policemen are people who show that they belong to groups known to be unpopular with the dominant political and economic powers of the community.

> An experiment conducted at UCLA in the fall of 1970 gives a remarkably clear example of this selective enforcement of our over-extensive system of laws for the purpose of controlling classes of people perceived as threats to the social order. A sample of black, white, and Chicano students with clean driving records placed Black Panther bumper stickers on their automobiles. The experiment had to be terminated after several weeks because the $1,000 fund that had been set aside to pay fines had been exhausted by the immediate rash of tickets received by all the students.[21]

Because of stress on aggressive power, police work attracts to its ranks many people with tendencies to enjoy using power against other people.

The immunities usually enjoyed by officers in uniform and the rewards of their aggressive behavior tend to increase these emotional tendencies.[22] Probably this explains the observation by Warden Lewis Lawes that while he "never had a request from a judge or district attorney to witness the execution of the man whom they had prosecuted or sentenced," on the other hand, "Numerous requests come from policemen."[23] Many policemen are humane and sensitive people. The problems of hostile or even sadistic aggressiveness are created by many others of callous temperament and by the system which so often puts a premium on aggressiveness.

An important problem of police conduct concerns policy relating to people with records of crime. Police have so much experience with recidivists that they become skeptical about the reform of any felon. When a crime is under investigation, therefore, their first thought is usually of men in the neighborhood who have served sentences for crime. Although every policeman knows that some people convicted of crime are later reformed, the police assumption regarding an "ex-con" is that having been once a criminal he will always be a criminal.

Even if a man formerly arrested has been found by the court to be "not guilty" the police are likely to take a dim view of that finding. Hence they feel free to stop and question on sight anyone with an arrest record on the presumption that even if he is not guilty of the crime being investigated he is probably engaged in some other illegal activity. In this general sense, from a police point of view, he is presumed guilty until he can establish his innocence.

Many men complain that when they have returned home on parole or after serving a complete sentence or even after being charged and found not guilty they find it almost impossible to take up the normal life of a law-abiding citizen because of the harassment from this sort of police action. When, in the presence of decent acquaintances or people with whom citizens "with a record" now have business relationships, the police are frequently accosting them and reminding them—and the other people present—of their records, the handicap may be so maddening that they soon return to crime.

Although the requirements of law do lay a heavy burden on the policeman, it is necessary to limit his activity by strict law. Otherwise citizens will soon find themselves abused, falsely arrested, blackmailed, and degraded by the very people they have engaged to protect them. Who will then protect them against their protectors-turned-oppressors? Police power, if not firmly controlled by law, holds the potential of despotism.

Even as it is, serious abuses of police power frequently occur in the United States. The police department in the District of Columbia, under Chief Jerry V. Wilson, was surely one of the better directed forces in the country, highly conscious of the need for good community relations and aware that its visibility was uniquely high when it made mistakes. Yet within the late 1960s and the earliest 1970s its activities included some quite outrageous actions.

As a method of controlling the May Day peace demonstrations of 1971 the police swept over 12,000 people from the streets and sidewalks and rushed them into confinement, most of them in a great fenced enclosure out-of-doors. Included were office people on ordinary errands, visiting tourists, observing bystanders, news reporters, and large numbers of deeply committed nonviolent protesters against the American belligerence in Vietnam, along with some people who had boasted that they would disrupt the traffic and normal business of the capital city. The courts threw out the cases, literally by the thousands, and repeatedly reprimanded the indiscriminate police action, although President Nixon praised it. Large numbers of law-abiding people remember bitterly the many hours they spent in confinement with no toilet facilities, no food, and no protection against the elements.

In August 1972, after a rash of bicycle thefts, the police deliberately set an unlocked, fancy, expensive bicycle in front of a supermarket, with plainclothes armed policemen stationed nearby. A sixteen-year-old boy whose own ten-speed bike had been stolen the preceding day was shot and killed by one of the policemen as it was alleged that he was riding away on the planted bicycle. The officer claimed that the shooting was an accident. To his credit Chief Wilson declared that the stakeout had been a mistake and would not be repeated.[24] But the boy was dead.

The overreaction of the police on May Day and in the bicycle stakeout were both due to the folly of deliberate plans of the police department. In both cases the police appear predominantly as foes of life and public order rather than as protectors. One tragic result is heightened hostility to the police, even to officers who are conscientious, self-disciplined, and humane. In a society permitting millions of guns in private hands, such hostility results not only in failure of public cooperation with the police, but in the killing of many fine officers.

On April 29, 1973, gangs of armed men dressed as hippies, but later identified as federal narcotics agents, were reported to have broken into two widely separated homes in Collinsville, Illinois, and terrorized the residents. In one home the man and his wife said the agents roughly bound them and ransacked the house, smashed the television set and left the house a shambles. The residents said the men refused to show identification, did not even mention a warrant, and made no apology when they confessed that they had "made a mistake" and gruffly left.[25]

Not much less serious in each case and highly disturbing in the aggregate is the eavesdropping invasion of privacy by both local police and the Federal Bureau of Investigation. An especially thorough study of wiretapping and other means of intercepting messages and listening to conversations in presumed privacy is the one reported in *The Eavesdroppers*, by Samuel Dash, aided by Richard F. Schwartz and Robert E. Knowlton.[26] According to this study, wiretapping began with the intercepting of telegraph messages before 1862. As early as 1895 the New York police were able to listen to any telephone conversation in the New York system and did listen even to supposedly private and privileged conversations of both lawyers and physicians.

Moreover, the investigation found widespread current use of eavesdropping devices by police, as well as by private detectives, in all the cities studied. Some were in jurisdictions where such invasions of privacy by police were legal, others where they were illegal. Even where legal orders were readily obtainable many policemen did not take time to obtain the orders. Many of the wiretaps were used by the police, not to fight crime, but in order to obtain payoffs by blackmail, mostly of gambling interests.

Eavesdropping and the evils which it could involve came to a climax in the "Watergate" and other scandals of the Committee to Re-elect the President in the national election of 1972. While these activities were not of policemen, some of the convicted conspirators were former CIA or FBI agents who had learned the techniques—and also, no doubt, the rationalizations—while in the employ of these investigative agencies. The Justice Department, too, was deeply involved. The FBI and CIA themselves did political spying also, as the public learned later, in 1975.

When violation of law and rank injustice are perpetrated by or on behalf of people appointed or elected as guardians of justice, we are in deep trouble.

5

Injustice in the Courts

A. Inequality in the Courtroom

Wide disparities in sentencing are equally maddening to defendants whether due to different laws or to different judges. Disparate laws were discussed in Chapter 4. We now turn to disparities and other injustices resulting from procedures and decisions of judges.*

If laws are so framed that the judge has little room for discretion

---

* Remedies will be discussed in Chap. 22.

when a defendant has been convicted, the result is bound to be unjust to persons for whom there are important extenuating circumstances and likewise in sentencing persons who are especially brazen recidivists likely to be continuing threats to peace and safety. On the other hand, when the judge is given wide latitude, as he is now in most cases, individual differences among judges may introduce other examples of flagrant injustice.

On January 26, 1973, this matter was put to a test. In a simulated but realistic court case, 43 District of Columbia judges, after hearing the same "evidence," handed down "sentences" ranging from probation to 20 years in prison.[1] Fortunately, the defendant so variably judged in this case was only hypothetical. But there are similar disparities of sentencing encountered in parallel real cases tried by different judges.

Consider the fate of men who evaded or refused drafting into the armed services during the Vietnam War and who were tried while American ground forces were still in combat. The maximum sentence possible under the law was five years and "twice as many defendants in Kentucky have received maximum sentences as defendants who have been put on probation. . . . On the other hand only two men were given maximum sentences in California, and 408 got probation during the same period." In the United States as a whole, in "the year ending in June of 1972, 1642 young men were convicted of refusing to submit for induction. All but 53 were put on probation. Of the 53 jailed 16 were given the maximum five-year sentence."[2] Of the 16 four were sentenced in just one of the 50 states, Kentucky. It is obvious that the main factor producing such gross disparities was not the degree of legal culpability of the defendants. All were tried under the same federal code. The figures disclose flagrant injustices resulting from the differing views of judges.

In a careful analysis for the *Texas Law Review* the relative severity of sentences was graded from 1 for a fine and 2 for a suspended sentence to 11 for life imprisonment and 12 for death. Wide typical differences among the judges were found. Judge K and Judge O averaged over four units difference. This meant that if a particular offender was sentenced by Judge K to a period of probation the same offender if sentenced by Judge O could expect to be sent to prison for six to ten years. Similarly, a man getting eleven to fifteen years from K should have expected the death sentence if he had been so unlucky as to be tried by O.[3]

Speaking of such disparities, George William Baab and William Royal Furgeson, Jr., comment, "Although this failure to achieve uniformity often has been attributed to efforts to individualize sentences, studies have indicated that the individualization revealed in practice has reflected 'more clearly the differences in judges than in convicted offenders.' "[4] Certainly this is a common belief among both prosecutors and defense lawyers. Hence a well-known practice of both is to maneuver the time and place of specific cases in such a way as to bring them before judges known to be severe or lenient in sentencing—a practice known as "court-shopping."[5]

Some of the differences in sentencing tendencies of individual judges may be due to personal temperament. A more important difference, sometimes related to temperament, is in basic philosophies of criminal justice. Most judges think of a just sentence as generally including retributive, deterrent, and rehabilitative aims, with temporary or permanent disablement also figuring in some cases, especially those of dangerous offenders. But the relative prominence of these various purposes in the judge's mind can make all the difference between probation and a stiff prison term, or between sentence to an institution known for its programs of treatment and training and sentence to a grim bastille with heavy stress on security where men simply "pay their debt to society" by suffering confinement in idleness for specified periods.

The very fact that there is no agreed policy and purpose of criminal justice opens the door to heavy influence from subjective and other factors which subvert justice. An especially important cause of injustice is the economic class of the offender. Related factors, such as race, education, and age, may also affect the ease or difficulty with which the judge identifies with the offender and hence may influence the sentence.

Simon E. Sobeloff, while Solicitor-General of the United States, described two cases which came before the same court. In one, the cashier of a small bank stole so much money from the bank as to wipe out all of its capital and surplus. He cleverly kept his crime hidden for many years but was finally discovered and indicted. The judge sustained a motion to quash because of the form taken by the indictment. The United States Supreme Court reversed his decision and returned the case to him for trial. The banker then pleaded guilty. The judge suspended sentence and the offender went free. In the other case the same judge gave a sixteen-year-old newsboy "an eighteen-month term for selling song sheets printed without permission of the copyright owners of the songs." Sobeloff adds, "Such fantastic vagaries tear down the mightiest sanction of the law—respect for the courts."[6]

Gus J. Solomon, Chief Judge, U.S. District Court of Oregon, wrote, in 1970, of a district judge who told him that he rarely imposed any fine, much less a jail sentence, on any income tax violator because the civil penalties were high and he found that most tax evaders "were intelligent, able, and public-spirited people." Solomon then asked him, "What do you do in a Selective Service case when the defendant was classified as a conscientious objector, but refused to perform alternative service because of his religious convictions?" Solomon continues, "I had hardly finished my question when he answered, 'I would give him 3 years; I give all draft evaders 3 years.' "[7]

Discrimination against the black and the young in the courts of Philadelphia was made dramatically clear by an investigation of 1971 records. A seven-month study by *The Philadelphia Inquirer* "showed there are two kinds of justice in Philadelphia—one for blacks and one for whites and one for persons under 30 and one for persons older than 30. . . ."[8] Among evidences of such discrimination, the investigation disclosed that

> Blacks who plead guilty of committing a violent crime or are convicted are sent to jail in 64 percent of the cases compared to 42 percent of the cases for whites. . . .
>
> Blacks accused of serious crimes against whites are found guilty by judges of the major charge against them in 49 percent of the cases, compared to 37 percent of the cases when both the offender and victim are black.
>
> Persons under 30 who plead guilty or are found guilty are sent to jail in 65 percent of the cases; persons 30 and over . . . are sent to jail in 48 percent of the cases.[9]

The reporters for the *Inquirer* were not concerned simply about sentences which were too long. They also noted that habitual offenders, because "wise in the ways of the system," were more likely to get out on bail quickly, often committing new crimes while awaiting trial. On the other hand, innocent people without resources "sit for months in jail unable to post bond while awaiting trials that will clear them."[10]

Economic status profoundly affects the treatment of offenders in other ways also. This is particularly obvious when the sentence is a substantial fine. As former Justice Arthur Goldberg comments, "The 'choice' of paying $100 fine or spending thirty days in jail is really no choice at all to the person who cannot raise $100."[11]

Imprisonment for lack of money to pay a fine is by no means rare. In fact, "In some state systems, as reported by the President's Crime Commission, as many as 69% of the inmates of local jails are there solely for the reason that they do not have the money to pay a fine."[12]

An important point at which economic status often deeply affects sentencing is the determining of an accused person's situation before trial. When bail is set and the poor person cannot secure the money he is remanded to jail for the weeks, months, or even years before trial. When other relevant factors were approximately equated it was found in an extensive study that "offenders without pretrial freedom are sentenced more severely than those with pretrial freedom." This fact is "seemingly explained on the grounds that lack of pretrial freedom often deprives offenders of both economic means and outside contacts. . . . Deprived of a means of income during confinement, these offenders have little chance of retaining counsel and of supplying the funds necessary to facilitate an adequate presentence investigation by a defense attorney."[13] It should be noted that the same factors could be expected to affect the likelihood of conviction as well as the severity of sentence after conviction. All this is in addition to the time spent in jail by the poverty-stricken defendant awaiting trial, time which very often is not counted toward his eventual term of sentence and which certainly cannot be returned if he is found not guilty.

The poor person charged with crime faces many other handicaps in his relations with the court besides inability to obtain release on bail. When a convicted offender is to be sentenced, the judge justifiably considers the resources which might be of assistance to efforts for reform if probation is used. Here the middle-class offender is more likely to have a good employment record, a good school record, and respected members of family or neighborhood to help him go straight.[14]

Jerome Hall speaks for countless people of limited means when he writes, "Anyone with actual experience in the administration of criminal law realizes that in the vast majority of cases the handicaps of fortune and intelligence are so great as to make 'equality' of the parties hardly more than a humbug."[15] Hall goes on to say, "The professional criminal undoubtedly has many advantages but they result from his greater knowledge, financial and political support, as well as from deficiencies in the substantive law."[16]

B. Plea Bargaining

Most people who appear before a judge for sentencing have not been convicted by either judge or jury, but have pleaded guilty. A Task Force of the President's Commission found that in the United States District Courts and the trial courts of general jurisdiction in eight states and the District of Columbia, 87% of persons convicted in the recent years studied had pleaded guilty without trial.[17] It is impossible to say how many of these pleas were obtained under the pressure of negotiations between the prosecutor and the accused person or his counsel, that is, by the process known as plea bargaining. It is certain that a large number of guilty pleas are so obtained.[18]

If all the people now pleading guilty had to be taken through the whole process of criminal trial before juries, or even before judges only, the burden on the courts would be greatly increased. Judges therefore encourage the effort to secure pleas of guilty. They give such encouragement unofficially by their generally known practice of pronouncing a lighter sentence to a person pleading guilty than to a defendant convicted of the same crime in court proceedings. The prosecutor does not have sufficient staff to prosecute in court all the persons he believes could be proved guilty of serious crime. He attempts to persuade an alleged offender to plead guilty by offering to seek a lighter sentence than would be expected after conviction in court or else by offering to change the charge to a less serious one in return for a guilty plea. When a good defense attorney negotiates such an arrangement with the prosecutor the result may be advantageous to the defendant as well as to the prosecutor and the court. The defense counsel can adopt a stiff bargaining posture if he thinks the available evidence is not likely to be persuasive in court. Even if the evidence is strong he can play on the prosecutor's misgivings about the uncertainty of juries and the various devices the defense can use to delay the trial and make the state pay a heavy price for the securing of a conviction.

On the other hand, if the defense counsel is a public defender or an assigned attorney, he may devote so little time to the case that he knows almost nothing about the trial assets held by prosecutor and defendant. The result may be, from the defendant's standpoint, no bargaining at all but a simple process of rushing him through conviction to sentencing and off to prison, in short "a sell-out" of the defendant's legal rights.

Until 1972 the potential injustice of plea bargaining was made worse by its doubtful legality and the conventionally accepted perjury commonly practiced in relation to it. In 1962 the United States Supreme Court had ruled, "A guilty plea, if induced by promises or threats which deprive it of the character of a voluntary act, is void."[19] In order to avoid running counter to this decision, when the defendant's plea of guilty was presented to the judge, the judge asked him to declare, under oath, whether he had been offered any inducement of any kind and the defendant swore that he had not. The conventional perjury involved meant that the negotiations were carried on in semidarkness without legal or public scrutiny. If the sentencing process showed that the defense counsel or prosecutor had failed to keep the bargain as the defendant understood it, the defendant was helpless because he had sworn that there was no bargain. In any event the judge might overturn the results of the bargaining and hand down a severe sentence on a charge which could not have been proved beyond a reasonable doubt in open court.

In 1971 the United States Supreme Court recognized the reality of plea bargaining and voided a plea of guilty obtained by an agreement which was violated.[20] However, the old practice often persists and in any case the defendant must depend upon his counsel to protect him from a violation of the agreement by the prosecutor or the overruling of it by the sentencing judge. If the defendant is poor his counsel is likely to be a broken reed on which to lean.

Is this justice? Certainly not in the sense intended by the Constitution. In Article III, Section 2, we read, "The Trial of all Crimes, except in Cases of Impeachment, shall be by Jury. . . ." Amendment VI, in the Bill of Rights, makes the following specifications: "In all criminal prosecutions, the accused shall enjoy the right to a speedy and public trial, by an impartial jury of the State and district wherein the crime shall have been committed, . . . to be confronted with the witnesses against him; to have compulsory process for obtaining witnesses in his favor, and to have the Assistance of Counsel for his defense."

The pressure on the accused to plead guilty, even if he is not, is maintained by the strong tendency of judges to pronounce heavier sentences on defendants who stand on their rights to trial than on those who plead guilty.[21] Another important pressure is the holding of the accused in jail while awaiting trial—a time often exceeding the sentence he is led to expect if he pleads guilty. Yet another is that the prosecutor, knowing that relatively few criminal cases actually go to court, often charges the accused with a serious crime for which he knows he could not convict him in court, in order to frighten him into pleading guilty to a lesser charge, actually the most serious which might, with luck, be provable. This tactic is not likely to be effective if the defendant has a good lawyer ready to devote adequate time to the case. The poor man, however, when represented by a lawyer who does not give him enough time either to hear his own story or to learn what evidence the prosecution holds, is helpless. Such poor men are legion. Some of them are the most bitter and cynical of inmates in our prisons.

On the other hand, men who have been ably represented by attorneys who have driven favorable bargains are often likewise cynical about the law. I have encountered both types of cynics in the prisons, some bitterly angry about their "raw deals" and others boasting of their "good luck." Inmates of both types regard the courts of justice as a public front for shady practices in which the important issues are money, influence, and personal bias, not justice.

A Task Force of the President's Commission rightly said, "Few practices in the system of criminal justice create a greater sense of unease and suspicion than the negotiated plea of guilty."[22]*

6

The Waste of Corrections

Seriously unjust as the laws and the courts are, the processes of so-called corrections are even more disturbing to a person concerned with a just and rational handling of crime.

---

* We will return to this subject in Chap. 22.

A. Financial Costs

In most states it is harder to secure money for corrections than for any other department of government. Who wants to spend money on criminals? What pride can a sponsor take in such a grim monument as a prison?

Yet people do want protection from criminals, so prisons are used and when they become sufficiently deteriorated from time or overcrowded by burgeoning population, new prisons are built. Because high walls and armed guards between a prison population and the public give the average citizen a feeling of security not otherwise obtained, most correctional appropriations go into prisons and the comparable institutions for juvenile offenders. The feeling of security is illusory, because a very small proportion of offenders can be found behind the walls at any time. Most of them have escaped arrest, otherwise "beaten the rap," or completed their time inside. Even fewer of the people now inclined to crime are behind walls. After all, punishment is not and must not be before the crime.

Twice as many adult and juvenile offenders are on probation or parole in the community as are in the institutions. Yet the operating cost of the institutions is over four times that of the community treatment programs. In 1965 the institutional operating costs were over $811 million and of the community corrections under $196 million.[1] The figures for the institutions do not include the very heavy expenditures for construction and amortization. It will be seen that the total was more than one billion dollars. By 1972 the figure had much more than doubled.[2]

The heavy weighting of expenditures toward institutions leaves community corrections seriously under-funded and short-staffed. As a result "Over 76 percent of all misdemeanants and 67 percent of all felons on probation are in caseloads of 100 or over, though experience and available research data indicate an average of 35 is about the highest likely to permit effective supervision and assistance."[3]

What do we get for the two billion dollars and more which we now pour into prisons and similar institutions each year? In order to answer we must first ask what kind of values we are trying to achieve. If it is direct protection from criminals, we are getting this to a very limited extent, since the fewer than 500,000 people behind walls are a small fraction of recent serious offenders. If we want to cause the people in this sample of criminals to experience personal indignities, loss of freedom, separation from families and friends, and other unpleasantness simply as retribution for their offenses, then this, of course, is accomplished.

Sometimes this purpose is described as making the criminal "pay his debt to society." However, it is a curious way of paying a debt. If we include in the taxpayers' expenditures the costs of constructing and amortizing the institutions, the expense of maintaining on welfare the families of those prisoners who were formerly supporting them, and other items, the total average price tag for keeping a man in prison for a year is likely to rise above $10,000.[4] If the prisoner is paying a debt to society, it is costing the creditor about ten thousand dollars per year to collect it!

B. Dehumanizing

The amount of overt physical brutality practiced by American prison guards against inmates has, by all accounts, diminished substantially since the early part of the century. It has by no means been eliminated. It is still common practice in many prisons for the guards to beat prisoners for disobedience, lack of respect, or offenses against other inmates, especially if the offender is relatively friendless and powerless, both inside and outside the institution.

Guards are poorly paid and the work of maintaining security in a prison is not pleasant for a healthy-minded person. For most state prisons training of custodial officers is minimal. The work therefore tends to attract disproportionate numbers of people possessing limited education and little promise for better paying work.

Antonio Sánchez Galindo, reformer and Director of the Penitentiary Center of the State of Mexico, says that one problem of the prisons is that many guards are similar to the violence-prone inmates. Rough, ill-educated men, they are inclined to attempt solution of their problems by force.[5] While there are wide differences among and within institutions of the United States, the statement would apply to large numbers of guards, now usually called correctional officers, in this country also.

Under these circumstances it is to be expected that officers will sometimes beat mercilessly inmates who have insulted them or devise more clever and long-lasting methods of torturing men who have aroused their special hostility. In *The Crime of Punishment* Karl Menninger documents many recent brutal practices in American prisons and prison camps, including such tortures as we commonly associate with distant times and places.[6] I have in my files news reports of a seventeen-year-old first offender literally tortured to death in the notoriously sadistic Cummins Prison Farm, Arkansas, following many similar tortures of other juveniles;[7] of the sadistic bludgeoning of prisoners at Attica, both before and after the revolt and its murderous suppression; of solitary confinement for months on end; of medical attention refused; of inmates left in cells with no clothing, toilet facilities, bedding, or light.

Psychological brutality is much more prevalent. The hardened criminal is lacking in sensitive humanity. So we put him in an institution where, more often than not, it appears that the main goal is to complete his dehumanization. Many people first come into prison avaricious, aggressive, and badly adapted to life in their social environments outside, but still very human. Sociable, witty, quick in sympathy and help toward a suffering neighbor, many are far from the common stereotype of "the criminal," despite their episodes of criminal behavior. The prison system seems as if designed to destroy their humanity.

They need to learn responsible decision-making: we deprive them of opportunity to make even petty decisions as we regiment nearly every move. We say they must be changed: we set them in an unchanging routine for days, months, years. If they are to live as free citizens in the future, they must learn to live in the world outside: we cut them off from nearly all contact with the outside world. Their gentler sensibilities need cultivation: the prison limits to the minimum all contacts with family or friends they love. They must learn to respect other persons and their rights: nearly all their contacts are with other criminals or with those representatives of law-abiding society, the officers, who, in most prisons, show little or no respect for them and for their rights. We would teach them the satisfactions of honest work: the prisons usually offer one dollar a day, or less, and most of the work is unlike anything outside and so does not prepare them for employment after release.

Daniel Glaser, in his extraordinary empirical study, *The Effectiveness of a Prison and Parole System*, writes,

> A necessary condition for a staff member's favorable influence upon a prisoner appears to be the capacity to treat the prisoner pleasantly. Such an attitude conveys to the prisoner the notion that he is accepted as a person even when his attitudes or actions are opposed. There is ample evidence that control can be achieved by the staff without assuming a hostile or superior attitude, and that positive leadership and influence is difficult to achieve unless one extends a minimum of friendliness and respect.[8]

Yet the role in which a prison guard finds himself placed tends to stifle such kindly impulses and aggravate any latent domineering or sadistic inclinations he may possess. Indeed, an experiment performed at Stanford University showed that even carefully selected, stable, well-integrated college students placed in roles merely simulating the work of prison guards soon became insufferably cruel. The experiment was terminated after only six of the planned fourteen days because the situation was having such a destructive effect on both the "guards" and the "prisoners."[9]

In view of such psychological influences at work even in a week of prison role-playing it is remarkable that so many real prison guards can retain reasonable normalcy. Yet many guards are good people and want to be as humane and friendly as possible. Prison inmates have told me, without dissent, that they knew many guards who would like to be decent.

But with accurate insight these inmates have said that the system and the prevailing attitudes of suspicion, repression, and hostility made it almost impossible for an officer in the usual custodial role to maintain an attitude of friendliness or even personal respect very long. In fact some new officers had told them, with apologetic embarrassment, that they were having to stop being so friendly as they had begun to act, because the other guards were getting down on them and had started to threaten their families or warn of accusations they would make if they did not stop "coddling the cons." "The older type of guard," the prisoners say, tries to do his job of keeping them in line while engaging in the least possible communication with them. The more sadistic and hostile officers even violate the regulations and the law frequently, making up their own rules as they go along. And this, say the inmates wryly, is the way respect for the law is taught in prison!

C. Prison Society

Even if all guards were the most winsome examples of praiseworthy humanity, they would be outnumbered and overwhelmed in social influence by the inmate's peers who share his own confined status. This dominant influence of other prisoners is due not only to their numbers, but also to the fact that the same ones are always there while guards come and go with the change of shifts, in addition to the fact that there is a natural fellow feeling for people who share one's own indignities and hardships. What is the prison society like?

A parent who wants sons and daughters to grow up good persons desires good companions for them, knowing that whatever autonomy any person has, social influences of good or evil companions are real. This is acknowledged in most American departments of corrections by the stipulation that offenders on probation or parole must not consort with other formerly convicted persons. Contrast the scene in a large prison: "Murderers, rapists, thieves, confidence men, and sexual deviants are the inmate's constant companions, and this enforced intimacy may prove to be disquieting even for the hardened recidivist. As an inmate has said, 'The worst thing about prison is you have to live with other prisoners.' "[10]

The evil influence of the "other prisoners" is not due to their attractiveness. Most prisoners have a rather low opinion of their peers. It is true that in juvenile institutions many boys admire the "big shots" among them who have committed crimes more daring than their own. But among adults the influence is exerted mostly through the general social atmosphere of low morals, the exchange of ideas for success in criminal adventures, and, above all, the inmates' code of conduct.

Such a code exerts a far greater effect on the formation of ideals and subjective moral sanctions in the minds of most prisoners than the official teachings of good citizenship. The formation of a counter-society of inmates, with its own mores, has for the individual prisoner the psychological advantage of supporting his defensive rationalizations of his situation.[11]

Daniel Glaser has found that many prisoners seek to avoid too much entanglement in the inmate social system for fear that such involvement would interfere with efforts to gain special privileges, early release, and favorable opportunities outside. However, he found that this trend "Becomes more true as inmates grow older; at younger ages, the reverse occurs."[12] It should be noted that it is precisely the younger prisoners who offer the larger potential for future crime and who are most subject to change for good or ill through the influence of their social environment. The inmates' code is very important for the understanding of prison influence on recidivism. What is the gist of the code? Sykes and Messinger, by a wide-ranging study of the matter, have arrived at some important general conclusions, while granting relative differences in various institutions and circumstances.

The maxims of the inmate code, they observe, "can be classified roughly into five major groups." These groups are characterized by the following account.

> (1) There are those maxims that caution: *Don't interfere with inmate interests.* . . . The most inflexible directive in this category is concerned with betrayal of a fellow captive to the institutional officials: *Never rat on a con.* . . .
> (2) There are explicit injunctions to refrain from quarrels or arguments with fellow prisoners: *Don't lose your head.* . . .
> (3) Prisoners assert that inmates should not take advantage of one another by means of force, fraud, or chicanery: *Don't exploit inmates.* . . .
> (4) There are rules that have as their central theme the maintenance of self: *Don't weaken.* . . . *Be tough; be a man.*
> (5) Prisoners express a variety of maxims that forbid according prestige or respect to custodians or the world for which they stand: *Don't be a sucker.*[13]

The inmates of a prison are usually not united, either by organization or a friendly network of relationships. Most of them would be especially happy to be disassociated at any time to their own personal advantage. They have many disparate interests and relationships outside and frequent conflicts of interest within the prison, having to do with homosexual pairings or with desirable work assignments or other privileges conferred by the prison staff. Some inmates who freely tell associates about their own crimes express utter moral contempt for other kinds of crime committed by other men in the group.

There is only one bond which unites them, though in a loose, unstable way. That is their common suffering of present imprisonment and their consequent need to cooperate for physical and psychological survival in the face of the indignities, espionage, and repression by their captors and the perils of close relationships with dangerous people around them. Even the dangers from other prisoners are blamed on the prison staff and system which keep them confined together.

An almost inevitable result of this situation is the development of an attitude hostile to the legal establishment and to the lawful society and its institutions which are perceived as together constituting the system under which they are suffering.

D. Prisons and Recidivism

Considering these evil influences which press hard on inmates, it is a wonder that so many are never convicted of any further crime after release. There is common talk to the effect that two-thirds of the people who leave prison on parole or termination of sentence return. Known facts do not support such a pessimistic generalization. Daniel Glaser reports that although there has been no national tracing of released prisoners to give us precise data, *"the few follow-up studies which have been undertaken point to a figure closer to one-third than two-thirds."*[14] In the various studies which have been made of the persons returned to prison, the majority were found to have been returned for violation of parole conditions, not as a result of convictions of new crimes. In New York only 7% were convicted of new crimes and returned to prison within the period of study which spanned five years from release. All other states studied showed substantially larger percentages returned, either as a result of new convictions of old crimes or after accusations of new crime.[15]

The figures on recidivism of youthful offenders are much worse. There is general agreement that "the younger a prisoner is when first arrested, convicted, or confined for any crime, the more likely he is to continue in crime. For those under 14 when first arrested, nearly half cling to a criminal path after imprisonment, compared with one in ten of those arrested for the first time over the age of 35."[16]

This is to expected for several reasons. The younger the boy the more susceptible he is to influences forming his self-image. If he begins thinking of himself as "a criminal" early in life, he is likely to act out that role and with each new episode confirm this self-identification. The young offender is more susceptible than an adult to the evil social influences in a correctional institution. Finally, since the law and the courts are inclined to try to avoid such launching of youthful offenders on criminal careers, it often takes a more serious offense by a youth than by an adult to bring about a formal conviction and sentence, and even more to induce incarceration.

Hence the studies of recidivism after release of youths from confinement do not include offenders who have committed some of the less serious offenses which would more frequently lead to imprisonment of adults.

Yet, in spite of these facts the recidivism of youthful offenders is not so high as two-thirds. When all the males with records of juvenile delinquency in the Philadelphia birth cohort study are included, it is found that "46 per cent of the delinquents stop after the first offense," and "35 per cent of the second-time offenders desist from then on." There the rapid drop ends. "Beyond the third offense, desistance probabilities level off."[17] This means that 64.9% of the boys who are arrested for one offense have no more than one subsequent arrest, if any.[18]

It would be a serious mistake to suppose that it was the influence of prison or comparable juvenile institutions which turned the nearly 65% of juvenile offenders away from further trouble with the law after the first or second offense.

From the same study the authors conclude,

> Not only do a greater number of those who receive punitive treatment (institutionalization, fine or probation) continue to violate the law, but they also commit more serious crimes with greater rapidity than those who experience a less constraining contact with the judicial and correctional systems. Thus, we must conclude that the juvenile justice system, at its best, has no effect on the subsequent behavior of adolescent boys and, at its worst, has a deleterious effect on future behavior.[19]

We have no way of knowing how many offenders of all ages experience no convictions after release only because they are not caught. In all probability some do not learn from their first experience not to commit crime but do learn to be cleverer in escaping arrest. A factor limiting this outcome, however, is that ex-convicts are watched more closely than other people, so they find it more difficult to avoid arrest.

One of the more extensive studies of adult recidivism was made by the United States Bureau of Prisons in 1949. It included 2,747 prisoners who had been released at least five years earlier and showed that "*about one fourth* of the men released from federal prisons in 1943 and 1944 were returned to prison during the next five years."[20] There are special reasons why Glaser regards that record as showing less than usual rates of recidivism. Among these reasons, many of the nonrepeaters were violators of Selective Service or of the new, sharply graduated income tax law and men coming out of prison in wartime found employment and motivation more readily than in most periods. After reviewing results of studies made in Massachusetts, Wisconsin, California, and New York, in various periods, he concludes tentatively: "In the first two to five years after release, only about a third of all the men released from an entire prison system are returned to prison," but there are specific conditions under which the rate tends to be higher.[21] Rates of return to crime are much higher among people originally sentenced for economic crimes not accompanied by violence than among violent offenders.

While rates of recidivism are much lower than is generally supposed, a small percentage of offending individuals repeat so often and so seriously as to add disproportionately to the total of crime. It was found in the Philadelphia birth cohort study that over 84% of all known offenses were committed by the 53.6% of the delinquents who were recidivists and more than half of the total offenses were committed by only 18% of the offenders who were especially persistent and frequent in delinquent acts.[22] The authors also found that when they carefully rated various offenses as to comparative seriousness, the more frequent the offenses by a particular individual the more serious the offenses tended to be.[23] There was a persistent trend toward ever more serious offenses, so that from the first to the fifteenth offenses, each tended to be more serious than the preceding one.[24]

It is common to find that the most incorrigible prison inmates were first brought into the penal system at ten or twelve years of age for small offenses such as breaking windows or stealing candy bars, or even for no offense of their own at all. The court may simply have put a boy in a reformatory because he was running loose with no parental guidance. From that time on, abuses by domineering men, severe punishment after escapes —normal responses to abusive confinement of an active boy—and associations in an antisystem society have led to deep embitterment and later serious crimes, sometimes including outbreaks of murderous violence.

One evidence of the evil influences exerted by associations in prison is provided by a study of released prisoners' associations outside. Glaser reports this finding: "Of the 54 men who never saw any prison acquaintances, only 9 per cent were subsequent failures. Of the 43 men who saw prison acquaintances only once, 21 per cent were subsequent failures. Of the 37 men who saw prison acquaintances more than once, 32 per cent were subsequent failures."[25]

That prisons are at the least ineffective means of turning people away from lives of crime is further indicated by the results of California's innovative system of probation subsidy.

California's Probation Subsidy Act of 1965 was an attempt to reduce radically the proportion of offenders serving sentences in correctional institutions, while simultaneously decentralizing and improving the supervision of offenders on probation. These aims are accomplished by providing from the state treasury a subsidy to any county which will take back for probation under county jurisdiction a wide variety of convicted persons, under supervision of specified quality. The original law has been supplemented from time to time in response to experience.

In 1964 it had been forecast that, with changes of population and projected increase in crime rates, the rapidly growing state of California would double its admissions into correctional institutions by 1975. This would require the state to spend billions of dollars for construction, as well as to expand rapidly current correctional expense. These facts inspired the inquiry out of which came the Probation Subsidy Act.

As a result of the new policy California spent on probation subsidy just under $60 million between 1966 and 1972. During the same years the state saved close to $186 million in construction and operation of new correctional institutions and operation of others not now in use. The total saving is much larger, for the figure of $126 million net saving does not include saved cost of supporting families of prisoners by welfare, in the many cases where the offenders placed on probation were able to earn support.

Did the turning loose of criminals by the thousands in the community result in a flood of additional crime? No. Thanks to the improved probation services, with the great reduction of caseloads per officer, and also because prisons and other correctional institutions are ineffective, the rate of recidivism seems actually to have dropped. Probation, rather than incarceration, was being used for a far larger proportion of convicted persons than formerly. In fact juvenile commitments dropped 41% and adult commitments 20%. Yet the proportion of probations violated dropped during the period.[26] Even so, Smith wrote in 1971, "California spends over $200 million per year for the correctional care of about 15 percent of those under State supervision or custody. The remaining 85 percent of the correctional population is cared for and paid by the counties at a cost slightly less than $200 million."[27] Yet it is in the counties handling offenders on probation "where 85 percent of the correctional population is, and where programs achieving the greatest success are found."[28]

The California experience would by no means lead to the inference that all use of correctional institutions should be discontinued. It does support the view that the heavy use of such institutions in the United States is so costly, both in terms of public money and in wasted human life, that it should be sharply reduced. The typical large American prisons are so costly, so dehumanizing, and so ineffective for the reduction of crime that to serve that purpose they are a dismal and tragic failure.

E. The Question of Purpose

Perhaps the purpose of prisons is not reform of the prisoner or, more generally, the reduction of crime. In the minds of some people it is rather the vindictive punishment of wrongdoers which, it is believed, justice requires.

We are driven again to the basic questions, What is criminal justice? What is a just sentence? What is the proper purpose of criminal law and the system of which it forms the basis? The current conflict and confusion over these questions make it difficult, if not impossible, to give the system rationally defensible structure and operation.

7

Confusion and Conflict of Purpose

Some of the contradictions and disparities of criminal justice in the United States result from the many different states, judicial districts, police departments, correctional institutions, and individual persons involved in its decision-making processes. This sheer diversity would bring about different decisions in similar cases even if all Americans agreed at all times on the purposes for which the system operates. Different police chiefs, legislators, judges, or prison wardens would be sure to choose different means to the same ends.

Actually, however, there are wide differences in the purposes for which the processes of criminal justice are being used. From popular discussions of publicized cases to the thoughtful exchange of views between judges concerning appropriate sentences, arguments often proceed from such contrary assumptions that there is little meeting of minds.[1] A few excerpts from conversations on the street and statements by judges to their colleagues will illustrate. In each of the following quotations, what purpose or meaning of justice is assumed?

(1) "It is the law. All the arguments whether marijuana is harmful or not are beside the point. Using marijuana is illegal and when people use it they deserve to be punished."

(2) "I don't care whether the death penalty reduces the number of murders or not. This guy killed a good man, the father of three children. I say we should send him to the chair. A guy like that doesn't deserve to live."

(3) "Every time he gets out on the street he soon goes back to his old trade as a burglar. He will have to be taken out of circulation for a good long time."[2]

(4) "What good will it do to put her in prison? Her problem is getting

drunk and then doing these reckless things. She needs help with her alcohol problem."

(5) "Robberies are increasing in my district. I am making an example of these people who are convicted in my court by giving them the maximum prison terms under the law."

(6) "This man was convicted of a grave crime. You gave him probation? Do you mean you just forgave him for what he had done?"

Of the above, "(1)" assumes the law as final norm of conduct and apparently recognizes no standard beyond it. If this were in the context of discussing the sentence of a convicted offender, it would not tell much about the basic philosophy of law held by the speaker, except, perhaps, to imply a rather harsh, vindictive attitude. Actually it was a sidewalk comment on an argument in the legislature for reducing the penalties for violating a marijuana statute. As such it implies an extreme form of *legal positivism*, the doctrine that justice is whatever the law requires and that there is no norm to which law ought to conform, excepting, perhaps, other statutory or common law. On this view a just sentence is simply a sentence which is according to law.

Statement "(2)" is the comment of a cab driver in Chicago on a case affected by the decision of the United States Supreme Court invalidating all sentences under which convicted persons were then awaiting the death penalty. The speaker was clearly affirming his belief in retribution as the dominant purpose of criminal justice, at least in this case. He thought it obvious that the severity of the penalty should be determined simply by the moral desert of the convicted offender.

The judge who made comment "(3)" was committing himself to the aim of incapacitation, at least in the case under discussion. In other instances he might support a different purpose, but he evidently believed that the only way which offered much hope of protecting the public from this burglar's depredations was to keep him behind bars.[2]

Comment "(4)," a question with added statements, implies that the purpose of a sentence is to rehabilitate the offender so that she will be prepared to live as a law-abiding citizen.

The judge who described his policy regarding convicted robbers "(5)" was declaring his adherence, in these cases, to the principle of general deterrence. He hoped that by holding an example of severe punishment before potential robbers he might convince them that this crime—at least in that district—would not be worth the risk.

In a negative way comment "(6)" by one judge to another appears to represent an assumption that a judge has the responsibility of giving a moral judgment upon the offender standing convicted before him. To fix just punishment is to give him what he morally deserves. Hence to assign no punishment other than probation for a serious crime is to "forgive" the crime. This is to make the purpose of sentencing the assessing of moral culpability and the imposing of a suitable retribution for that culpability. (Incidentally, it makes the further assumption that a sentence to probation is virtually no sentence.)

It must not be assumed that one purpose and one only is always the just and proper aim of a sentence and of criminal law. But when different aims or even different relative emphases are governing the efforts by various members of the criminal justice system the result is bound to be a working at cross-purposes, with much consequent confusion, recrimination, cynicism, and the reduction of the system to a "nonsystem." "Nonsystem" is exactly the descriptive term used, in 1972, by a highly responsible committee of the American Bar Association.[3]

In order to make an introductory appraisal of the principal suggested aims we will sketch the rationale of their defense by able spokesmen.

A. Legal Positivism

The term "legal positivism" is used in such varied senses that in itself it has come to convey no sure meaning excepting the negative one of rejecting traditional theories of natural law. Legal positivism is like the philosophical positivism of Auguste Comte (1798–1857) when it rejects a theological or metaphysical understanding of justice as norm of law. Comte announced that the ages of theology and metaphysics were ending and a new age of science was at hand. He was skeptical of all efforts to seek explanations of the world beyond the descriptive formulas of the empirical sciences. Similarly, the legal positivists call for an end to seeking some objective ethical norm or law of nature which prescribes right conduct and specifies just sanctions which human governments should use to enforce them. Beyond this negative, skeptical position legal positivists differ widely.

Hans Kelsen writes that his "Pure Theory of Law insists upon a clear separation of the concept of law from that of justice, be it called natural, true, or objective law, and . . . the Pure Theory of Law renounces any justification of positive law by a kind of superlaw, leaving that problematical task to religion or social metaphysics."[4] How then would Kelsen justify human or positive law? He replies simply that "legal positivism, as a science of law, refuses to justify positive law."[5]

The judge pronouncing sentence upon a convicted defendant in his courtroom has, on Kelsen's view, the sole duty of prescribing in accordance with the legislated and judicially enacted law. But what about the legislator? How will he know what proposed laws are just? Kelsen regards this as a misguided question. The question he should ask is rather what laws he and his constituents desire to have enacted. For human legislation is creating law; it is not an effort to discover or imitate some objective, natural, or divinely decreed law already in being.[6]

J. D. Mabbott maintains a less radical form of legal positivism. He insists that the justice of a punishment is not a function of the offender's moral desert nor of his damage to society.[7] Hence when a poor man's stealing of a loaf of bread was a capital offense the execution of a violator should not have been regarded as unjust. Mabbott's answer to all such complaints is: "That is the law."[8] Criminal justice is relative to law only; there is no norm of justice beyond that.

However, Mabbott does have much more to say than Kelsen on the problem of the legislator as he seeks to determine what the law ought to be. The business of the judge relative to the individual is simply to punish according to law. "Considerations of utility," on the other hand, properly relate to "two quite different issues. Should there be laws and what laws should there be? As a legislator I may ask what general types of action would benefit the community."[9]

Mabbott's absolute distinction between adjudication and legislation seems quite unrealistic for three reasons. First, judges often influence legislation. Is there to be no interplay in the judge's mind between his thoughts on useful legislation and his adjudication within the framework of law in the courtroom? Second, decisions of courts make law as well as enforcing it. When they develop strong convictions that the strict and literal applications of the law on the books to the cases before them are socially counterproductive—even leaving aside their possible belief in an objective justice—judges occasionally make decisions which sharply change the law under which other decisions will be made. As Jerome Hall says, judges do not merely legislate occasionally and "interstitially," for between any two decisions on similar cases there are significant changes which give new meanings even if old formulas may be used.[10] Third, much as judges participate in legislation, legislators participate in adjudication. They do this by setting the limits for sentencing under various statutes, and frequently even by legislating in direct response to recent particular decisions, including sentencings, in the courts.

Consequently, if considerations of social utility properly guide legislation as Mabbott thinks they should, they should also guide the sentencing by judges so long as they conform to the law. Both judge and legislator do their work in a social context and are inevitably influenced by similar public expectations of the law.

Many judges are legal positivists to a point. Probably few would go so far as to say with Kelsen that there was no ethical norm of justice to which the law and its application ought to conform. Few would be likely to agree with Mabbott's effort to interpret sentencing as purely retributive as contrasted with utilitarian law. Rather, judges frequently say that they simply set the sentence within the limits specified by law, inclining toward the maximum or minimum according to aggravating or ameliorating aspects of the particular crime. Such belief and practice do not get us far toward the defining of justice or the basic purpose of the law. Rather, they evade the question or refer it to the legislature.

When the radical character of Kelsen's view is fully understood it is unlikely that many thoughtful people would agree with it. One need not believe in a table of preexisting specific natural laws in order to insist that laws on the books do not exhaust the meaning of justice. The promulgation of a Nazi law depriving Jews of human rights does not make such deprivation just. We may be uncertain what laws on many subjects would be just, but we are convinced that many which are actual or conceivable are unjust.[11] This conviction is enough to deny Kelsen's thoroughgoing legal positivism.

Moreover, Kelsen's theory itself, in some of its aspects, implies a norm beyond the human law. He flatly denies what he calls "the usual assumption" that a sanction is assessed against a person because he has committed a delict (crime or harm). "That is not correct," he says. "It is a delict because it entails a sanction."[12] To say that a theory of the relationship between sanction and offense, which is a theory of justice, is "not correct" is to say that there is a norm of correctness.

At times Kelsen goes further and would appear to protest against such characterizations of his view as I have given. He says that "the effort to deal with law and justice as two different problems falls under the suspicion of repudiating altogether the requirement that positive law should be just. This requirement is self-evident; but what it actually means is another question."[13]

So understood, Kelsen's theory is not a theory concerning the proper purpose or function of criminal law or criminal justice at all, but rather an elaborate and explicit semantic exclusion of that issue from his "pure theory of law."

Sometimes "legal positivism" is used to mean simply a repudiation of belief in a preexisting natural law or revealed law and reliance instead on empirical studies of society to determine what positive law it would be wise to enact and apply. This would imply that the ruling ethical principle is one of social utility, as in a doctrine of deterrence, incapacitation, rehabilitation, or a combination of these.

B. Vindication of the Law

When a criminal statute has been enacted and publicized through the newspapers and other mass media, this process has pronounced formal public disapproval of the act thus prohibited. Such a pronouncement is expected to have some effect on people who had been engaging in the conduct now prohibited and other persons who might consider such conduct. But if they see that nothing happens when the new law is violated, most people will soon regard it as "a dead letter," not to be taken seriously.

If the effect of the law in the formation of conscience and the guidance of conduct is to be significant, the words of the statute must be *vindicated* by sanctions against convicted violators. Each time a judge imposes a sentence, according to this view, he is saying, on behalf of the society, "We mean it! We will not tolerate this kind of behavior."

Whatever reason one gives for having laws, one must want the laws to be real, and not idle words. There may be some which most people are willing to see fall into disuse and so, in effect, to become no laws. But no one save anarchists would wish to see all laws suffer that fate. The only way to prevent any particular law from becoming a dead letter or, in effect, a nonlaw, is to enforce it. This means that criminal laws—which ultimately back up all other laws—must be vindicated by the punishment of convicted violators. "Punishment," as the word is used here, does not imply retribution nor even a deliberate effort to make the convicted person uncomfortable. It does imply some legal interference with his personal convenience or liberty because of his offense.

Vindication, then, must be one purpose of punishment (in the broad sense) to which all who believe in criminal law should agree. What else are we trying to do when we punish, in addition to maintaining the credibility of the law as seriously meant? Arguments begin when answers are given to this question.

C. Education in Approved Values

In the Soviet Union and some other Communist countries the dominant aim of legal punishment, like the principal purpose of the laws and the courts, is to nurture in all the persons involved and in the public as a whole the active acceptance of the system of values approved by the government. Such education is evidently one of frequent purpose in the United States also, but in the context of different assumptions about people, as well as in the service of a different value system.

Harold J. Berman points out that in the adversarial model of adjudication, reinforced by "Western individualism and rationalism," it "has been assumed that the parties know their own interests and are capable of asserting them." This implies, further, "that they are independent adults who should stand or fall by their own claims or defences."[14]

In the Soviet Union, however, the government intends to teach the people how to live. This educational purpose of criminal justice—and of civil procedures also—is deliberately and intensively cultivated. Berman reports that in the Soviet Union, within "the thirteen years from 1958 to 1970 the three leading legal journals published approximately 400 articles on this or closely related themes."[15]

The educational responsibility of the courts is widely recognized in the theory and practice of American juvenile courts, though mainly relative to the individuals immediately involved. There may be an increasing recognition of it also in the criminal trials of adults. When a judge, in passing sentence, tells why the violated law has been thought important to the community, he is exercising an educational function. The influence of his statement is probably enhanced by his imposing a sentence which most of his hearers regard as fair, neither too harsh nor too weak.

In this country, however, there are many centers from which the nurture of value systems radiate. There is no one officially approved and all-inclusive philosophy as there is in the Soviet Union. Criminal law, with its court proceedings and correctional apparatus, is here only one of many sources from which approved values may be learned. In fact we should probably say that criminal law is not a source of nurture in a value system but rather a servant of all the others—economic system, religious institutions, political parties, public and private schools at every level, and innumerable free associations. Its function in value education should be limited to support of a certain minimum of values regarded as indispensable by nearly all of the public. The character education of the public is mainly left to the other, diverse institutions and associations. Among the other functions of law and courts in the United States, a critically important assigned task is the protection of precisely this right to diversity.

This situation and the traditions of freedom in the countries of the West limit the place of public value education in criminal law and its sanctions. Yet it is an important place. So discerning a philosopher of Western jurisprudence as Julius Stone writes of legal punishment, "Durkheim's explanation . . . is still basically the most attractive one, seeing it as a ritual reaffirmation of the outraged institutionalized values, which simultaneously strengthens the sense of value-solidarity of the whole group, and reinforces the conforming tendencies of any waverers in it."[16] I would not go so far. Yet, with due care to guard against presumptuous discrimination against life-styles which are unpopular but nearly or altogether harmless to others, a minimal educational function of criminal sanctions should be accepted along with other aims.

D. Retribution

The oldest and historically most influential concept of justice is probably the idea of giving a person his due. There are many references to this concept in the ancient Greek classics. The best-known and most graphic statement of it, however, is undoubtedly the *lex talionis* as it appears in Exodus 21:23–25, specifying punishment for harm done as "life for life, eye for eye, tooth for tooth, hand for hand, foot for foot, burn for burn, wound for wound, stripe for stripe."* The Bible generally represents divine justice also as retributive, though not in equivalence to harm done. It seems taken for granted that it is right for God to punish Israel or any individual in proportion to his moral desert, even though God is often represented, in both the Old Testament and the New, as mercifully withholding such just punishment.

The retributive theory maintains that the deliberate legal inflicting of pain or unpleasantness on a convicted offender in proportion to his moral desert is good in itself. If one regards the punishment as good only as a means to some other end, then one is setting forth a different aim—be it deterrence, rehabilitation, or other.

There is a strong common intuitive inclination favorable to retribution. This may be seen in the satisfaction felt and often heartily expressed by children when a villainous character in a story or in real life falls into unpleasant misfortune in direct consequence of his evil-doing. Such reactions indicate that a desire for vengeance, or at least for measured retribution, is deeply embedded in our culture. There is abundant further evidence of such widespread feeling. Among common expressions of it in adult life are the following statements often heard before or after the sentencing of a convicted criminal:

"I hope the judge gives him what he deserves."

"He had it coming to him."

"Death is too good for him."

While the motivation behind retribution is closely related to the desire for revenge, there are important differences. Both consist of returning evil for evil, but revenge is an angry, unmeasured striking back against a person or other agent believed to have done injury. The avenger is typically the victim of the previous wrong or a close relative or friend acting in place of the victim. Retribution, on the other hand, is a carefully measured and legally prescribed imposition of punishment. The Mosaic prescription of "an eye for an eye" was a merciful provision, displacing unlimited vengeance.[17] Among distinguished advocates of retribution are the philosophers Immanuel Kant and G. W. F. Hegel, the historian of English criminal law James F. Stephen, Pope Pius XII, and the Protestant lay theologian and essayist C. S. Lewis.[18] All of them distinguish carefully between retribution and revenge. In fact one of the common arguments for

---

* Scripture quotations are from the Revised Standard Version Bible, copyright 1946 (renewed 1973), 1952 and © 1971 by the Division of Christian Education of the National Council of the Churches of Christ in the U.S.A. Used by permission.

legal retaliation is that it serves to prevent outraged people from wreaking angry vengeance on the culprit, sometimes starting a blood feud.

We must return to this subject later for ethical evaluation.

E. Deterrence

When parents punish their children, in any society, they are usually seeking to change their behavior, not to balance scales of equivalence between moral deserts and inflicted pain. We should not be surprised to find, therefore, that even in ancient times the theory of retribution in criminal jurisprudence did not go without criticism or rival view. The ancient Stoic philosopher Seneca holds that for punishment "these three aims, which the law has had in view, should be kept in view also by the prince: either to reform the man that is punished, or by punishing him to make the rest better, or by removing bad men to let the rest live in greater security."[19] The first two of these purposes, as Seneca meant them, are now known as special and general deterrence, respectively, while the third is disablement or incapacitation.

Cesare Beccaria, in 1764, put the case against retribution and for deterrence very pointedly. "Can the shrieks of a wretch recall from time, which never reverses its course, deeds already accomplished? The purpose can only be to prevent the criminal from inflicting new injuries on its citizens and to deter others from similar acts."[20]

Special deterrence, that is the turning of the person punished away from repetition of his offense for fear of being punished again, does apparently have frequent effect. Many offenders do turn away from crime. They often report that, alone or with other influences, the sheer unpleasantness of the punishment turned them away from the prohibited conduct. "It wasn't worth it" is a typical comment. What proportion of nonrepeaters are so influenced by special deterrence no one knows.

Special deterrence seems especially effective against rationally planned property crimes with high likelihood of detection. Tax fraud and embezzlement are examples, provided the punishment after conviction was substantially larger than the profit of the crime. Unfortunately, deliberate white collar crimes, the kind most likely to be deterrable by such means, are especially likely to be so lightly penalized that the gains outweigh the losses of unscrupulous operators.

It is evident that severe punishments are often ineffective as special deterrents. The proof is in the fact that many thousands of chronic recidivists have been punished repeatedly by long and decidedly unpleasant imprisonment, often with complete deprivation of the pleasures they were seeking to gain by crime—whether of sex, material luxury, or illegal drugs.

It is impossible to know precisely how much influence our system of criminal justice exerts in general deterrence. Obviously, it does not deter hundreds of thousands of crimes which have been previously committed by others and punished. But who knows how many more crimes would be committed if there had been no such punishment?

We do have evidence of considerable general deterrent effect in some instances. For example, Judge Gus J. Solomon argues that in tax cases there is a substantial effect on potential offenses when jail sentences, usually of 60 to 90 days, are regularly imposed. In support of this conclusion he says, "In the State of Washington, defendants were sentenced to some time in 76–85 per cent of the income tax cases during the last 15 years. Even though Washington's population grew 20 per cent and its federal tax collections increased 400 per cent, there has been a steady decline in convictions."[21]

Further evidence is cited by Jerome Hall in this example: "Elmer L. Irey, Former Chief, Enforcement Branch, United States Treasury, describes the trial and conviction of Ralph Capone for tax fraud and reports that the next day and every day after that for several weeks many underworld operators went to the collector's office 'to pay Uncle Sam voluntarily $1,000,000 in taxes . . . they were afraid Uncle Sam would find out.' "[22]

Both Seneca[23] and Beccaria[24] recognized that moderate punishment was a more effective deterrent than severe punishment and Beccaria especially emphasized that the degree of certainty and the promptness were much more important than the amount of unpleasantness imposed. These relationships have been confirmed in recent empirical studies.[25]

A long prison sentence often increases the likelihood of more crime. Prison itself is usually demoralizing and much of crime is learned there. Among juveniles and youthful adults a severe sentence may give a kind of distinction in the society of the people whose opinions are most effective and who are in turn most likely to be influenced toward crime. Juvenile offenders especially often report that their greatest embarrassment when first institutionalized was that unlike "the big shots" they met they had committed small offenses and received light sentences. They also report frequently that their first days of incarceration were terrifying, lonely, and horrible, and they vowed never to get in trouble again. Then, as the days dragged into weeks, they adjusted to the new life and the standards of inmate society, formed new images of themselves, and learned to take all this for granted.

If we are to aim at achieving either special or general deterrence by legal punishment, it is obvious that we shall need to depend heavily on special studies of facts concerning the many factors involved. If we simply "punish the criminal to teach him and others a lesson," we are likely to teach lessons different from those we intend.[26]

F. Incapacitation

When a person is on a rampage of violent destruction he must be disabled in some way to remove the threat to life and property. When a sentence is pronounced for this purpose it usually consists of imprisonment. Sometimes the offender is so dangerous within the prison as to require confinement to special quarters there where he does not have access to other prisoners and to staff personnel.

Milder forms of incapacitation consist of removing from the convicted person the tools or other means of his crimes. One example is to disqualify a convicted embezzler for positions of trust. Another is to remove the driver's license of an individual convicted of operating a motor vehicle while intoxicated or of other dangerous driving practices.

Occasionally someone suggests that we should lock a persistent recidivist in prison "and throw away the key." The dominant idea in such suggestions is usually the permanent incapacitation of the offender so that he can never prey on society again. There may be people who, despite every kind of effort we are able to devise, will continue to be dangerous to life and property, although the occasional successful reaching and changing of men who had long seemed hopeless, by means of new approaches, should make us hesitant to pronounce anyone an incurable recidivist. If the kind of offense repeatedly committed by a person is especially grave—as criminal homicide, violent rape, or reckless armed robbery—continued incapacitation by imprisonment may, indeed, be the only way we can see of safeguarding the public. In the case of persistent offenses against property only, like larceny or even burglary, it will be necessary to weigh the human, social, and financial cost of incarceration over against the danger to property and seek for alternative methods of partial control.

Because there is a common popular faith in imprisonment as a disabling preventive of crime, its limits for this purpose must be indicated. As we noted earlier,* of serious crimes committed, only about 13% result in arrests and 2.9% in convictions of felonies. Even if all convicted were sent to prison, most would eventually be released. The final result, as matters stand now, is that only a very small fraction of people whose actions have shown them to be potential dangers to life or property are in prison at any given time. The biggest barriers to reversing this situation are the failure of the public to report crime, the inability of the police to solve most crimes on the basis of available information, and the unbearable cost in money and in liberty which would be required. If we chose to become a police state and make the control of crime the main business of our society it

---

* Above, Chap. 3, B, 1.

might be possible, but we should no longer have a democratic republic, be able to travel about freely, choose our places of residence and work, and have many other privileges we cherish as rights. In order to incapacitate most criminals by depriving millions of their freedom we should all have to give up a large proportion of the precious freedom we enjoy. In effect, all of us would live under conditions of imprisonment or probation. Even then there would be crime and the crimes of the government itself against the citizenry would be the worst of all.

A seventh purpose of criminal justice, namely rehabilitation of the offender, is the subject of the next chapter.

8

Rehabilitation in Many Modes

A. Rehabilitation Rising in Favor

About 98% of all the persons incarcerated in the United States will go free sooner or later. If the community is to be secure against further offenses by those who have committed crimes, they must be changed from the purposes and attitudes which led to their earlier offenses. Superficial changes of this sort may be produced, in some instances, by special deterrence. So long, however, as a person refrains from criminal activity only for fear of punishment, we must expect his inadequately socialized motives to take new forms less likely to be detected or run afoul of the law, but perhaps equally or more damaging to the community.

Deliberate effort to alter the intentions of an offender so that he will be a purposefully law-abiding citizen is commonly known as "rehabilitation" —a word which must not be understood as implying return to a former state.

Jeremy Bentham is usually credited with having exerted most influence toward making rehabilitation the chief goal in the state's response to crime. Adopting as supreme object of all legislation—as of life—"the greatest happiness of the greatest number," Bentham saw clearly that punishment must, then, be itself an evil. This evil could be justified only if it served to reduce evil (pain) and increase happiness by a greater quantity. If punishment of a lawbreaker is to be justified, it must predictably reduce *future* crime and with the least amount of pain possible. The state must therefore seek methods of humane reform of the offender.[1]

Bentham was not alone. His Italian contemporary Cesare Beccaria, while not distinguishing clearly between deterrence and rehabilitation, stressed as emphatically as Bentham—and 25 years earlier—the ethical requirement that punishment be designed to turn the offender and others from future crime, not to retaliate for past offenses.[2]*

In recent years there has been a strong tide of opinion and practice moving from preoccupation with punishment to support of rehabilitation as principal goal of criminal sanctions. This does not imply advocacy that punishment should be abandoned. The enforced subjection of an individual to rehabilitative measures constitutes punishment.[3]

Moreover, advocates of rehabilitation recognize the need for incapacitation and deterrence in some cases. But in answer to the question what a penal institution should be trying to do with the individual who has been placed in its custody under sentence for crime, most of the higher ranking officials would now agree in saying the goal should be rehabilitation. Directors of the United States Bureau of Prisons have long held this view, especially from the extended tenure of James V. Bennett through the current administration of Norman A. Carlson. Even prison superintendents who have the reputation of being especially stern and rigid in their attitudes and methods of control usually place rehabilitation high among their aims within the prison community.

Winston E. Moore, Executive Director of the Cook County Department of Corrections and thus responsible for Cook County Jail (later called Division Number 1) and House of Corrections (or Division Number 2) assumed office at a time when the prisoners in the Jail were largely out of official control and consequently under the corrupt and abusive domination of "barn bosses," i.e., strong and violent convicts. He boasts that now "The staff runs this place; the inmates do not."[4] He insists that inmates be treated with respect so long as they obey the rules—which are unusually rigorous. He states his priorities as follows: "(1) Keep them in; (2) Feed and care for them; (3) Protect them; (4) Then begin the other work of rehabilitation."[5] This appears to put rehabilitation far down the list and I suspect that it appears so to the inmates. However, Mr. Moore shows most pride and pleasure when he tells about the improvements in medical care and the educational programs of the Jail, especially the Pace Program of college-level instruction. He would like to expand the rehabilitative programs. But he complains that resources are severely limited because the public does not adequately appreciate that it is permanently protected from a criminal only when he has been reformed.

Norman A. Carlson lays greater stress on rehabilitation and since it is more often accomplished with persons on probation, he favors placing first offenders "nearly always" on probation. However, he, too, finds his work

---

* Cf. above, Chap. 7, E.

obstructed chiefly by lack of resources for rehabilitation, although improving somewhat. He attributes the lack to the fact that correctional work has no effective political constituency and the further fact that the public has a mixed view of aims. The various purposes urged for just treatment of the lawbreaker are all in the public mind and are in paralyzing conflict. Yet even the general public is becoming more receptive to appeals for rehabilitative measures, he says.[6]

This current trend is supported by the vigorous recent efforts of such traditionally conservative organizations as the American Bar Association and the Chamber of Commerce of the United States.

The American Bar Association has carefully prepared, revised, approved, and published a series of volumes proposing "Standards" for many kinds of laws and procedures in the system of criminal justice. The largest volume of the series, approved and published in 1968, is *Standards Relating to Sentencing Alternatives and Procedures*. In that volume there is little explicit statement about the philosophy on which the recommendations are based. Yet most of the Standards presented imply the high priority of rehabilitation or are consistent with it.[7]

The Chamber of Commerce of the United States is distributing a 20-minute slide-and-tape program entitled *Modernizing Corrections*. The cover of the accompanying script states the purpose as follows: "Explains why business has a stake in rehabilitating offenders; modernizing jails and prisons." The position of the Chamber and the argument for rehabilitation are stated succinctly in the tape and script as follows: "Ninety-eight percent of all convicted criminals eventually return to society. The ultimate goals of any correctional system must be to prepare these people to become constructive, functioning members of society."[8]

B. Various Modes of Rehabilitation

If we accept rehabilitation, in a broad sense, as the prime goal, or as one of the main goals, of sentencing, we must still decide among a number of different forms or models. Some have so little in common that even the use of the common name "rehabilitation" may be questioned.

1. Therapeutic treatment.

Karl Menninger makes a well-informed and eloquent plea for therapeutic treatment as both rehabilitative of convicted criminals and preventive of crime.[9] He does not advocate assigning every convicted person to a psychiatrist, but from his own wide experiences as a psychiatrist he does advocate approaching the whole problem of crime from a therapeutic point of view.

Menninger would leave psychiatrists out of criminal trials. When we have dropped the retaliative, punishing motif from our system of criminal justice, he contends, the question of moral responsibility will not determine the treatment meted out to the convicted person. The question for the court to decide should be simply the question whether the defendant performed a morally unacceptable *act* legally defined as criminal. Menninger cites with approval Sheldon Glueck's proposal that after a criminal court has decided that a person is guilty, "procedure thereafter should be guided by a professional treatment tribunal to be composed, say, of a psychiatrist, a psychologist, a sociologist or cultural anthropologist, an educator, and a judge with long experience in criminal trials and with special interest in the protection of the legal rights of those charged with crime."[10]

Indeed, Menninger would apparently make much larger room than is now provided for control and treatment of persons dangerous to society *before* they commit crime—a proposal fraught with great peril to our civil liberties.

The American Friends Service Committee makes a documented attack upon the kind of treatment advocated by Menninger and formerly urged by the Friends.[11] In that book, *Struggle for Justice*, we read such statements as this: "Not only has treatment not produced any desirable changes, it has increased the numbers and suffering of those receiving the treatment."[12] The authors object especially to the indeterminate sentences which confine some persons guilty of relatively minor offenses for inordinate periods because some board members are not convinced that enough change has yet taken place in the offenders' personalities. Having a person with unpopular life-style or unpleasant personality in their grasp, they determine not to let him go until they remake him according to their desires. In fact the emphasis on therapy tends to be hardest on people "who most offend against middle-class morality or who refuse to knuckle under to prison authorities," rather than on those who are most dangerous.[13]

While the authors reject therapy as the inclusive guiding principle, they also reject retribution as firmly as ever and recommend therapy as an alternative which a prisoner may freely choose. However, they would have the sentence comply strictly with a law fixing a moderate maximum for every kind of case. Within the maximum period the convicted person would have to be released whether the therapists were satisfied or not. In addition to psychotherapy there would be a wide range of other rehabilitative services also from which the offender could choose.[14]

Therapy on such voluntary terms would escape the harshest criticisms leveled against rehabilitation in general and therapy in particular. As an example of such criticism we may take the caustic assault by C. S. Lewis: "To be taken without consent from my home and friends; to lose my liberty; to undergo all those assaults on my personality which modern psychotherapy knows how to deliver . . . who cares whether this is called Punishment or not?"[15]

The danger that a person once committed to psychotherapy may be left there long past any reasonable or needed period is emphasized by an experiment in which eight normal adults submitted themselves for treatment in psychopathic hospitals. Acting normally and talking truthfully throughout their hospitalization, all were quickly spotted by other patients as "not belonging" there. But all were given diagnoses as mentally diseased, the psychiatrists took from a week to 52 days to decide that they could be released, and not one was declared well, even when released.[16]

Finally, we must ask whether we should accept the assumption that all criminals are ill and therefore need therapy.[17] By any norms of medicine and psychiatry many appear to be altogether healthy as individuals and even in their intolerable criminal acts to have responded rationally to the experiences they have encountered.

Such observations lead to consideration of rehabilitation in a second mode.

2. Education.

Our prison population seems to differ little from the general population in average mental ability; it falls very much lower on the scale of average education. The inmate should be offered all the education he can master, for better employment and wiser handling of relations with other people. A wide variety of courses at high school and college level can be found in many prisons, with the intention of providing inmates with preparation for a crime-free life outside.

Some penologists observe that academic courses do not usually provide ex-convicts with marketable skills, so they would emphasize vocational training. In various prisons I have observed programs in carpentry, upholstery, masonry, automobile mechanics, plumbing, television and radio repair, music, typing, nursing, printing, leatherwork, visual arts, and agriculture, as well as the usual cooking, laundry, shoe repair, and sewing. Important obstacles encountered are the lack of motivation among the majority of inmates, absence of modern equipment which one must master to be employed outside, and political pressure from private industry and the labor unions to prevent the doing of much useful and marketable work in the correctional institutions.

3. Behavior modification.

The work of B. F. Skinner and other psychologists on schemes of behavior modification is generating considerable interest and some correctional experiments. One scheme is to place every newly admitted inmate in bare surroundings, with minimal means of life. Immediately after desirable acts he receives small rewards, and by attaining preannounced standards of conduct and achievement, he advances to better furnished quarters with more privileges. Through such "reinforcement" he is encouraged in the attainment of ever higher standards of conduct and accomplishment until he has such privileges as work release and home furloughs, and, at last, his freedom. Unfortunately, outside the artificially manipulated situation of such a "Skinner-box" prison, good conduct and socially desirable achievements are not quickly and reliably rewarded. Indeed, it often happens in the outside world that antisocial activities are rewarded, while the generous and conscientious citizen must be prepared to pay a price for goodness. While reinforced patterns may become habits with self-generating rewards, in some cases, it may be questioned whether behavior modification will achieve much reliable and stable improvement of conduct. Early experience confirms the doubt.[18]

4. Religious conversion.

In the curing of drug addicts involved in crime, some organizations of religious people have had many striking successes. One organization especially praised by some students of the drug problem is Teen Challenge. This theologically conservative organization receives teenage youth and some more mature men who have requested transfer from prisons, other correctional institutions, or drug treatment centers. They live in large houses in urban residential neighborhoods, or on special farms, under strict regimen, but without locks or guards. All must daily attend chapel and engage in Bible study, as well as keeping regular hours of work, academic study, recreation, and group therapy. Efforts are made to convert every person to evangelical Christian faith. However, the staff members seek also to discover and overcome the emotional and social problems which first drove the boys or men to drugs and crime. Of course many young offenders would not want to enter such a program and some who do soon ask to be sent back to state institutions or violate the strict rules and are ordered returned. But among those who stay the success rate is high. The youth themselves say the big keys to their success are God and the genuine caring and lovingkindness shown by the men who are in charge— some of them men who themselves have come up through this or a similar rehabilitative experience.

5. Moral awakening.

Whereas behavior modification is concerned solely with outer activity —whether or not its users agree with Skinner's own denial of any such thing as inner character—and religious conversionists seek the transformation of the soul, some correctional officials use various other devices aimed at training and strengthening the offender's conscience. Dr. Miriam Van

Waters, who made a remarkable record of rehabilitation as Superintendent of the old Massachusetts Reformatory for Women, had a fertile imagination in the devising of schemes for this purpose. Her own motivation was profoundly religious, but usually her approach was not explicitly so. When she had some inmates who seemed to have no moral scruples of any kind, she placed two of them together in a kind of enforced partnership of mutual dependence. When one failed to get the food or clean clothing or to perform other chores for which she was responsible, the other suffered the resulting deprivation with her and bitterly condemned her for her failure. Assignments were frequently reversed and soon the lesson became internalized. When a social conscience in the tiny society of two persons was well developed, three or four persons were placed together, and so on to the acceptance of responsibilities for a whole block or dormitory. Other women were startled into responsibility by being placed in Dr. Van Waters' own home within the prison yard or otherwise shown a degree of trust which they found almost incredible. A necessary key to her amazing success was the strong, mature lovingkindness she showed invariably toward everyone. Women who came to know her wanted, above all, not to betray her trust in them.[19]

6. Social readaptation.

An idea widely accepted among the ablest correctional officials in Mexico is that the problem of crime cannot be properly handled by concentrating attention on the crime, nor even on the criminal. The criminal may be neither mentally ill nor lacking in normally rational control of his conduct, although he may be both. The one need of which we may be sure is the need for a new adaptation of this individual and the social milieu with which he has come into conflict. The very name of the national correctional administration is a sign of this approach, for it is called *la Dirección General de Servicios Coordinados de Prevención y Readaptación Social*; that is, The General Administration for Coordinating Services of Prevention and Social Readaptation.

When we understand the task as social readaptation, rather than simply the rehabilitation of the individual, we must make two especially important changes in usual practice. First, we must make an effort to maximize the inmate's meaningful relations with other people and especially the family members and neighbors to whom he will presumably return. Second, we must make simultaneous effort to prepare his family and neighborhood to receive him. We must not assume that the fault is all his. In fact it may even turn out that he has been "more sinn'd against than sinning."[20] The social workers in his community and the staff in the correctional institution must carefully coordinate efforts so that the bad relations which led to crime, and may have been aggravated by it, will be surmounted in a mutually acceptable readaptation of interests and activities.[21]*

Similar ideas are sometimes advocated in the United States, but they are rarely put into practice. Social workers out in the community operate under one department of government and the prison staff under another. Organized, continuing cooperation is usually difficult under such conditions. In addition, the individualistic emphasis in this country and the strong tendency to self-righteousness support the notion of concentrating attention and treatment on the legally identified individual. But George Bohlinger III, former Superintendent of Massachusetts Correctional Institution, Norfolk, is surely right when he insists that the terminating of a criminal career requires that we discover the problems in social relations of which the crimes are symptoms and that we deal with the problems. Hence Bohlinger does not like "the rehabilitative model," but would prefer "the reintegration model," which requires "getting back on the street and learning how to function on the street."[22]

C. The Basic Current Issues in Criminal Justice of the United States

From our description of current practices, trends, and ideas it would appear that there is a fundamental issue which must be resolved if we are to have a coherently organized and effective system of criminal justice. If that issue is resolved in the direction almost universally advocated by serious students of the problem and the facts, a second basic issue emerges.

1. Past-oriented retribution or future-oriented purpose.

It is obvious that rehabilitative efforts stand in the way of the objective, impersonal balancing of accounts which is the ideal of retributionists. Free psychiatric care, academic or vocational instruction, religious or moral awakening, and assistance with problems of social adjustment are seen by retributionists as rewarding or "coddling" the criminal. Resources for all such constructive efforts are held back under political pressures generated by public desire to "crack down" on crime and retaliate against the criminal. Moreover, effective efforts of rehabilitation are often thwarted by the retributive aspects of the process, vindictive attitudes of guards and the public, and pejorative labels which are attached permanently to the offender. In the face of such influence it is hard for him to accept caring efforts to help him as genuine and to form the kind of positive self-image which is necessary to his living as an upright, law-abiding citizen.[23]

---

* See below, Chap. 17, D, for an account of this philosophy in practice.

The clash between retribution and future-oriented purpose is most conspicuous in relation to rehabilitative themes. But it comes frequently into opposition also with the other future-oriented aims of prevention. Questions of prevention are different from those of punishment for the sake of retribution or what would often be called justice. A parking meter which rejects most slugs more effectively incapacitates meter cheaters than a system of fines, short jail sentences, or short license suspensions. But the concentration of massive public attention on "just punishment" for crime diverts inventive effort away from such commonsense solutions.

We need to answer unequivocally the question whether we want our handling of crime to be directed to leveling the scales for past events of crime or to concentrate our attention on preventing future crime by such devices as disablement, deterrence, and especially rehabilitation—in the widest sense. If we decide for the latter, then we face a second question.

2. Rehabilitation: of individual alone or in community.

Again we find a working at cross-purposes. We know that one cause of high crime rates is a disintegrating or alienated neighborhood. When individuals feel that there are weak ties or none binding them to family, neighborhood, or fellow workers, they are especially likely not to have conscientious scruples against injuring or wronging them. When members of a minority group—whether set apart by skin color, national origin, low education, or small economic means, or by all these together—have little sense of common humanity with the larger society, the condition is ripe for crime. Especially if there is a sense of oppression by the larger community, so that the law, with its police and courts, is viewed as a hostile force, crime rates are high. When such an alienated individual or a member of such an alienated group is arrested and convicted of crime, what is to be done?

If attention is concentrated on that individual, even if it be in therapy or other supposedly helpful measures, the state is saying with a voice loud and clear, "Here is where the fault is. This is a bad, or sick, or ignorant individual who must be changed. The victim, the family, the neighborhood, and the larger society are acceptable." If the individual is a member of an alienated minority, many other members of that minority may feel identified with him. In either case the sense of alienation, embitterment, and anger is likely to be increased, whether on an individual or a group level. By aggravating that feeling we are working against all the positive influences for rehabilitation and a crime-free life.

Hence the question: Are we to concentrate attention on the individual alone or at least almost exclusively, or shall we attempt to readapt him to his social environment while trying hard also to make the society itself whole? Should we combine the two? Can we do so?

Where the United States stands at present on these issues, as compared with other industrialized nations of the Western world, is clear. As pointed out earlier, we use imprisonment more often, for more kinds of crimes, than any other industrialized nation. Besides, crime for crime, our prison sentences are longer than those of any other of these comparable countries.[24] This practice of heavy emphasis on isolating the individual from the rest of the people states more emphatically than any words could declare that we believe the primary trouble is with the individual offender so that he must be isolated from the rest of us while we punish or change him. On the other issue, the question of retribution versus preventive, future-oriented measures, we have seen that we are trying to go in opposite directions at once and making little headway.

How did we get into this condition? Does the history of American culture explain our present peculiarly American predicament relative to crime? Are there American ethical resources to guide us into sound policies for solving our crime problem or at least reducing it to manageable proportions? To move toward answers to these questions we must examine the historical roots of American crime and of American legal ethics, then assess our contemporary cultural resources for finding better ways to advance.

PART III

FORMATION OF THE
AMERICAN CONSCIENCE

9

Puritanism: a Paradoxical Heritage

James Russell Lowell wrote, "A strange hybrid, indeed, did circumstance beget here in the New World, upon the old Puritan stock, and the earth never before saw such mystic-practicalism, such niggard-geniality, such calculating-fanaticism, such cast-iron-enthusiasm, such sour-faced-humor, such close-fisted-generosity."[1] Undoubtedly every nation, and especially every large one, has contrary inclinations and ideals within its culture. The United States, however, holds to sharply contrasting norms with unusual tenacity and not only fails to resolve the resulting tensions, but ardently promotes opposing ideals as moral obligations. In fact some opposites are often defended by the same people.

It is only by noting the historical and present developments of these inner tensions that we may hope to understand both the special character and magnitude of crime in America and also certain unique characteristics of our largely futile efforts to deal with it. One unique aspect of crime in the United States, relative to other industrialized nations, is, as we have noted, the amount and seriousness of violence. We have noted also the unusual severity with which we punish criminal offenders. The roots of crime and of our harsh and ineffective methods of dealing with it are alike to be found in strands of our cultural heritage.

Erik H. Erikson, while well acquainted with stresses in other nations, says of the United States, "This dynamic country subjects its inhabitants to more extreme contrasts and abrupt changes during a lifetime or a generation than is normally the case with other great nations."[2] Michael Kammen cites many foreign observers to similar effect.

It is not enough, however, to remark that there are unusually severe cultural paradoxes in American life. If we would understand and ameliorate the crime and the unusual ways of handling it in the United States, we must know the precise character of these paradoxes, their origins, and our cultural resources for handling the resultant problems. We must study the historical and contemporary formation of the American conscience and especially of the American legal conscience.

To a degree unique among the larger nations of the world, most of us Americans are descendants of immigrants who deliberately broke away from their older cultural traditions. They began a process which, unlike the course followed by the Canadians or Australians, took them rapidly on an independent course out of the British Empire and later British Commonwealth.

Most of our American forefathers were selected or selected themselves as among the most aggressive and discontented people in the Old World. Some were in serious trouble with the law and either fled or were expelled. Much larger numbers were so seriously dissatisfied with religious, political, or economic conditions at home that they underwent great risks to solvency and to life itself by embarking on the adventure of colonization in America. When they came, their neighbors of more passive temperament remained east of the Atlantic. Most of our immigrant ancestors, then, were aggressive malcontents.[3]

The immigrants from Africa were, of course, tragic exceptions, since nearly all were brought against their wills. However, much more than the Europeans, they were broken off from their cultural roots. The slave traders and many slave owners not only broke up tribal groupings but also, with cold indifference or deliberate purpose, divided their families. The slaves were thus left forlorn, detached individuals, without familiar language, with few shared customs and ideals, dependent upon the culture of people who looked upon them as scarcely human. It is small wonder that their descendants find it difficult or impossible to identify themselves with the culture which perpetrated such savage cruelty upon them. Under the circumstances it is remarkable that they have contributed so much as they have to the majority culture.

The original Americans have been permitted to participate very little in the dominant culture. The Indians at best have faced the choice of submerging themselves as individuals in the customs and institutions of the white immigrants, thus giving up their "Indianism," or accepting places in reservations deliberately barred from genuine participation in the wider society.

The formation of ideals and institutions which have shaped the effective legal conscience of America has been almost exclusively the work of European immigrants. In that work English Puritans, including Separatists, Puritan Anglicans, and Calvinistic nonconformists, along with religiously similar Calvinists of the Continental Reformed and Scotch Presbyterian churches, have played the dominant roles. Especially was this so in the formative colonial years.

A. Importance of Puritanism in the United States

1. Great influence on American culture.

Some historians have been reluctant to concede to religious impulses much influence on political affairs. Human motives are notoriously mixed. In every considerable social movement it is possible to find economic and other influences. On the other hand, if the historian is to judge by the letters, advertising, contemporary descriptions of daily practice, laws, and other documents of the founding colonists, religion played an exceedingly important part in the colonizing of America and in the determining of its culture and laws. We shall have occasion to stress heavily some economic factors which have made us Americans what we are.[4] But first we must speak of Puritanism, kindred religious movements, and Jeffersonian humanism.

By Puritanism we mean, not the general popular stereotype of joyless prudery, but the 17th-century movement of English Protestants who, obeying the Bible as they understood it, rebelled against episcopal and royal oppression. Frustrated from achieving their aims in England, many of the Puritans came to the New World to establish "holy commonwealths" on the biblical plan.

When reference is made to Puritanism in America, readers generally think immediately of Massachusetts. While this response accurately reflects the origins of the Massachusetts colonies, it fails to recognize how wide and deep were Puritan influences in other regions. Actually, Puritanism dominated the early colonization of such different regions as Virginia, Long Island, Newark and East Jersey. The Presbyterians and many Baptists represented similar traditions, all based on the teachings of John Calvin and the Westminster Confession. In influence upon civic affairs they readily joined with the Anglican Puritans of New England and Virginia. Through the Great Awakening (roughly 1725–1775) all these influences were merged in a common ethos.

Sydney E. Ahlstrom says of the American colonies before the Revolution, "Among other things they had become the most thoroughly Protestant, Reformed, and Puritan commonwealths in the world. Indeed, Puritanism provided the moral and religious background of fully 75 per cent of the people who declared their independence in 1776."[5]

2. Special influence on legal ethics.

Two characteristic beliefs made the influence of Puritanism on the law especially strong. One was the belief that a rigorous rule of law was necessary to the survival of any human society. Totally depraved as human beings were believed to be, they would destroy the social order if not strictly restrained. The second was the idea that the laws of the state should conform wholly to the laws of God as set forth in the Bible and interpreted in the church by his ministers. In the Puritan commonwealth the minister's calling was to study the Bible and teach the people what God required. The calling of the magistrate was to hear the Word and then to frame "godly laws" and ensure that the divine will was obeyed.[6] Indeed, under Puritan influence, the Connecticut Colony used the Mosaic code as its only law for 24 years.

Roscoe Pound wrote of seven factors which had contributed to the shaping of American law:

> (1) An original substratum of Germanic legal institutions and jural ideas; (2) the feudal law; (3) Puritanism; (4) the contests between the courts and the crown in the seventeenth century; (5) eighteenth-century political ideas; (6) the conditions of pioneer or agricultural communities in America in the first half of the nineteenth century, and (7) the philosophical ideas with respect to justice, law and the state that prevailed in the formative period in which the English common law was made over for us by American courts.[7]

It should be observed that Puritan influence, besides being one of these factors, strongly affected three others, the fourth,[8] fifth, and seventh. Moreover, the Puritan influence proved to be especially deep and enduring. In his invaluable history of American criminal law scholarship and its inpact on practice Gerhard O. W. Mueller speaks of the limited remaining effect of the Germanic institutions and the feudal law by the middle of the 19th century. He continues, "Puritanism, however, was still paramount in American criminal law, especially in legislative enactments."[9]

When we ask what *kind* of influence Puritanism had on the development of American criminal justice we come face to face with paradoxes rooted in the very purposes and goals of many early colonists.

B. Commitment to Form an Ideal Commonwealth

Both the Plymouth Pilgrims and the founding Puritans of Massachusetts Bay sailed to America with the purpose of establishing an ideal commonwealth. Economic motives were frankly acknowledged. But they were embraced in a more ambitious purpose than the mere making of a better living. John Winthrop, founding governor of Massachusetts Bay Colony, and father and grandfather of Connecticut governors of the same name, stated this purpose in a lay sermon preached during the Atlantic passage, on board the *Arbella*. Said he,

> For wee must Consider that wee shall be as a Citty upon a Hill, the eies of all people are uppon us; soe that if wee shall deale falsely with our

god in this work wee have undertaken and soe cause him to withdrawe his present help from us. . . . wee shall open the mouthes of enemies to speake evill of the wayes of god and all professours for God's sake; wee shall shame the faces of many of gods worthy servants, and cause theire prayers to be turned into Curses upon us till wee be consumed out of the good land whether wee are goeing. . . .[10]

The English Puritans regarded England as God's modern chosen people in solemn covenant with him.[11] But the covenant had been broken. It was now the special errand of the Puritans who had come to America to fulfill the covenant as a sacred remnant people, establishing here the ideal commonwealth so that their shining example would call England back to her holy destiny. In view of this sacred task the New England Puritans believed that any deviation within their colonies was a treasonable threat to all the people in them. Hence the Quakers and other dissidents were called "enemies of the people of God" and the like.[12]

Virginia is often described as motivated by solid economic goals as contrasted with the religious professions of New England. This is a gross exaggeration. Admittedly, the promotional literature often falsely represented Virginia as offering fantastic opportunities for wealth, even while wave after wave of immigrants were decimated by hunger, Indian attacks, and disease. Yet "the colonizing impulse was fulfilled within the same frame of universal relevance as the Puritans assumed."[13]

The idea of a divinely destined purpose has entered into the patriotic assumptions of American culture and persisted through the succeeding centuries. Henry W. Longfellow, beloved poet of the 19th century, still strikes a responsive chord when he writes,

> Sail on, O Union, strong and great!
> Humanity with all its fears,
> With all the hope of future years,
> Is hanging breathless on thy fate![14]

In his famous State of the Union message to Congress in 1862 Abraham Lincoln called the United States "the last best hope of earth." When Woodrow Wilson took the United States into World War I he sounded this theme again and again as he called the nation to a holy crusade "to make the world safe for democracy."[15]

C. Democracy, Generosity, and Community

John Winthrop's famous sermon on the *Arbella,* en route to the Massachusetts Bay Colony, setting forth the model of the new ideal commonwealth, was significantly entitled "Christian Charitie. A Modell Hereof." He pleaded for brotherly love and the helping of one another.[16] William

Bradford tells of the remarkable ways in which similar hopes for the new community to be planted at Plymouth were fulfilled, both at sea and after landing.[17] The colonists denied that their governments were democracies because they were governed, not by the people, but by rulers whom the people chose and thereafter obeyed. Moreover, the franchise in Plymouth and Massachusetts Bay, though broader than in England, was limited to church members, and membership was subject to strict requirements. Nevertheless, the Mayflower Compact represents government as formed by the people and everywhere trends were soon established toward more inclusive franchise and limited discretion of the rulers.[18]

So appealing was the ideal model of community that socialistic communities frequently developed. Plymouth had communal ownership and cultivation of the land at first, as did also Jamestown before John Smith. There were strong tendencies to socialistic organization among the German sects like the Mennonites. In the 18th and early to middle 19th centuries more than 120 such communities were formed, the Shakers, New Harmony, Oneida, and Brook Farm among the most widely known, and the Mormons by far the largest and most enduring—with gradual, but never total, departure from communal principles.[19]

The voluntary generosity which was so urgently preached by the early Puritan, Baptist, Quaker, and other leaders of church and community became a strong American tradition. It has given rise to great numbers of privately supported institutions, such as hospitals, all the churches, many colleges and universities, associations for many causes, and agencies for domestic and foreign relief. But there is another side.

D. Self-Righteous Intolerance and Vindictiveness

The Puritans who came to America seem to have had almost unlimited belief in the power of criminal law. It is frequently taught that the early colonists brought the English common law with them so that it continued to govern the handling of crimes without a break. As Gerhard O. W. Mueller points out, this view is contradicted by the very purpose of their coming. They meant to establish in America true biblical commonwealths, unlike the apostate society from which they had come. Their belief in the equal authority of all the Bible, to be understood in literal and absolute terms, led them to take much from the Old Testament Books of Law as a model for their own criminal codes.[20]

The Jewish rabbis had, for some 1,500 years, interpreted the more vindictive passages of the Pentateuch in terms of the historical trend which they represented—mitigating unbridled vengeance—and in the Mishnah had deprived them of their harsh, retaliatory aspect. But to the Pilgrims and the other New England colonists "an eye for an eye . . . a life for a life" was intended as a standard of retributive justice. When the magistrates and governors softened the law of retaliation with mercy, they were likely to be scolded by the clergy. Thus the ministers of Massachusetts Bay, on January 19, 1636, solemnly declared that John Winthrop had been too lenient. He promised that thereafter he would be stricter.[21]

The effort to erect laws of the state on a biblical foundation was not new. "The laws of Alfred (871–899), for instance, begin with the Ten Commandments, an adaptation of considerable parts of Exodus, extracts from the Acts and a historical statement as to the diffusion of Christianity."[22] But, as Mueller says of the men who first determined the direction of American criminal law, "All were versed in the Bible and took its strictures and commands more literally than their fellow-Englishmen."[23]

The deliberate intolerance, wide scope, and harshness of the laws in colonial New England are proverbial and need not be detailed here. It should suffice to mention the hanging of Quakers in Boston and of "witches" in Salem, and the death penalties (though rarely inflicted) for blasphemy, adultery, homosexual acts, and false witness. The Puritan ministers taught that every destructive storm, epidemic, Indian attack, or other calamity was a divine punishment for the presence of sin in the colony. Hence every kind of heresy or immorality was regarded as a threat to the very lives of all the people and must be crushed or banished by any means required.

Similar provisions in other colonies are less widely known. Literal enforcement was more often achieved and the harsh rigors were longer lived in New England than elsewhere. Yet similar presuppositions were generally assumed and the same seeds of vindictive, self-righteous intolerance were sown very widely.

Virginia, for example, under rule of the Virginia Company (1607–1624), maintained compulsory church attendance, while "idleness, gaming, drunkenness, excess in apparel were heavily fined." "Observance of the Sabbath was enforced by laws as rigorous as those of New England, in fact even more rigorous."[24] Saying anything against teachings of the Bible or "the known Articles of the Christian faith" was punishable by death.[25]

Even William Penn, establishing a religious refuge for Quakers and other persecuted people in Pennsylvania, declared "the divine right of government beyond exception and that for two ends: *first, to terrify evil doers*: secondly, to cherish those who do well. . . ."[26]

E. Justice with an Uneasy Conscience

It seems strange that under leadership which spoke so much of kindness, community, and brotherly love the early colonies could practice and defend such vindictive cruelties in punishment as were to be found everywhere. But every deviation from orthodox doctrine or approved practice was likely to be regarded as endangering the community and so putting the deviant outside the pale.[27]

The paradox of generous lovingkindness and harsh cruelty within the colonial communities gave rise to much uneasiness and tension. In New England strong protests against efforts by the civil power to enforce religious conformity were made by a number of strong leaders, especially Thomas Hooker, Anne Hutchinson, and Roger Williams. As far as Hooker was concerned, however, his differences with John Cotton and Massachusetts Bay were only in shadings of essentially the same Puritan severity. In Hooker's Connecticut the death penalty was established for witchcraft, blasphemy, adultery, and for a child over sixteen who cursed or struck a parent.[28] The intolerant Puritans were bound to be disturbed at times with the memories of their own sufferings from similar intolerance. They tried to quiet their misgivings by such arguments as were stated by Nathaniel Ward in *The Simple Cobbler of Aggawam* (1647), for example: "He that is willing to tolerate any Religion, or discrepant way of Religion, besides his owne, unless it be in matters merely indifferent, either doubts of his own, or is not sincere in it."[29]

Yet the discrepancy between the lovingkindness professed and the harsh judgments on many unpopular members of the community could not be altogether stifled. One sign that the severe laws drawn literally from the Pentateuch ran afoul of the more humane sentiments in the Puritan conscience is the difficulty encountered by the more austere clergy in securing their enforcement. Many sermons complained of laxity in legal efforts to stamp out immorality. Indeed Rowland Berthoff even states that the death penalties prescribed by law "for adultery and for youthful disobedience . . . were never actually inflicted."[30]

Even though the courts were not so severe as the letter of the ancient Hebrew law and the preaching of some ministers commanded, they were still too harsh for much popular sentiment.[31] An especially dramatic surfacing of the conflict in conscience and the beginning of more moderation occurred in 1692, the year of the horrible witchcraft delusions in Salem. Judge Samuel Sewall, a justice of the Supreme Judicial Court in Massachusetts, stood during a public fasting service of Old South Church, Boston, while Rev. Samuel Willard, the pastor, read a statement written by the Judge. In it he confessed to his own responsibility in the horrors and says he "Desires to take the Blame and shame of it, Asking pardon of men. And especially desiring prayers that God . . . would pardon that sin and all other his sins. . . ."[32] The witchcraft hysteria embarrassed the clergymen who had urged on the persecution and reduced clerical influence in the colony.[33]

Other movements and events, however, were to give renewed vigor and wider dissemination to vindictive, individualistic self-righteousness. They would strengthen also generous humanism and community spirit, both within the churches and in the secular culture and law of the country. The paradox would continue and intensify.

10

The Great Awakening and Jeffersonian Humanism

The 18th century witnessed two major developments profoundly affecting the ethical ideals and expectations of Americans. One was the series of religious revivals collectively known as the Great Awakening. The other was the intellectual Enlightenment which formed the main convictions of the men who led in fashioning the national independence and Constitution of the new republic. The two movements were so deeply related that it is appropriate to consider them successively in this one chapter.

A. Significance of the Great Awakening

The religious leaders of the early New England colonies believed that every true Christian had passed through an experience of conscious conviction of sin, forgiveness, and spiritual rebirth. Profession of such experience was therefore a prerequisite to church membership. However, through the "halfway covenant" and generations of routine church life, such requirements and expectations had fallen away by 1700. In the years that followed there were many lamentations of the dullness and powerlessness of church life in New England. Elsewhere there were wide local differences but there was generally little religious vitality.

Then, after anticipatory revivals under the preaching and leadership of Solomon Stoddard and some others, a series of revivals led by Jonathan Edwards in Massachusetts spread from one region to another. George Whitefield deliberately carried the torch from England to Georgia and in rapid succession to all the American colonies. Gilbert Tennent and many lesser figures promoted the movement. Between 1738 and the Revolution few communities in the colonies remained untouched.

Not only did the waves of revival bring new life and influence to the churches and cause new denominational divisions to occur. They also popularized new social ideals and did much to forge the peculiar kind of unity in diversity which changed a number of separate colonies into a people with national self-consciousness.[1]

B. Reinforcement and Dissemination of Puritan Ideas

Although many ministers of non-Puritan traditions actively participated in the Great Awakening, everywhere it went it carried certain characteristic Puritan doctrines. These included the doctrines of God's awesome sovereignty, the sinfulness of all human beings and their eternal damnation by divine judgment, the necessity of repentance, forgiveness and regeneration by God's merciful grace, and the gathering of the regenerate persons into a saved and saving community of faith—the church.

Some revivalists laid more stress on one of these elements, while others stressed a different idea. Yet all who had much success in "soul-winning" included all these doctrines, whatever their various proportions in the message. Not only were the ideas taught; they were driven deep into the subconscious recesses of people's minds by the soul-shaking emotional responses which accompanied their declaration.

The Great Awakening thus strengthened in American culture attitudes of severe judgment toward acts regarded as evil and belief in the justice of harsh penalties. After all, no penalties which human courts could exact would come close to rivaling the eternal tortures of hell which were declared to be God's just punishment of sin. At the same time the proffered mercies of God provided a model of human mercy to the lawbreaker. Such mercy, however, was not regarded as justice and no offender could claim it as a right nor presume to expect it.

Though it had important connections with evangelical movements in Britain and Europe the Great Awakening was a distinctly American phenomenon. It emphatically revived and extended to all the colonies the belief in a special divine calling or errand. As Ahlstrom says, "Above all, it awakened millennial hopes that a covenanted nation, repenting its sins and trusting in God, could become an instrument of Providence in realizing the Kingdom."[2] We have observed earlier that such lofty expectation, in combination with a strict moralism and grim notions of the ever-present divine judgment, has led, in America, to an especially broad scope of criminal law and has supported severe punishments for its violation.

C. Nationalistic and Revolutionary Fervor

The Great Awakening was the first social movement to sweep through all the colonies. It contributed much of unity and free, revolutionary spirit to the whole.[3] Ahlstrom writes, "Vital for the political future of the colonies, the Awakening also made the people aware of their common spiritual heritage, and of their existence as an American nation."[4]

The influence of the Great Awakening in the forming of conscious national unity made it especially important in establishing the mood of the nation. Since it established throughout the colonies a sense of national mission, it tended to make the people increasingly impatient of domination or interference from outside the colonies. At first this sense of national evangelical Protestant identity stirred militant action against the presence of Spanish and French power in the region, and so tended in favor of British interests. But once the other powers had been driven back to a safe distance, the hostility was turned against the British rule. This revolutionary spirit was closely joined with the individualistic emphasis of the revivals.

D. Humane and Democratic Themes of the Awakening

Despite occasional anti-intellectual aspects of the Great Awakening, especially in some extreme appeals for undisciplined outpourings of emotion, the main thrust explicitly favored intellectual training. The churches which it revitalized and extended strongly supported broadened educational opportunity.[5] Churchmen working in the revivals and missions of this period founded many institutions of higher learning including such later famous ones as the University of Pennsylvania (1740), Princeton (1746), Brown (1746), Columbia (1754), Dartmouth (1769), and Rutgers (1766), among others.

Jonathan Edwards was one of the towering intellects of American history. His philosophical work joined a modified Calvinism with a carefully wrought metaphysics relying heavily on the science of Isaac Newton and the philosophical writings of John Locke.

The democratic political ideas of Locke were reinforced by the popular experiences of the revivals. One who has experienced the personal favor of God is not likely to stand in awe of human royalty or aristocracy. The sense of personal autonomy gained in the Awakening first expressed itself within the churches, where lay people exercised greatly increased activity and authority. But it did not stop at that point.

Edwards himself knew well the political implications of the doctrines he was preaching. He made this clear at the 1748 funeral of his uncle, Colonel John Stoddard, the strong civil authority who had until then protected him from the wrath of the wealthy "river gods" of the Connecticut Valley. With many of these men before him, he described the qualifications of a ruler. First of all he placed "great ability for the management of public affairs." Good rulers must have the power to discern "those things wherein public welfare or calamity consists." Not only must they be keen observers and students of human nature; they must understand particularly well "the state and circumstances of the country or people that they have the care of." It is to be noted that Edwards does not represent good rulers as men who will simply obey the commands of Scripture or support eternally valid virtues. He is stressing pragmatic attention to observed needs and capabilities. In further realistic emphasis he warns that the good ruler must take special care to oppose persons who would serve their selfish interests by "little tricks and intrigues," and who would thus "grind the faces of the poor, and screw upon their neighbors."[6]

The Great Awakening renewed a broad scope of criminal law to enforce religious observance and Puritan moral standards, but new attempts to impose conformity were ably challenged. Elisha Williams, who opposed the emotional excesses of the Awakening, but led in the more sober renewal of Puritan orthodoxy which accompanied the revivals, wrote a letter from Massachusetts Bay in 1744 to a Connecticut friend in which he powerfully defended religious freedom for all but "papists." Despite the exception he made, the arguments he employed for the right of private conscience in religion implied freedom of religion for all without exception. Vigorously opposing interference by the state with the preaching of itinerant evangelists, however obnoxious, he went much further to define the proper scope of law. Said he, "That greater Security therefore of Life, Liberty, Money, Lands, Houses, Family, and the like, which may all be comprehended under that of Person and Property, is the sole End of all civil Government."[7] Similar views were expressed by Abraham Williams in his sermon to the General Court (legislature) of Massachusetts Bay, May 26, 1762.[8]

E. Thomas Jefferson and His Times

Thomas Jefferson, besides being the principal author of the American Declaration of Independence,[9] an important promoter of the Bill of Rights, and third president of the United States, was an especially influential writer on the philosophy of government in America. Anyone who would understand the cultural context of American law must take account of his work.

The best-known and most important single writer in exerting influence upon Thomas Jefferson was John Locke. As Charles M. Wiltse says, "He knew Locke so well that the very phrasing of the second *Treatise* recurs in the *Declaration of Independence*, although Jefferson protests that he 'turned neither to book nor pamphlet' while writing it. . . ."[10] Locke was a major source among influences on Jefferson's doctrines of human equality and the responsibility of government to support the natural law rights, including the right of revolution against tyranny.

Wiltse finds reason to believe that Jefferson was also influenced by his reading of Cicero, Hugo Grotius, Lord Kames, and the legal code of Alfred. The Great Awakening and the spirit of the times had prepared much of the populace to respond to his appeals to Locke and claims of inherent human rights. But according to Wiltse, "the leaders of the Revolution . . . gave equal weight to the argument from legal precedent" in England.[11] Some decisions by Sir Edward Coke, Chief Justice of the King's Bench, were especially congenial to the revolutionary cause and to Jefferson's thinking.

In his thought about the punishment of crime Jefferson was particularly influenced by Beccaria, as the very title of his "Bill for Proportioning Crimes and Punishments" suggests and as footnotes in that document prove. This influence, again, encouraged his own bent in the direction of moderation and humaneness.[12]

Jefferson did not stand alone. Several of his colleagues in the founding and building of the new nation shared the direction of his own political philosophy, particularly Benjamin Franklin, James Madison, and George Mason. But because of his great learning and the scope of his writings it is especially convenient to see the contribution of the Enlightenment at the birth of the nation through the evidences which he affords.

F. Jefferson's Concept of Government

The early American ideas of government were concerned predominantly with its negative function of restraining wrongdoers, including domestic and foreign enemies. Beyond that, to be sure, the colonial regimes were expected to provide machinery for resolving serious disputes, sometimes the building of roads, and, in some colonies, the collecting of support for the churches. But the emphasis was on the providing of security against evil. Indeed, one reason for the support for religion was the hope of diminishing sin.

Jefferson was no friend of big government. He was always wary of the threat to freedom when it extended its functions too deeply into the lives of its citizens. But Americans have appreciated insufficiently his shifting of concern from exclusively negative to include positive tasks of government.[13]

If, as Jefferson and the signers stated in the Declaration of Independence, all men are "endowed by their Creator" with the "unalienable Rights" to "Life, Liberty and the pursuit of Happiness" and "to secure these rights, Governments are instituted," there are consequences reaching much further than Jefferson may have intended. Particularly in relation to our present concern with criminal justice, they affect the purpose, scope, and sanctions of criminal law. The purpose will not be to compel virtue or orthodoxy or to prevent sins of all kinds, but rather to prevent or diminish acts which threaten or reduce the life, liberty, or seeking of happiness by other people. Hence the scope will be limited to prohibitions of such acts only. The sanctions must be limited so as to interfere no more with life and liberty than may be necessary to prevent more interference with the lives of others by criminal acts than is caused by the punishment inflicted.[14]

I do not find that Jefferson ever drew out these implications for criminal law as did Jeremy Bentham, his slightly younger English contemporary. However, in his writing of legislation and his arguments concerning it he showed a strong impulse in these directions. Like Bentham he emphatically rejected retaliation as a meaning or goal of justice. Writing in the last years of his life, he speaks of the *lex talionis* as a "revolting principle" and says he cannot remember how the Virginia Assembly of 1776 had come to give approbation to it, for "the modern mind had left it far in the rear of its advances."[15] No abstract notion of balancing the moral culpability of a criminal by a quantity of suffering inflicted as punishment could stand before his concept of government.

G. Qualified Egalitarianism

One of the worst and most pervasive features of criminal justice is the unequal treatment of the rich and powerful as over against the poor and weak. Jefferson had an important part in developing the uneasy conscience of Americans relative to such inequality.

When he wrote in the Declaration of Independence that "all men are created equal" he had no notion that all were created with equal abilities. He was saying that all had equal *rights*—and specifically that they had equal rights in human society to life, liberty, and the pursuit of happiness.[16] Writing a letter shortly before he left the presidency, in 1809, he spoke of his earlier doubt about the abilities of black people, which he had even then thought might be based on too narrow observations of them in the unfavorable circumstances of slavery. He now welcomed accumulating evidence that his doubt had been ill-founded. Then he added, "but whatever be their degree of talent it is no measure of their rights."[17] He drove the point home by commenting that the superior understanding of Sir Isaac Newton did not give him the superior right of being "lord of the person or property of others."

Jefferson wanted to see his state and his country ruled by the true *aristoi* of character and ability, as selected by popular vote. While having no illusions about the infallibility of the common populace, on the whole he had more confidence in their general integrity and sound judgment than he had in the upper classes of society. In 1795 he wrote that he disagreed with the judgment of such men as Rochefoucauld and Montaigne that fourteen out of fifteen men were rogues. The proportion among the general populace would be much more favorable. However, he thought the proportions about right for "the higher orders"![18] On the other hand, he did not wish to see all the complex and often emotion-charged issues which governments must decide subjected to popular vote.

His egalitarianism was qualified, and yet it was true that, as Wiltse says, "An aristocrat by birth, by temper and by culture, he yet denied all but the natural aristocracy of talent, and based his state on the equality of men."[19]

H. Jefferson and Slavery

If Jefferson was such a champion of universal rights, how did it happen that he was a slaveholder to the end? When he spoke of all men being created equal was he mentally excluding people of African origin from the human race? Such questions were asked with growing intensity in the decades before the Civil War and Jefferson was cited as authority by abolitionists and defenders of slavery alike.

There are many passages in his writings in which he vigorously condemned the whole institution and practice of slavery, not only for its denial of human equality, but for its corrupting effect on the slaveholders and their families and its degradation of the black people.[20] After describing with passionate eloquence these and other iniquities inherent in slavery, he wrote, "Indeed I tremble for my country when I reflect that God is just; that his justice cannot sleep forever. . . ." Foreseeing the likelihood of a future reversal of fortune, he says, "The Almighty has no attribute which can take side with us in such a contest."[21]

In the Virginia legislature Jefferson's first action was the successful introduction of a bill to outlaw importation of slaves into Virginia. He tried hard to secure passage of a law to permit slaveowners to free their slaves, but in this he was unsuccessful. He tried through several days of debate to secure inclusion in the Declaration of Independence of a denunciation (part of his original text) of the king's imposing on the colonies the slave trade, which he calls

cruel war against human nature itself, violating its most sacred rights of life and liberty in the persons of a distant people who never offended him, captivating and carrying them into slavery in another hemisphere, or to incur miserable death in their transportation hither. This piratical warfare, the opprobrium of INFIDEL powers, is the warfare of the CHRISTIAN king of Great Britain. Determined to keep open a market where MEN should be bought and sold, he has prostituted his negative [veto power] for suppressing every legislative attempt to prohibit or restrain this execrable commerce.

The fact that this passage with more of similar import was in Jefferson's draft of the Declaration and removed only by a stubbornly fought amendment should end all doubt that Jefferson intended to include black people among the people who held equal human rights.

On the other hand, he did continue to keep slaves, he wrote of his doubts that they had native abilities equal to those of other people, and he thought that when the slaves were freed they must be resettled apart from the white people, preferably in their African homelands.[22] It can be replied that he could not legally free his slaves, and if he had done so illegally they would not have been allowed the status of free people; that he tried repeatedly to change the law so that they could be freed; that there are testimonies to his extraordinarily generous treatment of his slaves; that he later thought his doubts about their native abilities ill-supported; and that his proposals for colonization did not imply unequal rights. Such replies are not wholly convincing and the debate has taken many turns.[23]

Beyond doubt, however, is the fact that he believed slavery to be an immoral institution. It is certain that when he taught that all men are created equal he put into American culture a tradition which would forever set the American conscience both against slavery and against every form of discrimination before the law on account of race or any other accident of birth or status. In the civil rights movement of the 1960s it would be used effectively on many occasions to stir patriotic American pride against the evils of discrimination.[24]

I. Tolerance and Human Moderation

Jefferson asked that only three items appear in his epitaph and his wishes were respected. By his choice, one of the three was his authorship of "the Statute of Virginia for Religious Freedom."[25] Although he did not write the United States Bill of Rights, he had a hand in the Virginia Bill of Rights which served as a model. When he first saw the Constitution, as written while he served in Europe, he thought the guarantees of personal liberty inadequate and said they must be supplemented by a bill of rights. The first ten amendments allayed his doubts and won his strong support for the whole.

The separation of church and state was especially important to Jefferson because it guaranteed the freedom of the individual's personal thought and convictions from interference by government. Actually government could not control a person's real beliefs if it tried. It could only make weak men hypocritical pretenders to orthodoxy, while subjecting honest men to persecution.

Jefferson was by no means indifferent to religion. Even his many expressions of anticlericalism must be placed alongside his generous annual subscription to the support of a patriotic Episcopal pastor, the Rev. Charles Clay of Williamsburg[26] and his lifelong church membership.[27] His belief in God and personal immortality were clear and earnestly held. He called himself "a real Christian."[28] He was highly unorthodox. Today he might be viewed as a theologically conservative Unitarian or as a liberal Christian.

His lifelong championship of religious toleration was not due, then, to religious indifference. Quite the contrary. He had such high regard for the inner, spiritual life of the individual and his relationship with God that he wanted no invasion of it by doctrinaire and arrogant clergymen or an inquisitorial government.

To Jefferson and Madison more than to any other individuals we owe the civil liberties entrenched in the Bill of Rights, and particularly the constitutional abolition of all that attempted enforcement of orthodoxy and of church support which had widely prevailed in the early colonies. As Earl Warren has rightly said, "The heart of any constitution consists of its bill of rights. . . ."[29] This is especially true as far as the criminal law and procedures are concerned. Hence Jefferson's impact upon the philosophy and basic structures of the American system of criminal justice is incalculably great.

At the same time we must be reminded that in these matters Jefferson was expressing ideas which were widely prevalent among thoughtful Americans and also among intellectual leaders of France and England. Furthermore, the moods of toleration and love of liberty which motivated such ideas were widespread at all levels of American society. They had been stimulated by the increasing rapidity of movement to the frontier, the diversities of the Great Awakening, and the uniting of widely variant people in the common cause of the Revolution.

Jefferson and like-minded colleagues moved explicitly for the moderation of some punishments prescribed for criminal offenders. In the spring of 1776 he introduced into the Virginia Assembly the draft of a proposed constitution. According to this draft, the death penalty would be abolished excepting only for murder and certain offenses in the military services. Torture would be absolutely forbidden. These provisions and most others of the proposal were not adopted, but they showed Jefferson's concern for humane moderation in the punishment of crimes. Later, however, he introduced in the Assembly his "Bill of Rights for Proportioning Crimes and Punishments," a compromise of which much was enacted into law.

The tolerant, generous community-mindedness of Jefferson's ideals, even though widely shared, did not resolve the American paradox. Slavery persisted even in his own Monticello. Most of his efforts to limit it and move toward general emancipation in Virginia, in the new territories, and in the United States were defeated. His more liberal efforts to moderate the punishment of criminal offenders failed. The Virginia laws, after all of his proposals were amended, prescribed such punishments as castration and other forms of mutilation and burning of hands. Witchcraft and sorcery were still to be punished, not, it is true, by hanging, but by ducking and whipping.[30]

Despite his cultivated rationality Jefferson represents the paradox of American idealism and selfish cruelty. In his case the idealism is expressed in the most memorable language, especially the great clause, "all men are created equal," which was to serve again and again as text for movements of reform. Yet he built his privileged life on a foundation of slave labor which belied his language and contrasted meanly with his protests against British violations of American rights. A free American son of a black African, Benjamin Banneker, pressed this point home in a 1791 letter to Jefferson, as he wrote, "but, sir, how pitiable is it to reflect, that although you were so fully convinced of the benevolence of the Father of Mankind and of his equal and impartial distribution of these rights and privileges which he hath conferred upon them, . . . you should at the same time be found guilty of that most criminal act, which you professedly detested in others."[31]

Meanwhile, forces quite different from the better features of the Great Awakening and the Enlightment were gaining momentum. The vicious inhumanity of slavery would undermine much of the good. Within the 19th century this and other economic forces would bring aggressive and ruthless individualism to greater dominance, release new violence, and develop new illusions of power and self-righteousness. The better influences of the Great Awakening and Jeffersonian humanism would persist in the American psyche and find frequent expression. But the opposing forces of relentless individualism would be mightily reinforced and leave to the 20th century a dark heritage nearly unmanageable in its later decades.

11

The Rush for Riches: Its Social Cost

A. The Early Race for Land and Opulence

The greatest single attraction of America to Europeans from the beginning was the vast amount of land, much of it good land, which appeared to be here for the taking. To farmers being squeezed into ever smaller acreages as population increased and to other laboring people who saw no prospect of escape from poverty in the Old World, the prospect of land ownership west of the Atlantic was a powerful magnet. Much of the promotional literature featured this prospect. The passion for land was to be a powerful factor for three centuries in determining the ideals and forms of American culture.

1. Restrained in early colonies.

In the 17th and early 18th centuries the desires and rewards for land ownership in the colonies were subject to several restraining influences. Such economic factors as poor soil and distance from markets made the ownership of land much less profitable than most immigrants had anticipated. However much land the king and his chartered proprietors might sell or otherwise assign to new immigrants, ownership was likely to be contested by the earlier inhabitants, of whom more must be said later. Both work and daily living might be hampered by lack of certain manufactured goods.

There were also some cultural restraints. The Puritans and many others brought with them class structures in which they had formerly lived. Such men as John Winthrop and later Cotton Mather tried to dissuade people of the lower classes from moving upward alongside or past people of higher class.[1] Climbing often took place nevertheless, but the old social structures were persistent and changed so slowly that there was little disruption of social stability. The most lucrative business in most of the colonies through the mid-18th century was land speculation, which was highly competitive. "At the same time, . . . Americans who plunged into that universal enterprise did not also explicitly disavow the old-fashioned values of harmony and mutual responsibility between social classes,"[2] which were the traditional obligations attached to landed estates in England.

Cotton Mather and other Puritan ministers saw what was happening and tried to restrain the growth of materialistic selfishness. Mather lamented that *"Religion* brought forth *prosperity,* and the *daughter* destroyed the mother." He went on to say, "There is danger lest the *enchantments* of the world make them forget *their errand into the wilderness."*[3] Actually, the lure of riches made the descendants forget much more than that as the old sense of noblesse oblige diminished.

The pace quickened and in 1773 an editor in Charleston, South Carolina, complained that the lives of the planters were "one continued Race: in which everyone is endeavoring to distance all behind him; and to overtake or pass by, all before him."[4] Farmers in other colonies were not making so much wealth from the soil at that time, but other means, such as land speculation and trading overseas, were similarly employed. Before the end of the 18th century the pattern of competitive, capitalistic individualism was well established. In Europe most people were settled in their own niches and unless disturbed by war or natural calamity they lived in a well-structured system of mutual responsibilities, however restricting or unfair. In America "Men and women, as in no other country, were on their own with their niches to carve."[5]

2. The rush to the West.

After the War of Independence the drive to conquer the wilderness and claim fortunes in land rose to a high pitch and continued throughout the 19th century. The race for land in the West reinforced individualism, while constantly breaking up groupings of relatives and neighborly friends. As a result "the perennial land rush so confirmed Americans in their earlier inclination toward the individualistic pursuit of material ends that they soon came to see their own society in terms of the single value—always necessary but hitherto ranked much lower—of economic progress."[6]

By 1900 what remained of social unity was principally a sense of common interest formed by converging private interests of individuals, all trying to get ahead. The degree of such convergence was, of course, constantly fluctuating. For many individuals, part or all of the time, it dissolved altogether, leaving them with no sense of loyalty to a social purpose curbing their private economic aggressions.[7]

Most of the thousands and later millions of people who moved west were seeking riches, or at least more prosperity than they had previously achieved. Yet the old spiritual sense of a national mission was deep enough in the American psyche to require that the people come to terms with it in some manner. To be sure, some did go west to establish religious communities free of persecution or incompatible influence. But even when primary economic motivation was evident it was thought necessary to give an idealistic account. Many writers and speakers obliged by picturing the westward movement "not as inspired by a calculus of rising land values and investments but (despite the orgies of speculation) as an immense exertion of the spirit."[8] The novels of J. Fenimore Cooper and the volumes of Theodore Roosevelt's *The Winning of the West* contain many examples of such idealization. President William McKinley's doctrine of "Manifest Destiny" made political capital of a slogan first popularized in 1834, to justify further national expansion.[9]

When a mantle of piety was thus cast over the pursuit of wealth in the West, it by no means served to place a restraint on individual aggressiveness. Rather it served to make the uninhibited accumulators of wealth self-righteous exemplars of "the American way."

3. The great waves of immigration.

The population of the United States in 1775 was about two and a half million. With very little immigration in the next 40 years the number of Americans had nevertheless grown to about nine million by 1815. Then came a great surge of immigrants—more than nine million between 1815 and 1875. Nearly six million came from Ireland and Germany alone.[10]

Most of these people were fleeing the terrible famine in Ireland, the economic dislocations and unfulfilled expectations produced by industrialization elsewhere, or the military conscription on the Continent. Whatever the push from behind, nearly all were attracted to the United States by the same forces which were drawing Americans to the West, the lure of space and the prospect of land and wealth. By and large they were radical individualists, in process of becoming ever more extreme in their resistance to social controls of their economic aggressiveness.

This radical stance, when taken by the more successful members of society, has come to be known in the United States as politically conservative.[11] For example, wealthy holders of oil and gas resources resist government controls of their methods and prices in the name of conservative resistance to "socialism," "communism," or "statism."

Most of the European immigrants had lived previously in structured societies with status, relationships, and responsibilities relatively stable, though recently threatened or breaking under the strains of growing industrialization. In the United States the prevailing individualism plunged them into bewilderment. Often the immigrants settled close to others from the same background and tried to reestablish the familiar network of social relationships as far as possible. But their children, attending public schools and identifying themselves as Americans, broke away from their parents' way which they found embarrassingly "old-fashioned" or "foreign." It became even easier for them than for other young Americans to fall into a radical individual irresponsibility and delinquency.[12]

B. High Rewards for Ruthless Individualism

Nowhere else on earth has individualistic economic aggressiveness with a minimum of social restraint been so handsomely rewarded for so many people as in the United States of the 19th and 20th centuries. It would be strange if a social trait so richly compensated had not become uniquely accentuated.

Many Americans among the moderately wealthy have contributed substantially to society by invention, innovative organization of industry, discovery of resources, or entertainment. Some families which became very wealthy in the 19th or early 20th century have given on a large scale to education, social research and service, religion and art. Such names come to mind as Carnegie, Ford, and Rockefeller. The founders of these fortunes won their wealth at tragic cost to numerous exploited workers, consumers, and competitors. Yet they did compensate in part by their services and gifts to society.

As the ideal of community service has continued to weaken and the idealization of individual "success" has gained, the making of great fortunes has become increasingly crass and lacking in compensating social service. The careers of recent big money-makers are characterized much less by invention or conspicuous service than by stinginess, sharp dealing, big tax breaks, special privileges from government, lucky gambles, and a single-minded interest in the accumulation of wealth. Of the 25 biggest "new wealth holders" listed in 1957, eleven were said to have made their money principally in oil. In the process they had profited enormously by the oil-depletion allowance and political deals for offshore drilling rights or exploitation of public land.[13] Most of them are unknown as benevolent contributors.

In the complicated economic and political life of the middle and late 20th century individual efforts are often combined in predatory groups. United by nothing but the commonality of their individual desires for money or power, they may develop codes of secrecy in intrigues against the public interest. If the policy of the leader is then in conflict with the public interest or even criminal law, loyalty to this "game plan" may inhibit impulses even to question or criticize, let alone withdraw.[14] The criminal conspiracies in the Nixon White House became what Shana Alexander aptly calls "the American Dream in ruins" and "a nightmare."[15]

In one notorious business conspiracy 29 manufacturers of heavy electrical equipment, including all the largest companies, participated. High executives held clandestine meetings under false names at isolated resorts and conspired to rig supposedly competitive bids and to fix prices far above fair levels. In the 1960 trial 45 officials pleaded guilty or *nolo contendere*. The criminal conspiracy involved hundreds of millions of dollars.[16]

On a much smaller scale sharp trading and shady deals take place in local communities everywhere in the country and many of the practitioners not only rise to the top of the financial scene, but are accorded places of honor in local society. What do such examples teach American youth about acceptable American ideals and conduct? The vision of brotherhood is not altogether lost, but alongside and in conflict with it is the approval of unscrupulous individual initiative to "get ahead."[17]

C. Idealization of Selfishness

All societies make room for individual acquisition of some private possessions, at least, and in many societies it is given wide opportunity for
development. However, it has usually been accompanied by recognition
that with larger means go larger responsibilities to the community and
particularly to its less fortunate members. Certainly such recognition is a
vital part of the traditional Christian, Jewish, and humanistic culture of the
American people. This pole of community responsibility has been weak-
ened in the United States and the pole of individualistic initiative strengthened by the race for riches in the 19th and 20th centuries.[18]

Usually the hard-driving competition for wealth, idealized as "the
American way," is not called by so crass a name as selfishness. But the
fact that it often is precisely that came dramatically into the open in a
speech by Senator Henry L. Dawes of Massachusetts in 1883. The debate
concerned the Cherokee Indians who had been forced to move from Appalachia to Oklahoma and appeared to be doing well there. Senator Dawes
noted that the communally organized tribe "owned tens of thousands of
horses, cattle and hogs"; and "there was not a family in that whole nation
that had not a home of its own. There was not a pauper in that nation, and
the nation did not owe a dollar. It built its own capitol, and it built schools
and hospitals." But the Senator perceived a fatal flaw. "They have got as
far as they can go, because they own their land in common. . . . *There is
no selfishness, which is at the bottom of civilization.* Till this people will
consent to give up their lands, and divide them among their citizens so that
each can own the land he cultivates, they will not make much more progress."[19] The Senate hastened to correct this sad state of affairs by dividing
the land. It also demonstrated that the white Americans practiced the
selfishness they preached by expropriating more than half the Cherokee
land and making it available to white settlers.

During World War II, in an effort to spread the burden and eliminate
war profiteering, President Franklin D. Roosevelt proposed a 100% income tax on all income of an individual above $25,000 or of a couple
above $50,000. However, many Congressmen were troubled lest the eco-
nomic system break down under an arrangement by which people of high
income would not be constantly lured by the hope of yet higher gains.
Defenders of the President's proposal said they were confident that at a
time when millions of young Americans were risking their lives without
hope of reward, businessmen would do their utmost without profits above
the levels—very high in the buying power of those days—which Roosevelt
had set. "The American way" won as Congress defeated the presidential
proposal and protected profits as usual.

D. Breaking Down Social Structures

1. Urbanization and mobility.

The rush for wealth in the 19th and 20th centuries has introduced or greatly increased a number of social trends, especially urbanization and high mobility, which have both aggravated crime and strengthened pressures for vindictive responses to it.

Statistical studies have shown that "(1) more criminals are born in urban centers, (2) more criminals live in the cities, (3) more crimes occur in the metropolitan areas, and (4) as cities become larger rates of crime tend to rise."[20]

Urbanization may be observed in many countries as an accompaniment of industrialization. But in the United States its effects have been added to other forces, already described, peculiarly present or strong in this country. Together they weaken to the breaking point the fabric of the social order.

Closely related to urbanization is the high mobility of the American population. On the average, about one-fifth of the people move to different homes in any given year. Some massive movements are especially significant. Between 1950 and 1960 there was a net emigration of 323,000 or 32.8% of all the black population from Mississippi to other states, mostly in the North and Far West. An even larger proportion of the smaller number in Arkansas moved out of that state, while all the southern states excepting Florida experienced a heavy exodus.[21]

People who move to a new social environment tend to feel less moral restraint from social pressures, more often feel alienated, and more rapidly develop unrelieved and unbearable anxieties and tensions. Whether among ghetto dwellers or middle-class suburbanites any or all of these conditions raise the rate of crime.[22]

2. Individualism weakening the family.

Strength of the family is important to the moral health of the community. It is the first and potentially the strongest line of defense of the social order. As we saw earlier, the person growing up without strong family ties is especially likely to develop attitudes of personal alienation and covert or open hostility which lead to criminal offenses and are exceedingly difficult to change.*

The weakening of the family as a social institution in America is so well known that the point need not be labored here. The high rates of divorce and desertion, the problem of schools in handling otherwise undisciplined and unguided children, and the number of young people who are

---

* Cf. discussion and references above, Chap. 2, B, 2.

choosing to live together without marriage are all signs of the embattled family.[23]

Many things have been blamed and doubtless several factors are involved. It must be recognized that the stereotyped roles of men and women (aggressive breadwinner and fighter vs. passive ornament, sex-object, and indulgent mother) which had developed in American society were misguided and destructive. Not only in the literature of women's liberation and of sociology, but also in real life, various new styles of marriage and family life are being tried.[24] Patterns must be found which will enable men and women of an advanced industrial age to develop fully and make the largest possible contributions both to their children and to the wider community. During this experimental, transitional period much disorganization is inevitable. Other factors include contraceptive pills, the population explosion, urbanization, mobility, and the lessened authority of religion relative to sexual morals. One major force, underlying and penetrating others, is the rampant individualistic hedonism of our culture. The individualistic search for pleasure tends to inhibit the socializing functions of the family, whether the parental roles be in the old patriarchal, sexually stereotyped styles or in new and genuinely egalitarian ones.

Families have taken many effective forms in human history. Especially well-known examples are the traditional larger families in many lands and the older American farm families in which everyone above infancy participated both in earning the livelihood and also in household chores. But no orderly society has long existed without a strongly communal family structure of some kind. It is this, and not merely a traditional stereotype, which is now threatened in America by excessive individualism.

In too many homes, father, mother, son, and daughter all look for their pleasures in their own individual ways in radical disregard of other members. Each one who earns money goes his or her separate way to do it and of course the children go out to their own school classes and peer groups. Many a home thus becomes little more than a place to sleep most nights and to eat most days, often at individually variant hours.

The individualism strong in America from the beginning and reinforced by the rush for riches in a geographically and industrially expanding society has thus literally come home. As it undermines and often altogether destroys the family it gains that much more force. When even the family is held together only by the uncertain ties of convergent individual interests the social order is in serious trouble.

3. Youth culture.

The continuity of order in any society depends upon close relations between successive generations. If any generation is to abide by norms of conduct necessary to peace, orderly life, and freedom within the society, it must be because such norms have been inculcated by precept and example.

Although complaints of the "generation gap" in communication occur in every age, they are especially characteristic of the present time and the complaints come both from the young and from their parents. Both verbal and enacted expressions of contempt for traditions of religion, sexual morals, property rights, education, the law, and the government understandably reached an all-time high on university campuses in the late 1960s, at the height of the Vietnam War. In the 1970s the expressions have become much less dramatic and there appears to be a somewhat wider student acceptance of norms so explosively rejected a half decade earlier. Yet there continues to an extraordinary degree a youth culture relatively separate from the adult culture. This youth culture—by no means including all youth—has its own characteristic language, music, style of dress, life goals, and attitudes toward property, all of which are frequently the despair of parents and other concerned elders.

More accurately, one must say that there are several youth cultures or subcultures in the United States which are alike in their relative discontinuity with the adult cultures of their social environments.[25]

One major cause of this discontinuity is that with the great prolongation of formal education most youth are kept from sharing with adults the responsibilities of daily work. Rather, most of their hours are spent in a social world of youth to the ages of eighteen, twenty, and beyond. Another cause is the extremely rapid pace of technological change which means that the youth have grown up in a kind of world faced by adults only after their basic attitudes have been formed. The war in Southeast Asia, eventually opposed by a great majority of the American people, drove a wedge between the generations because the young men were being compelled to fight in it while most older people remained emotionally aloof. The youth have grown up in a world gravely imperiled by a combination of overpopulation and nuclear armaments which threatens the end of civilization and possibly of the human race itself. Many young people, especially among the best educated and most humane, have come to feel nearly desperate because of most adults' continued preoccupation with individual achievement. Their parents often complain that they lack ambition.[26]

While some of the youth subculture emphasizes strongly humane and community-building goals which give promise for the future, others are of a different stripe. As Daniel Glaser says, "life in an adolescent group with deviant standards frequently instills habits and values inconsistent with the requirements for a legitimate and self-supporting adulthood."[27] When members of such a deviant adolescent group are cut off from meaningful communication with parents and other adults they are likely candidates for delinquency and crime, sometimes moving into addiction to alcohol or drugs on the way.

Unlike other social phenomena stressed in this chapter, the youth cultures usually stress group life rather than individualism. The youth cultures are often in reaction against excessive individualism and so a symptom of a fractured, individualistic society rather than a cause. Yet they exacerbate division and distrust and in some of their forms incubate much delinquency and crime.[28]

4. Destructive responses to social disorganization.

There are many current attempts to heal the alienations, divisions, and general disorganization of society. Such efforts include formation of small groups in the churches, neighborhood organizations of wide variety, various measures to equalize opportunity and to relieve poverty, and direct challenges by youth and by churches to individualistic materialism. Other responses are very different.

The high and rising rate of crime, from the ghetto to the White House, and from the poorest of the unemployed to the top executives of many great corporations, represents a breakdown of social order. The person who violates others' basic rights, bodies, or property is obviously lacking in an adequate sense of oneness in community with the injured people. Serious crime is usually a symptom of alienation. Violent crime signifies an especially high degree of alienation and often also a latent resentment and hostility breaking out into destructive expression.

A reaction to the disorganization even more popular than crime is a vindictive effort to set the forces of law against people viewed as responsible for the disorganization or as not conforming to the social order. Sensing that the ordered unity of society is breaking down, many people call on criminal law to restore it. When the disorder persists they become increasingly hostile and call for ever more severe and often for mandatory penalties to impose order by force.

It is seldom adequately appreciated that the angry calls for the death penalty or mandatory life sentence arise from motivation strikingly similar to the motivation of violent crime itself. Both represent individuals lashing out against other people who are seen as obstructing or threatening their own way of life, and both exhibit a tendency to see the other person as an impersonal thing or as an enemy, not as a fellow member of a single human community. If the angry person sees himself as alone or as a member of a group powerless to use the machinery of society for his purpose, he commits crime. If he sees himself as a member of the established order, he is more likely to call for harsh reprisals of "law and order" against the objects of his anger.

It is not strange that the very people who most loudly call for harshly enforced "law and order" often are or become criminals. They seek to use the police, the courts, and the prisons to attack the demonstrators, other nonconformists, or political opponents who annoy them. But when these efforts are frustrated by the courts or legislatures or when they want to attain other goals to which their way is blocked by law, they organize their own private "police" or gangs or economic conspiracies in attempts to circumvent the law.

The disorganization of society by division into estranged ethnic minorities has an especially important part in the high rate of crime and in the vindictive reactions to it in the United States. We now turn to this subject.

12

Race, National Origin and Violence

A. The Indians

The violence and lawlessness which so gravely infect our national life cannot be properly understood apart from the long, tragic history of relations between Americans of European origins and the American Indians.

1. Three centuries of dishonor.

It is a disgraceful irony that white Americans, who think of themselves as a peaceful and democratic people, have shown to the indigenous population such wanton violence, perfidy, impatient greed, and cruelty as belie the most rudimentary professions of civilized conduct. Helen Hunt Jackson's exposure of a part of this record in 1881, under the title *A Century of Dishonor*,[1] might well be extended to cover three centuries of dishonor. She especially indicted a persistent pattern of "cheating, robbing, breaking promises," and refusing "protection of the law to the Indians' rights of property, of life, liberty and the pursuit of happiness."[2]

At the very beginning the survival of the colonists sometimes depended on the generous hospitality of the Indians, as at Plymouth in the winter of 1620–1621. Even after the increasing numbers of the settlers, their exclusive occupation of land, and the dishonest greed of some had worn out their welcome, relations with the Indians continued to be conciliatory while the newcomers were an evident local minority. However, when the colonists were more firmly established, their occupation of land was more extensive, and their destruction of forests and game threatened the very existence of the Indians on their traditional tribal lands, the typical relationship became a kind of uneasy truce, broken by raids and massacres from both sides.

There were vigorous protests by some English settlers against the usual assumption that the British throne had a right to assign vast tracts of land to proprietors or companies without regard to prior claims by the inhabitants. Roger Williams was one of these protesters and it was one principal reason for his expulsion from Massachusetts Bay. He moved to Rhode Island where he tried to base colonial policy on fair and mutually advantageous negotiated agreements.[3] William Penn and the Quakers demonstrated that it was possible to build a large and successful colony on mutual understanding and fair compensation, with no fighting or massacres so long as the Quakers maintained control of the colonial government.

These examples stand out, however, as rare exceptions. Usually, even when the colonists went through the motions of paying for land and negotiating treaties there were radically different understandings on the two sides. Never having known such a thing as exclusive and permanent personal possession of land, the Indians often thought they were granting shared temporary rights of land use, while the colonists claimed lasting and exclusive tenure. Worse still, even after the newcomers had negotiated for specified lands and guaranteed Indian rights beyond the frontiers without any encroachment or interference, it was usually only a short time until these rights were violated as the settlers moved west.

The pattern continued. Methods gradually became more subtle, but violations of treaties, exploitation of resources on Indian lands, paternalism, and unequal treatment continue even in the 1970s.

2. Denial of human rights.

The most extreme denial of human rights has been practiced by white colonials and later governments against the Indians. From 1641 the Dutch settlers offered and paid bounties for the scalps of Indians; later the Puritans did so. "The last American scalp bounty was offered by the Territory of Indiana in 1814." No need to plead self-defense for homicide there! No discrimination between hostile or dangerous individuals and unarmed, friendly, even sleeping ones. No horror of the barbaric practice of scalping. Any scalp would be paid for by the Territory of Indiana so long as it came from an Indian head. This, it was stated, was for "encouragement to the enterprise and bravery of our fellow citizens."[4]

Occasional expressions of respect for Indian character and achievements appear in all periods of white American life. Felix S. Cohen claims that Benjamin Franklin and Thomas Jefferson learned some of their own ideas of government from Indians like the Iroquois Canasatego, but this is doubtful.[5] Jefferson condemned the enslavement of Indians and defended them against charges of inherent inferiority.[6] Yet he supported the policy of driving them west in front of the settlers' advance.[7] Thomas Paine, with all his passion for freedom, was indifferent to the rights of Indians.[8] J. Fenimore Cooper has good Indians and bad Indians in his tradition-making novels, but the good Indians are the ones who helped the whites as they took the country.

It seemed acceptable to ride roughshod over Indian rights and even to slaughter them wantonly because they were widely viewed as subhuman or at least so evil as to have no human rights. In my Nebraska boyhood I often heard the old western saying, though usually with limiting conditions, that "the only good Indian is a dead Indian." Theodore Roosevelt's published comment on that murderous insult is horribly revealing. Said he: "I don't go so far as to think that the only good Indians are dead Indians, but I believe nine out of ten are, and I shouldn't inquire too closely into the case of the tenth. The most vicious cowboy has more moral principle than the average Indian."[9] With such ideas abroad in high places it is small wonder that even while Roosevelt was writing, in 1890, the United States Army "massacred ninety-eight disarmed warriors and two hundred Indian women and children" in the Sioux Reservation of South Dakota and this disgrace went into American military annals as "the Battle of Wounded Knee,"[10] poignantly echoed in the 1973 Indian occupation of the village bearing this name.

3. Legends of lawless American violence.

Fights between white settlers and neighboring Indians became legendary. Until the middle of the 20th century it was seldom pointed out that after the early colonial years, while the Indians might win local skirmishes, in the larger context they were so heavily outnumbered and facing so much heavier firepower that early disaster was everywhere a foregone conclusion. We must not detract from the courage of white individuals and groups in particular episodes. But the popular tradition of heroic cowboys and treacherous but inferior Indians should be seen as a grotesque distortion of the long struggles of the native Americans to defend their homelands.[11]

One of the most shameful episodes occurred after the federal government settled with the Cherokees a long series of quarrels and fights by the treaty of 1785. The Cherokees, under its provisions, relinquished all rights in the large settled areas, but in turn were guaranteed security against any encroachment on other prescribed territories to the west. They settled down there, took to farming with skill and industry, and generally maintained friendly relations with their nearest white neighbors. Indeed, according to the 1825 census, 147 white men were married to Cherokee women and 73 white women were married to Cherokee men. They even adopted a government and a system of schools patterned after those of the United States.[12]

In his painstaking study of Cherokee law John Phillip Reid writes, "The Cherokees' triumph was that they turned to American common law, converted it to their own use, and made it work. Their tragedy was that not all men shared their respect for the rule of law."[13] Unlike the Cherokees, large numbers of the white frontiersmen, including President Andrew Jackson, had more respect for their own interests and violent power than for constitutional law. In direct and declared defiance of the United States Supreme Court they forced the Cherokees out of the ancestral lands they had still retained.

Wilbur R. Jacobs concludes that "harsh living conditions, contact with Indians both in peace and war, and remoteness from central authority, all influenced the emergence of a tough new American breed among the white settlers."[14]

The toughness of this new national character included readiness for quick resort to force, especially gunfire, an inclination of citizens to take the law into their own hands, and an idealization of vindictive response to wrongs, fancied or real. This tradition would be expressed later both in a high rate of violent crime unique among developed nations and in an exceptionally harsh treatment of convicted offenders.

B. The Blacks

1. Slavery.

The slave trade, the institution of slavery, and the whole aftermath of Reconstruction, with the subsequent resubjection of black people and continued racism, have done much in hardening American character, and establishing barriers of alienation among us. This tragic history of black-white relations has consequently contributed heavily to violent crime and irrational, vindictive responses to it.

The North, especially New England, and the South, alike, were deeply involved in the inhuman slave trade. Corrupting tribal chiefs in Africa to sell their more unpopular or feared subjects or prisoners of war, and packing the masses of men, women, and children in the holds of their ships, with no sanitary facilities, with minimal and often unclean food and water, the traders seem to have limited their cruelty only by their desire not to have so many slaves die in passage as to reduce their net profits.

Once in America, the survivors of the terrible ocean passage were sold, with much deliberate separating of families as well as of tribal compatriots the better to divide and control, and much other separation merely incidental to profit-seeking.[15] By 1860 there were over four million slaves in the United States, about one out of seven persons in the total population.[16] In the South slave labor was so profitable that even after the legal importation of people to be sold as slaves was abolished, a lively smuggling traffic continued at St. Augustine and elsewhere right down to the Civil War.

While slaveholders differed greatly in their treatment of slaves, the whole institution itself was so extreme a violation of elemental human rights as to go beyond any rational defense in modern times. It seems strange that it could have been practiced by people who made any profession of Christian faith, with its doctrines of the universal fatherhood of God, the Golden Rule of conduct, and the call to lovingkindness. Yet, excepting a few isolated individuals, there appears to have been no protest among white colonists until 1688, when four Germantown Quakers presented the first American group resolution against slavery to the Monthly Meeting in Dublin. The document was sent on to the Yearly Meeting where no action was taken. Not until 70 years later, in 1758, did a larger group go on record. Then the Philadelphia Yearly Meeting opposed both slave trading and slaveholding by Quakers.[17]

The Anglican bishop and philosopher George Berkeley lived in the American colonies for three years and in 1731 said in a sermon that the slaveholders in America had "an irrational contempt of the blacks, as creatures of another species, who had no right to be instructed or admitted to the sacraments."[18] In some states the denial of induction into civilization and the Christian life went further. "It became a crime to teach these men and women to read and write; it became a crime to give them a Bible."[19] Fathers were taken away from their wives and children. Slaveholders compelled men and women of their selection to live together for highly profitable breeding purposes. "Vice, immorality and brutality were institutionalized. The sanctity of the family was violated; children were sold from mothers and fatherhood, in effect, was outlawed. The rape of a slave woman, a Mississippi court ruled, is an offense unknown to common or civil law. The 'father of a slave,' ruled a Kentucky court, 'is unknown to our law.' "[20]

If it was really so bad, then, it is sometimes asked, why were there no revolts? There *were* revolts! The fear of uprisings among the slaves was a constant dread in innumerable farmhouses and with good reason. Herbert Aptheker has collected accounts of 250 slave revolts in the area of the continental United States.[21] The fear became acute after the fiery and bloody revolt of the slaves in Haiti in 1791, with the battles there leading finally to independence in 1804.

A revolt involving several thousand slaves was organized by Gabriel Prosser in Virginia, but on the very day, August 30, 1800, was betrayed by two informers. The governor called out the militia and after a short delay caused by a sudden downpour and disastrous flood the state moved in for the arrest and hanging of the leaders. A second large revolt under the leadership of a prosperous freedman, Denmark Vesey, was similarly betrayed and crushed in 1821. The fierce and deadly, though short-lived reign of terror imposed by Nat Turner and his 70 followers on Southampton County, Virginia, in August 1831 is history and legend. Bennett says "at least fifty-seven whites" died in 24 hours, before the militia put down the insurrection.[22] He tells also of the terror which spread to plantations and farmhouses near and far as slaves were killed in panic on the slightest suspicion.

Less dramatic but more effective in liberating slaves and arousing antislavery sentiment and action in the North was the "Underground Railroad." Brave black and white guides led countless thousands north, past the terrible police arm of the Dred Scott Decision, to Canada and the fugitives told their stories to ever larger circles of sympathizers. As the full horror of slavery dawned on minds not closed by a lifetime of indoctrination, sentiment for abolition grew.

But in this nation of violence, despite many political approaches to the issue, it was only by the most deadly war of American history that the violence of slavery itself was ended. Even after that the legacy of violence continued to bedevil race relations and the annals of crime for a century. How much longer?

2. Reconstruction.

After the Civil War and the passage of Amendments XIV and XV, the former slaves voted while all southern whites who had actively participated on the side of the Confederacy were excluded from the polls. Federal troops kept watch. In many places the former slaves were in the majority. Even so, most of the higher offices continued to be in white hands. Many men from the North, some conscientiously supporting the rights of black people and others in quest of personal political preferment and power, went south and worked with the former slaves to control local governments and a number of state legislatures. The common traditional picture of "Carpetbagger government" as a wild orgy of corruption, squandered funds, and mismanagement was much overdone. The southern whites were outraged by the necessity of living under mayors and councils who had recently been their slaves, and under legislatures influenced or even dominated by them. Northern friends of the black people who were their political allies were hated as "nigger lovers." Hence the history of Reconstruction as written by southern whites has been deeply affected by hostility.[23]

However that may be, most southern whites regarded the situation as intolerable and were determined to put an end to it. "By 1871 the invisible empires of the Ku Klux Klan had a membership of over half million, and a Congressional investigation that year uncovered hangings, whippings, shootings and mutilations in the thousands. In Louisiana alone, two thousand persons had been killed, wounded or injured in a few short weeks before the election of 1868."[24]

The supposed justification of lynching was the protection of white women from black rapists. Actually, a 1942 study discovered that of 3,811 blacks lynched between 1889 and 1941, less than 17% were even accused of rape or attempted rape. The actual accusations were mostly for attempts to vote, labor union activities, and the like.[25]

After President Rutherford B. Hayes withdrew the federal troops in 1887 and the long concealed racism in the North blocked any further protection of the blacks by the federal government, white violence in the South had a field day. The Ku Klux Klan and other vigilante groups throughout the former Confederacy tortured, lynched, and terrorized the black people in a long regime of violent repression. Combining economic forces with brutality, the whites drove most blacks out of political activity. State constitutional amendments, despite the federal Amendment XV, "legally" deprived nearly all blacks of the franchise by hard literacy tests from which whites were exempted if they, their fathers, or their grandfathers had voted before 1861.[26] The *Plessy v. Ferguson* decision of the Supreme Court in 1896, approving "separate but equal" facilities for the races, completed the general reassignment of black people to a lower caste status, for the equality formally presupposed was not taken seriously.[27]

3. Persistent race prejudice.

Race prejudice in all sections of the United States deeply affects the incidence of crime and also the measures of crime control.

Hans von Hentig in his classic work of 1948, *The Criminal and His Victim*, says, "Racial minorities do not receive the same protection of the law as is given to the dominating class."[28] This continues to be a problem in the 1970s. It is widely publicized that ghetto blacks often complain of police brutality and harassment. But in the 1960s the blacks in Harlem and south central Los Angeles mentioned "inadequate protection more often than brutality or harassment as a reason for their resentment toward the police."[29] A study of police records showed that in Cleveland it took "almost four times as long to respond to calls concerning robbery from the Negro district as for the district where response was next slowest."[30]

In the efforts to solve reported crimes, in the treatment of suspects, and in the punishment of convicted persons there is also much racial bias, in the North as well as in the South. In 1972 Wolfgang, Figlio, and Sellin reported their observation that Philadelphia boys committing offenses were sometimes given "remedial disposition" and not taken to juvenile court. Other boys were put through the full process of formal criminal justice. What were the principal factors enabling the observer to predict which process the police would use in a given case? Was it the seriousness of the offense? A record of repeated offenses? Low socioeconomic level? No. The study showed that "the most significant factor related to a boy's not being 'remedialed' by the police, but being processed to the full extent of the juvenile system, was his being nonwhite."[31]

Many state prisons housing large black populations from urban ghettos are located far out in the country and manned almost or altogether exclusively by rural white officers. Given the history of black people and the personal experiences of many convicted individuals, the living under absolute control of white prison staff beyond reach of frequent visits by family and friends is bound to create a highly alienated and defensive mood. Add various coarse, sometimes lawless and cruel actions by the officers against the inmates, such as occur in every large prison, especially between white staff and black inmates, and we have a condition of racial tension often rising to an explosive level. So it was that the stage was set for the tragedy at Attica in 1971.

The average family income of black people in the United States is little more than half that of white people, while black unemployment is much higher.[32] There are many factors involved, including inferior education, lack of personal and family contacts with employers, an air of hopeless resignation in some families, and, especially among the young males, a deep hostility toward the business and institutional life of a white-dominated society. It is not easy to overcome such forces, but that is the task which the white people of the United States have brought on themselves by the centuries of abuse, exploitation, indignity, and neglect which they have heaped upon their black neighbors. At present we are making various compensatory efforts in education, employment in some corporations and institutions, and various special funds for the seeding of economic improvement. Yet at the same time we continue to perpetuate the problems by various patterns of prejudice, especially segregated housing.

The whole experience of dominating black people, using them, pushing them aside, and assuming superiority over them has expressed and increased white Americans' tradition of aggressive, hardhearted ruthlessness. At the same time it has had an even more intense effect on black people because it has been concentrated on their much smaller numbers and they have had to live with it as a force affecting every aspect of life, social, economic, political, religious, and residential.

Like every social influence, these forces have elicited a wide variety of responses from different individuals. Some have developed self-abasement into a fine art in order to please the dominant whites. Others have taken such jobs as they could get, however far below their potentials, accepted segregated housing, and gone about their own living as best they could. A few have made personal efforts of heroic dimensions, and investing superior talents, won places of affluence and considerable power. Many others have sullenly accepted residence in the ghetto, poor jobs or unemployment, and lived off welfare funds with such supplements as charity of friends or community might provide. Large numbers, especially among the young, live in chronic rebellion against the whole society which has so unjustly treated their ancestors and now confines their own families in scarcely habitable ghettos. There they feed on their angry resentment. Some of them feel that they have a right to "get theirs" in any way they can. Sensing no stake of their own in the present social order, they feel no obligation to abide by its rules or to respect its institutions and property.[33]

By such social and psychological processes many blacks have come to mirror the most ruthlessly aggressive traits in the whites who have been most exploitative. If they were on the inside of big business they would probably do what some white insiders do: pad expense accounts, engage in dishonest advertising and selling practices, cheat on their income taxes, and perhaps engage in embezzlement. None of these practices, even if exposed and punished, would put them into the FBI statistics of Index crimes. Since they are actually on the outside, they engage in purse snatching, burglary or robbery, all noted with alarm in the FBI reports.

Basing their judgment on exact statistical analysis of public records, Wolfgang, Figlio, and Sellin found that among Philadelphia youth, "nonwhites in their seventeenth year inflict more social harm, through delinquency, on the community than do whites from age 7 to age 18."[34] Most kinds of unprincipled and financially profitable behavior open to the black person on the outside of our business institutions can be carried out as effectively by a sixteen-year-old boy as by an adult—probably with less risk. Hence *his* form of antisocial behavior is likely to begin early. On the other hand, the white-collar crime of white exploiters can achieve its desired results only after they have gained positions of power and trust.

Which kind of misconduct does more harm to the whole social order? To answer we should need to weigh the atmosphere of fear and hostility which hangs like a pall over our inner cities against the general distrust of government, resentment against the oil companies and others, enormous waste of resources, and loss of confidence in the future of America which poison our national life.

We do not need to answer the comparative question to see the monstrous price in crime, violence, and repression which we are paying for the long, chronic aggression against the black people of America.

C. Nativism and the Immigrants

All Americans, of course, are immigrants or the descendants of immigrants, excepting only American Indians. But after the Anglo-Saxons established clear dominance they determined who would be welcome and who would not. At first, much as the blacks were welcomed as slaves, most immigrants, including the great influx of refugees from the Irish famine in the mid-19th century, were welcomed as additions to the supply of labor. For the most part this positive attitude prevailed until after the Civil War.

Then, while employers continued to encourage immigration, the labor unions began to resist it because of the added competition for jobs. As the numbers of Irish and Germans, and later the great influx from southern and eastern Europe, thronged the ports of entry, circles of opposition spread to the middle and upper classes.

In the last decades of the 19th century there was much American praise of the vigorous Anglo-Saxon or Teutonic blood of the older American strains, with their devotion to the strenuous, self-reliant life. Protestant religion was often corrupted into an identification with this combination of racist pretensions and individualistic aggressiveness. Thus Madison Grant's book, *The Passing of the Great Race* (1916), praised and recommended by *The Boston Transcript* and even, with reservations, by *The Nation* and the *Annals of the American Academy of Political and Social Science*, lauded the Nordic race and warned of the danger that it would be inundated and lost in America. He described the Nordics in very ambiguous and flexible terms as to physique. But in personal characteristics they were heroic fighters, self-reliant, aggressive, and eminently fit to rule. The book was enormously popular and was followed by others, riding the tide of nativism.[35]

The Know-Nothing movement of the 1840s and 1850s deeply entangled racist themes with anti-Catholicism. This combination—always latent —came to the surface in a great surge of hostility to all who were not "WASP" (white Anglo-Saxon Protestant) in the 1920s and 1930s. The Ku Klux Klan was reorganized and grew to considerable size before some of its leaders were convicted of misappropriating funds and liberal opposition to all that it represented brought about its reduction to relative impotence. However, this was not before the Klan and the whole anti-immigration movement had mightily reinforced the self-righteous, vindictive, and even violently aggressive strain in American tradition.[36]

This time there was an eventual positive gain. In the 1930s and the following decades a loose coalition of Jews, Roman Catholics, blacks, leaders of other minority groups, and broad-minded Protestants fought back with massive propaganda for true "American brotherhood." The frightful Nazi racism and its deadly fruits added to popular revulsion of feeling against racism. The election of John F. Kennedy, an Irish Catholic, as President, in 1960, was made possible by this broad movement away from bigotry. Yet the atmosphere of bitter hostility in Texas at the time of his assassination and the intense hatreds which provided the backgrounds, at least, for the assassinations of Martin Luther King, Jr., and Robert F. Kennedy showed how fanatically strong were the continuing bigotry and racism in some segments of the population. The violence of these assassinations greatly reinforced the violent trends in the urban black communities and among many disillusioned white youth, which had been held in check by the nonviolent civil rights movement. With new disorder and talk of violence from these quarters came new repressive violence from the police—in the "police riot" at the Chicago Democratic Convention in 1968 and the subsequent decimation of the Black Panther leadership by police gunfire. So the cycle of violence has continued.

D. The Tradition of Violence

Karl Menninger asserts that all of us are instinctively violent, destructive, and criminal at heart and that this is the reason we are so intrigued by stories, pictures, and the realities of violence.[37] On the other hand, Marvin E. Wolfgang says, "Man is not innately criminal, violent, or aggressive. He responds to people, events or other kinds of stimuli that precipitate violative, violent or aggressive behavior."[38] Both would agree that violence is widespread throughout the world. Wolfgang insists that it is not uniquely American and cites the aftermath of the French Revolution, the horrors of Nazism, and the high incidence of individual and group violence in several Latin American and Asian countries as examples.[39]

Richard Hofstadter acknowledges such violence in other lands and points out that apart from the Civil War we have no such wholesale massacres in our history as attended and followed St. Bartholomew's Day of 1572 in France or the slaughter of Communists and their sympathizers in Indonesia in 1965–1966.[40]

Yet there are two characteristics of violence in the United States which are unique among developed nations. Hofstadter points out that especially "impressive to one who begins to learn about American violence" are "its extraordinary frequency, its sheer commonplaceness in our history, its persistence into very recent and contemporary times, and its rather abrupt contrast with our pretensions to singular national virtue."[41] We must add that among the educationally and economically developed nations it is also unique in its institutionalized and idealized character.

The large scale perpetuation of slavery into the last half of the 19th century could not have been maintained without the acceptance of widespread personal violence among respected people in the community and before the law. Violence of white people toward black people continued to be widely practiced with impunity in the deep South even into the 1960s. Many neighborhoods and communities of the North proved to be no less violence-prone when large numbers of blacks migrated into them. In short, violence of white people against black people has been a traditional American institution for over three centuries and has been breaking up only in the last two decades.

Little less traditional is the violence attending disputes of industry with organized labor and between rival labor unions. In the record are the riots and murders attending the deadly railroad strike of 1877; the drawn battles of strikers, strikebreakers, company guards, and troops in the mining country of Idaho in the 1890s; the bloody steel strike of 1919; the violent confrontations met by efforts to organize tenant farmers in the 1930s and later; the many attacks on the United Farm Workers of America organized by Cesar E. Chavez in California, in the 1970s; the murder of three Yablonskis (discovered January 5, 1970) after Joseph A. Yablonski dared to challenge the political machine of Tony Boyle for leadership of the United Mine Workers in 1969; and the deadly attacks on truck drivers during the work stoppage of independent truckers in 1974. The list could be extended indefinitely, especially if we included stone throwings, slashed tires, arson and threats of arson.

A broader survey of violent episodes with wide support in the "respectable" community would include accounts of Bacon's Rebellion (1676), the tortures of Loyalists before the American Revolution, battles on the Underground Railroad, especially in Pennsylvania, as slave owners tried to recapture fugitives with the aid of northern marshals, the Know-Nothing political riots against the Irish and other immigrants, especially in Baltimore (1854–1860), and many more examples.[42]

American violence has been further institutionalized by movies which have placed images of gun-fighting cowboys and Indians and cops and robbers among our most popularly known exports abroad.[43]

When so much of bloodshed among our people has been accepted, institutionalized, and even glorified, is it any wonder that crime often takes such violent forms or that the processes of criminal justice among us are more often harsh and destructive than among other nations of comparable development?

13

Minority Religions

Although on the whole the dominant religious influence in the formation of American culture has been Protestant, especially from churches of Puritan tradition, several minority religions also have exercised important influence. From the early colonial years Roman Catholicism has played a prominent role in American life. The Friends have exerted influence, particularly on criminal justice, far out of proportion to the small Quaker population, from the time of their first appearance in New England in 1656. Jewish immigrants were few in the colonial period. However, the influence of Hebrew tradition on common law came with the earliest English settlers and as Jewish people entered the country rabbinical teachings and the views of Jewish lawyers, judges, and scholars made important contributions to American criminal justice.

A. Roman Catholic Ambivalence

Catholics, like Puritans, have pushed American legal tradition in opposite directions—toward wider tolerance and toward the legalizing of intolerance, toward moderation of legal severity and toward harsher penalties.

1. Widened tolerance and legal intolerance.

After several earlier vain efforts to found permanent colonies in coastal lands of the present United States, Spanish Catholics under Pedro Menéndez de Avilés established a fort, church, and settlement at St. Augustine, Florida, in 1565. When French Protestants (Huguenots) settled 35 miles to the north the Catholics massacred them.

It is well known that Lord Baltimore, founder and first proprietor of Maryland, sought to establish that colony as a refuge for his fellow Catholics. Probably for prudential motives, but nevertheless to his credit, he enacted the principle of toleration, so that Protestants were welcome and were, in fact, numerous from the beginning. Yet the toleration included no adherents of non-Christian religions.

The "Act concerning Religion," passed in 1649 and commonly known as "The Maryland Toleration Act," specifies that any person who denies the doctrine of the holy Trinity or denies that Jesus is the son of God "shall be punished with death and confiscation or forfeiture of all his or her lands and goods. . . ."[1] Also, any person who utters "any reproachful words or speeches concerning the blessed Virgin Mary the Mother of our Savior" is to be fined "five pound Sterling" for first offense. The penalty is doubled for second offense and for the third the culprit is to forfeit all property and be permanently banished.[2]

The toleration of any form of religion other than Roman Catholic ran counter to the old and dominant tradition of the Church. As the acceptance of religious pluralism was defined in the United States, this became the subject of much controversy in the Vatican. In the late 19th century efforts were being made in France and elsewhere in Europe to gain Catholic acceptance of the American principle of separation of church and state.

Pope Leo XIII responded by denouncing "modernism" and "Americanism." To many Catholics, as to earlier Puritans, religious tolerance looked like an expression of doubt about one's own professed faith or at least indifference about its importance. While the Vatican was willing to accept religious toleration and even separation of church and state as prudent compromises where Catholicism was in the minority or held a small enough majority to make establishment and banning of "heretical" movements impractical, it still plainly held that only "truth" and not "error" had the right to civil protection.

2. Moderation and vindictive severity.

Roman Catholicism has been less perfectionistic than Puritanism in its expectations of human conduct outside the monastic orders. Hence, regarding many practices, especially gambling and the use of beverage alcohol, most Catholics have opposed criminal sanctions. On the other hand, in the 1960s and 1970s Catholic officialdom led the effort to maintain the prohibition of contraceptive information and devices by criminal law, and later to prohibit abortion, even in earliest pregnancy, as "murder."

As for the penalties in the criminal justice system, Catholic influence has generally come down in favor of retribution as primary meaning and purpose of justice, hence in favor of the death penalty for murder and severe sentences for other crimes.[3] In taking these stands Catholics have often spoken of the severe divine retribution after death, emphasized by their Church, as a model for human justice. On the other hand, many Catholic chaplains have ministered to prison populations with sensitive understanding and humanity, and many nuns identify impressively with the alienated poor.

B. Paradoxes of Quaker Influence

The great and rapid success of Penn's colony made it especially conspicuous among the British colonies. So far as his charter permitted, Penn made the laws of Pennsylvania "a code of Quaker principles applied to actual government."[4] Largely as a result of this example the Friends became "the most potent religious movement in the colonies outside Puritan New England."[5]

1. Stress on love and forgiveness.

The respectful and honorable dealings of the Pennsylvania Friends with the Indian inhabitants of the area are in sharp contrast with the haughty, treacherous ruthlessness which other colonies displayed toward their indigenous neighbors. The "Great Treaty" which Penn made with the Indians in 1683 was described by Voltaire as "the only treaty not sworn to and never broken." When there were disputes between colonists and Indians they were resolved by juries representing both groups. There were no hostilities until policies were changed after Penn's death.

There was complete religious freedom, although only Christians meeting certain property qualifications had the vote. In penal policy the death penalty was restricted to murder and treason. The other colonies maintained long lists of capital offenses.

The humane policies of early Pennsylvania and the Quaker leadership in renouncing slavery are sufficient to gain for the Friends recognition as far in the vanguard of humane tolerance and enlightened social policy. The noble intentions of the Friends have been sustained at a high level. Unfortunately, intentions and consequences are not always in harmony.

2. Perfectionism and reforms gone astray.

The Friends represent a radical form of Puritanism. They are second to none in their exacting ethical demands. Since they brought to America less confidence in the character-producing power of law and more confidence in the power of love than the Puritans themselves held, the Quakers did not produce such excesses of zeal in enforcing conformity. Yet they did contribute to the expectation that Americans would be better than other people and their governments would merit special divine favor. When lovingkindness faltered, this moral perfectionism would contribute to unfortunate results in the form of self-righteousness and national pride.

About 1790 the Friends espoused the holding of convicted serious offenders in solitary confinement, without labor. The first institution built and operated under this policy was Eastern Penitentiary, opened at Cherry Hill, near Philadelphia, in 1829. The theory was that a prisoner kept in solitude would not be subjected to the degrading influence of other prisoners. With distractions limited to eating the meals brought to him and receiving occasional moral instruction or medical attention he would be left to meditate on his sins and, it was hoped, repent.[6] At the time this seemed to many people a big humanitarian reform, in view of the contemporary floggings, torture, and capital punishment. More advanced proposals had been made by Beccaria and Bentham, it was true, but the Quaker proposal of the penitentiary was actually adopted in Pennsylvania and soon in many places throughout the world.[7]

The penitentiary movement brought results not anticipated by its advocates. One result was to establish imprisonment for specified terms as the usual method of dealing with persons convicted of crimes in wide variety. Nowhere had this method prevailed until adopted in the United States. But once the example was set it was attractive. When a person became a social problem the easiest course other than capital punishment was to shut him away out of sight. Let him sit alone with his sins until by silent meditation and perhaps prayer he was reformed. The church, neighbors, and local government could thus disclaim further responsibility for him. Since the death penalty had become unacceptable for most offenses, the penitentiary seemed the simplest way for ridding the community of crime. Soon the first penitentiaries were overcrowded, more were constructed, and the whole prison system grew far beyond expectations.

A second result was that enforced solitude, when long continued, more often resulted in madness than in reformation.[8] The advocates of penitentiaries had failed to appreciate how profoundly social a human being is by nature. Without significant social relations an individual is unlikely to be transformed in character for the better. When it is understood that moral character consists of habitual attitudes and actions toward other persons, it is strange that anyone should suppose it would be likely to develop in solitary confinement. Any human being finds it difficult even to maintain sanity through extended isolation from all human relations. Persons whose emotional life is already poorly integrated find it especially difficult.

In the 20th century the Friends, like many other humanitarians concerned about the cruelty and ineffectiveness of the correctional system, have supported the therapeutic model. Instead of punishment, rehabilitative treatment should be employed. As soon as an offender seems to be rehabilitated, let him be released. People who are sick are released from the hospital when well or when sufficiently recovered to continue convalescence at home. Similarly, the therapeutic approach to corrections indicated that terms of incarceration should be indefinite, the time of release depending on the pace of therapeutic rehabilitation.

The Friends have recently taken the lead among prison reformers in recognizing and exposing abuses which have resulted from the therapeutic approach. A special committee studying the matter for the American Friends Service Committee found that in ten years after California adopted the rehabilitative ideal and indeterminate sentencing "the median time served has risen from twenty-four to thirty-six months, *the longest in the country.*"[9] Moreover, it was found that the prisoners themselves hated this approach and for a reason which the Committee thought sound, namely that the coercive treatment denied the prisoner's autonomy and personhood.[10]

In the conflict between vengeful cruelty and more humane dealings with criminal offenders Friends have nearly always been on the side of humanity, at least in intent. On the other hand, on the issues of individualism versus social understandings of responsibility and of corrections they have been deeply divided and remain so. For example, in the thought-provoking and highly useful report which has just been cited, the special committee of Friends vigorously attack the therapeutic model of corrections, because it is based on theories which "share a more or less deterministic premise, holding that man's behavior is caused by social or psychological forces located outside his consciousness and therefore beyond his control."[11] Later, objecting again to rehabilitative treatment in corrections, they say, "In fact, the whole deterministic view of man that underpins these strategies contradicts the values of free choice, individual autonomy, and self-determination that we embrace."[12] Here there appears to be a wholly individualistic sense of responsibility. On the other hand, in the same report, there is much evidence of deep and active concern about social institutions because of their influence on people.

In much ameliorated form the old Puritan paradoxes are present in the Quaker community.

C. Judaism

Jews in considerable numbers were late in coming to this country. We are told that two Jews, and perhaps more, were on the ships of Columbus in 1492. Some Jews invested in the Dutch trading companies and a few came to New Amsterdam to live in or soon after 1654. Before 1700 a congregation had organized there. By 1776 there were communities in at least a half dozen American cities, including 30 families in New York and 500 Jews in Charleston. Ahlstrom says that in 1800 the total number in the United States "probably did not exceed two or three thousand."[13] Nearly all of them were Sephardim, that is, Jews of Spanish or Portuguese ancestry.

In the 19th century, encouraged by the superior freedom and economic opportunity offered in the United States, large numbers came from Germany and elsewhere in northern Europe, so that there are estimated to have been 250,000 Jews in this country by 1880. Even larger numbers have come from eastern Europe in the past century. The total Jewish population in the United States is now about six million, a number greater than can be found in any other country and nearly half of all in the world.

The Jewish influence on American law, however, has been far more than proportionate to population. Some reasons for this will become evident as we examine the kinds of influence exerted. But others can be mentioned at this point. They would include (1) the emphasis on law in Jewish tradition, (2) the resultant disproportionate numbers of Jewish lawyers, and (3) the extraordinary stress on education and lifelong continued learning in Judaism, which is at least partly responsible for bringing many Jewish lawyers into positions of power in the judicial system and in the law schools.

1. *Ancient retributionism.*

Important as has been the influence of American Jews upon the law and particularly the system of criminal justice, probably the influence of ancient Israel has been even greater. Especially was this true in the colonial period. As we have observed, the Puritans used the retaliatory laws of the Pentateuch literally to form the basis of early American criminal justice. We have never recovered from that harsh beginning.

The principle of the oral Torah prevented the Jewish people from thus freezing the severe penal standards of the ancient desert. The Mishnah and later writings of the Jewish scholars present a much more moderate and humane spirit.

Christianity, to be sure, holds a similar doctrine, the belief in the revealing power of the ever-present Holy Spirit. Unfortunately, the Puritan immigrants had made the printed page of Scripture their sword and shield in battling against both the papacy and their political persecutors and in doing so had crystallized a rigid biblicism. While they had found in the Bible grounds both for vindictive legalism and a community of lovingkindness, they lacked means of moving beyond the paradox. That remained for later biblical and theological scholars and the task is still incomplete, among some Christians, despite Jesus' own explicit repudiation of the *lex talionis* (Matt. 5:38–39).

In Judaism, too, the idea of retributive punishment, though moderated and sometimes abrogated among the scholars, is tenaciously held among many of the relatively unlearned and the written Torah can always be quoted in its support.

2. *Liberal contributions of Jewish jurists and legal scholars.*

Jewish contributions to the humanizing of American life and particularly criminal justice have been important. Several Jewish lawyers have served well as Associate Justices of the United States Supreme Court as well as in other capacities. As we mention Justices Louis D. Brandeis, Benjamin N. Cardozo, Abe Fortas, Felix Frankfurter, and Arthur Goldberg, we notice at once that they have differed greatly. Yet all have had in common a remarkable breadth of concern for equitable treatment of all people, and especially protection of the relatively weak against abuses by the strong.

We must admire the massive scholarship of the distinguished contemporary writer on the philosophy of criminal law, Julius Stone. Although a professor in Australia, he is also at home and has received signal honors in the United Kingdom and the United States. His broad humanitarian interest and detailed linking of law with the social sciences are especially noteworthy. Among the Jewish scholars and law professors we are bound to think also of the historian of American law Lawrence M. Friedman, of the legal philosopher W. Friedmann, and of Milton R. Konvitz who has done much to relate explicitly the traditions of Judaism to contemporary American problems. Others who come to mind include Morris and Felix Cohen, Paul Freund, Edmund Cahn, Jerome Frank, and that remarkable husband-wife team Sheldon and Eleanor Glueck. Many more should be mentioned, but just now we cannot omit Samuel Dash. He is principally known to the public as Chief Counsel and Staff Director of the United States Senate "Watergate Committee." Apart from this he is the distinguished Director of the Georgetown University Institute of Criminal Law and Procedure. To these tasks he brought extensive experience as prosecutor and as defense counsel. His teaching and writing show a special concern for protecting common citizens against mistreatment by the powerful devices of government.

The broad concerns for the whole community and especially for its weaker members, which characterize all these persons, are not accidentally related to their Jewish heritage. These relationships will become evident as we seek an emerging ethical consensus in Chapter 16.

An exhaustive treatment of our subject would, of course, include many additional minority religious groups, such as the Mormons, Pentecostals, Christian Scientists, Bahaists and others. However, for various reasons such as smaller numbers, late development in this country, or relative separation from public life, none has influenced criminal law to a degree comparable to those discussed and none has provided a comparable ethical input into the formation of the American conscience as it affects common ideals of criminal justice.

14

Time and Space in American Culture

"It is not too much to say that in America space has played the part that time has played in the older cultures of the world."[1] This is an important thesis of Sidney E. Mead in his interpretation of certain peculiar characteristics of religion and culture in the United States.

A. European Use of Time

Any American who lives and works in a European country, even for a short time, is likely to be impressed with the patience of the people. He may even be annoyed with their seemingly easygoing ways. The differences among actively campaigning political parties in some European countries, especially France and Italy, are very much greater than any observable in most parts of the United States. Yet the people endure the extreme attacks on their accustomed ways of life, believing that *in time* matters will be straightened out.

In England, especially, the quiet good-natured waiting of turns in any of many long queues encountered in an ordinary day is a wonder to American visitors. More marvelous is the rational coolness with which most English people accept more serious disruptions of life, whether from wartime bombing of their cities or from an energy shortage suddenly aggravated, in early 1974, by an oil embargo and then raised to critical proportions by a coal miners' strike. The people generally expect that somehow they will "muddle through" *in time.* Time is a commodity of which there appears usually to be an adequate quantity.

That this characteristic European belief in time as resource for resolving tensions and solving problems is particularly strong in England is significant for American history. Most early American immigrants were English and might have been expected to bring this belief in time with them. But the new environment quickly changed their attitudes.

B. The American Wilderness

1. Sense of short time, limitless space.

From the beginning the time has always seemed to Americans already too late. The Pilgrims landed at Plymouth in early winter. They desperately needed houses, a harvest of food, the friendship of the Indians, and, in case that should fail, defenses. There was not time enough and half of them died before the next year's harvest. Americans at Plymouth, Jamestown, New Amsterdam, and even St. Augustine were dropped on this continent already running to catch up and they have never stopped.

As Mead stresses, the peoples of Europe—and it was particularly true of England—had found themselves confined in space. Such freedom as they could find must be discovered in time. "But when the first white men from Europe set foot on the new continent with the intention to remain as settlers, this relative significance of time and space was reversed."[2]

2. Frontier community.

Even in the 19th century Thomas Carlyle was to characterize America as "A vast deal of land for a verra few people."[3] The immense areas of unused or sparsely used land which lay before the settlers gave the illusion of infinite space and resources. Many people were always eager to move west and claim large tracts of land before others did so. Other people who were pulled along were always struggling to conquer the wilderness, build shelter, and get seed planted. There was never enough time, but there was always space. There was so much new land available that for several generations little effort was made to fertilize, plow deeply, or rotate crops. When the thin soil became less productive, the people moved west again and the restless struggle was renewed in another area.[4] When population began to be congested and problems of city life appeared, the West beckoned. In about 1799, in Boston, Rev. Joseph Stevens Buckminster "expressed gratitude on Thanksgiving Day that the country had an inexhaustible supply of unsettled western lands. It seemed to him that the escape they offered from the city's festering problems was the only sure hope for American democracy."[5]

3. Frontier violence.

The sense of limited time had much to do with the violence of the frontier. There was not time to carry on seemingly endless negotiations with Indians to achieve mutual understanding about land use and occupation. Often time seemed lacking even for reaching agreement with white neighbors. The threat or actual use of the gun was faster and speed of solution seemed essential. Likewise in dealing with crime—the stealing of provisions, cattle or horses, or the seduction of a wife—there was no time for judicial sifting of evidence and thoughtful weighing of penalties. Instead, the "swift justice" of vigilantes forcing the offender to ride on a sharp rail, the tar-and-feathering, or the shoot-out was the answer adopted.

C. American Use of Space to Relieve Tensions

From the very beginning American space was used to relieve European stresses. Religious dissenters under pressure to conform and suffering minor discrimination or even active persecution in Europe relieved both themselves and their tormentors by putting the Atlantic Ocean between them.[6] Others were banished to America or, especially in the 19th century, came to escape economic pressures or disasters. In effect they too were using American space to relieve European tensions. Since economic stringencies often produce political upheavals, space on this continent thus served as a safety valve for Europe.

1. Formal or informal banishment.

Such processes have been repeated countless thousands of times within America. In the 17th century there were strong pressures for conformity, especially, but by no means only, in New England. While succeeding generations brought a willingness to accept broader deviance, tolerance in religion and life-style has continued to be limited. But because of available useful space, "people who thought 'otherwise,' like Roger Williams or Brigham Young, could go 'elsewhere' and do so with impunity."[7] Sometimes they were officially commanded to leave or threatened by vigilantes and ordered to "move on."

Thus Anne Hutchinson and Rev. John Wheelwright were condemned in a solemn synod meeting at Newtown in 1637 and banished from Massachusetts Bay in 1638.[8] Nathaniel Ward was probably speaking for most people in Massachusetts Bay when, in 1647, he wrote, "All Familists, Antinomians, Anabaptists, and other Enthusiasts, shall have full liberty to keep away from us, and such as will come to be gone as fast as they can, the sooner the better."[9] Banishment was easy and accomplished without much offense to conscience, because, as John Cotton pointed out, there was so much pleasant, fruitful land that to be sent out into it was "not counted so much a confinement as an enlargement."[10]

A Virginia law of 1662 instructed "the Governor and Counsel" to compel "all nonconformists to depart the colony with all convenience."[11] As noted earlier, the Maryland Toleration Act of 1649 specified that banishment was to be the penalty for a third offense of certain heretical or irreverent utterances.

Even in the 1970s it is not uncommon for a person who has been repeatedly arrested on relatively minor charges, so that he has become a chronic nuisance, to be told by a prosecutor that charges will not be pressed if he moves out of the town, county, or state and does not return. During American fighting in Vietnam the notion that protesting nonconformists should leave was expressed in the sign displayed on many automobiles, "America: Love it or Leave it" and others of similar import.

2. Voluntary exile within America.

When persistent disagreement arose between Thomas Hooker of Newtown and John Cotton of Massachusetts Bay Hooker and his people moved out to Connecticut. Hooker said the towns in Massachusetts were too close together, and the economic advantages of more space may have provided an important incentive. But Hooker certainly considered it desirable to put space between himself and Cotton, and their relations were more friendly after this had been accomplished.

Such voluntary escape from uncongenial surroundings fast became so common that it has been and is today part of the American way of life. Many people who have trouble with their neighbors or simply find few friendly associations look for a new location, even if moving is not required by changes in place of employment. A family may repeat this process frequently within a short span of years. Many Americans do not try to settle down anywhere, choosing rather to live on wheels. "The trailer-house hitched to an automobile is as fitting a symbol of the American's concept of freedom today as once were the saddlebags, the rifle and the ax."[12]

As we observed earlier,* such high mobility tends to increase crime by weakening the sanctions of social approval and censure. At the same time Americans highly prize their own personal freedom and view it as including their privilege of living their own lives untrammeled by the opinion of their neighbors. The distinctive American personality is in part due to the fact that for so long he and his ancestors have been able readily to escape the physical proximity of other people. Hence the controls of social custom have long sat lightly on the American's shoulders. As Mead says concerning such controls of a person, "their formative influence depends finally upon his inability to escape the society of his peers."[13]

D. Running Out of Space

Today, unclaimed land is in short supply. As an observer travels across the country the shortage is not obvious. There are still millions of acres which bear no houses and are not cultivated. However, when a family proposes to seek independence by moving to some of the unoccupied lands the available space quickly shrinks nearly to zero. Great areas are desert, while most of the remainder is privately owned for grazing, mining, or lumbering or is reserved by government for purposes of conservation or recreation. Land sufficiently fertile and otherwise suitable for occupation and support is so expensive that few individuals can afford to buy enough to provide for a family. The great majority of Americans are able to live at or near present standards only by participating in a highly industrialized society. This means that they must live near the sources of their livelihood, usually urban. Even the flight to the suburbs of our large cities is hampered by problems of sewage disposal and transportation. We are increasingly crowded together at home, at work, and on the road. Our long-established customs of doing as we individually please make us resentful that other people's automobiles, the trucks essential to our commerce and industry, the neighbors' loud radios or television sets, and unruly children or dogs hamper our freedom and interfere with our own life-style, while we may be equally loath to curb our own activities which annoy our neighbors.[14]

The energy shortage which was suddenly accentuated by the Arab oil embargo at the beginning of 1974 posed an especially frightening threat to

---

* Above, Chap. 11, D, 1.

American ways of life. For to find liberty by use of space one must have transportation, and to go in any direction at any time we choose we must have private vehicles with enough fuel to operate them at will. The gasoline shortage did more than interfere with our going to work and home again. In a few months or years that problem could be solved by car pools and a wide variety of public transportation. We perceived in the energy crisis the beginning of a threat to our traditional American liberty, the liberty of individual movement in space, whether for a Sunday afternoon escape to the country, or a family vacation in the mountains, or a cross-country trek with tent or trailer.

1. Crowding and crime.

Konrad Lorenz, in his famous best-seller *On Aggression*,[15] disturbed the reading public with his evidence that human beings, like many other creatures, are instinctively aggressive and under certain conditions become dangerously violent. Particularly, he stresses that crowding induces violent aggression and that, within limits, aggressive reaction to crowding has survival value because it spreads out members of the species so that they do not compete for the same resources. Human beings, however, have developed such dangerous weapons that aggression may now exterminate them.[16]

In the United States crowding is especially difficult for people to accept. When people of radically different traditions and life-styles compete for the limited jobs, housing, and elbow room in our crowded urban centers, their crowding and frustration lead, with frightful frequency, to the vain escapes offered by alcohol or other drugs, or to a violent lashing out against unfortunate victims who happen to be near. The effort to escape by means of drugs aggravates the problem by requiring so much additional money as to make it impossible for most people to support a drug habit by lawful means. Drug addiction combines with the hostility engendered by abrasive crowding, with tragic results.

2. Substituting walls for space.

Since we no longer have much available space to which criminal offenders or strongly disliked nonconformists can be banished, and we cannot readily move away from them, we resort to the use of walls. The majority of incarcerated people have given no evidence of being dangerous.* But a prison wall, like empty geographical space, serves to put people offensive to us out of our sight.

However, the device of imprisonment is not a satisfactory substitute. It is obviously unsatisfactory to the prisoners, but that is not all. People who

---

* See above, Chap. 1, B.

are imprisoned do not make their own way as the banished were wont to do. They are a heavy burden on tax-paying citizens. Besides, most of them cannot be kept behind walls indefinitely. Life terms for most offenders would not only be flagrantly unjust; they would impose an insufferable burden on the rest of society. Finally, putting people behind walls does not remove them from society. A part of society is there with them in the persons of officials, secretaries, professional staff, security officers, and other prisoners. The more people we imprison the more of our society is there with them. We like to forget this and put the inside of prisons both out of sight and out of mind. But we forget only by self-deception. Rude awakenings come when prison riots break into the news and much more frequently when people brutalized in the prisons come out by escape, completion of their terms, or on parole and put into practice what they have learned "inside."

3. Living with social problems.

No longer can we solve our problems of tension between races, peoples of different national origin, or groups with clashing customs, values, and life-styles by moving away from one another. Although I see no way to avoid some use of incarceration for dangerous individuals, we cannot continue to regard separation by prison walls as the normal and usual solution to problems of deviant behavior. Unclaimed space is in short supply and large-scale use of imprisonment is a wretched substitute.

After two hundred years the United States of America confronts a new necessity, the necessity of living with its social tensions and resolving them right where they are. We have, at this bicentennial period, a rendezvous with destiny. We are called upon by the realities of a settled national area to face our problems at home and learn to live with one another. This coming of age nationally will demand of us such maturity, rational sobriety, and patience as will be exceedingly difficult to muster. But today there is no way to escape.

15

Two Americas

By what standard are the laws and processes of American criminal justice to be judged? American tradition of national and personal purpose does not speak with one voice. The vexatious problem does not arise from

our plural heritage of diverse religions and professional moral philosophies. On most issues concerning the defining of justice in the courtroom,
authentic Judaism, Christian theology, and our major heritage of secular
political philosophy are on the same side.

The problem of establishing an ethical foundation for criminal justice
in this country rises largely from the presence of a strong American tradition flagrantly contrary to our heritage of great religions and secular
humane philosophy. Indeed, this contrary tradition has much to do also
with the high rate of crime in this country.

There are two Americas. We work in the ever-present context of both,
and they often affect the thought and action of the same people.

A. America A

America A is generous, community-minded, benevolent, and humane. All
three of our high ethical traditions have contributed to it. Christian teaching emphasizes lovingkindness, fellowship, active concern for the weak,
and the sacred dignity of every human individual, regardless of his age,
ancestry, condition, or moral worthiness. Judaism stresses the justice of
opportunity for all, the need to embody concern for the poor in law, the
obligation of public benevolence, and the responsibility of every individual
to serve the community according to his means and ability. From the best
political philosophy of our founding fathers, especially Thomas Jefferson,
we have drawn the doctrine that "all men are created equal" in political
and civil rights, that science and technology should be put into the service
of all people, that there should be no discrimination on grounds of religion
or race, and that justice and peace should be sought with self-restraint,
patience, care for the truth, and generous consideration of others.

After his famous 1831 visit to America Alexis de Tocqueville wrote
about the amazing propensity of Americans to form "associations . . . of a
thousand . . . kinds" in order to cooperate for a wide variety of purposes.[1]
This characteristic has persisted. Kammen observes that despite their "social philosophy of individualism" Americans are "a nation of joiners and
have developed the largest associations and corporations the world has
ever known."[2] Much "joining," to be sure, is for profit or for trivial or
even nefarious purposes, but much of it has great value both for specific
high goals and for weaving a network of mutual social support.

America A offers a truly magnificent heritage. It has produced the
Mayflower Compact with its pledge of mutual loyalty to the community as
a whole, and the Declaration of Independence based on acceptance of the
"self-evident" truths "that all men are created equal, that they are endowed by their Creator with certain unalienable Rights, that among these
are Life, Liberty and the pursuit of Happiness." America A gave us the

Bill of Rights, the ten precious constitutional amendments which guarantee our civil liberties. It offers education to all our children.[3] America A has developed popular higher education, public philanthropy on an unprecedented scale, Abraham Lincoln's pledge and actual policy of "malice toward none" and "charity for all," the return of the Boxer Indemnity to the Chinese people, and magnanimity toward the Japanese and all of Europe following World War II. It has been expressed in the cooperation of our pioneers in sharing the little they had in the face of hardship, in united community funds, in unparalleled voluntary support of our religious institutions, in the founding of the Red Cross—and so we might continue.

America A is truly "America the Beautiful" and it rightly claims the pride and devotion of all citizens.

B. America B

Unfortunately, over against America A stands America B. I do not refer to a mere frequent failure to live up to the high standards of our best utterances and deeds. America B is a tradition deliberately promoting, urging, and glorifying ideas directly contrary to those we have been considering.[4] That they *are* contrary is too seldom recognized.

America B is tightfisted, individualistic, self-righteous, materialistic, aggressive, impatient, vindictive, and prone to violence. In international and interethnic relations America B is quick to resort to arms and Theodore Roosevelt often praised that propensity to violence as a sign and stimulant of American character. In economic affairs it possesses abundantly the "selfishness" which Senator Dawes said was necessary to civilization* and which is sometimes called "the American way."

One historical explanation of it is doubtless the fact that so large a proportion of our population is sprung from people who, in the Old Country, were among the most discontented and aggressive. That is why they came while others chose to stay. Most of us in the United States are descendants of malcontents. It is not strange that there should be a disproportionate share of aggressive, individualistic impatience in our temperaments.

The hard struggle to tame the wilderness and the violent conquest of the Indians strengthened this heritage. Many American pioneers and the economic adventurers of the 19th century were able, by hard work, fast aggressiveness, and ruthlessness, to gain fabulous riches. Never, anywhere, have so many people been lured by such great natural resources. We should not find it surprising, then, that we Americans are known all round the world for our hard-driving, individualistic aggressiveness.

---

* See above, Chap. 11, C.

Some qualities of America B account for much of American achievement. Impatient discontent with things as they are and a quick readiness to seek actively for better ways can, when well-directed, lead to useful inventions, to rapid exploration and taming of the wilderness, and to discovery and progress in every sector of life.

Unfortunately, our rugged individualism and vaunted tradition of aggressive effort to "get ahead" and "win big," whatever the obstacles, produce other results which are less savory. America B perpetuated slavery and struck out of the Declaration of Independence the denunciation of the slave trade which Jefferson's draft had included. It voted down his bill in the Virginia Assembly to permit slaveowners to free their slaves voluntarily. America B, in our Puritan past, defended the *lex talionis* of eye for eye, life for life, drawn from the Old Testament, many centuries after Jesus had denounced it and the Jewish Mishnah had so redefined and circumscribed it as to substitute moderate penalties for vindictive retaliation. In the 1970s the vindictive voices are heard again ringing through our legislative halls in the scramble to make political capital out of efforts to restore the death penalty.

America B produced massacres of poor straggling remnants of the Indians and the scrapping of many Indian treaties. It spawned the Know-Nothing bigots to attack late European immigrants. It urged on the night riders of the Ku Klux Klan and barbarous lynching parties. Recently it has produced the notorious 1960 conspiracy of the largest manufacturers of electrical goods, My Lai, aerial bombing massacres in Southeast Asia—and "Watergate."

Former President Richard M. Nixon exemplified and expressed with special clarity the norms of America B. He frequently extolled the virtues of people doing things "for themselves" (not for others). Even while he was accumulating wealth, his benevolent contributions were paltry. He showed little or no sympathy for people who were unable to support themselves. The "Watergate" investigations have exposed a circle of conspirators in his Oval Office for whom winning an election was not enough. They must "destroy" the opposition even if they must use forgery, burglary, misdirection of official agencies, and criminal concealment of evidence for the purpose.

It was precisely the egomania of that Oval Office which led to the automatic taping of all that was said there "for history" and so provided the most decisive evidence bringing about Nixon's downfall. So strong was the self-righteousness of the President himself that after publication of the incriminating tapes, his resignation and admissions of guilt by several staff members, and even as he accepted his successor's official pardon, he continued to maintain that he had only made some errors of judgment in his efforts to serve the country. America B, in the special form of lust for personal power and glory, self-righteousness and the converging of individual ambitions in a conspiratorial "game plan," was thus exposed for all to see.

C. America B as Source of High Crime

Is it any wonder that America B has produced the highest rate of murders and other violent crimes in any developed nation? Ruthlessly competitive advertisers sponsor television shows featuring violence, without regard to the public good. Between scenes of violence they use every device they can contrive to persuade the viewer that this or that luxury is the indispensable requirement of a healthy, successful life. For millions who are persuaded, there is no lawful way to obtain these things. Many have insufficient sales resistance and America A character to live without them, while there is much of the America B aggressive ethos in their own personalities also. So they get the things they were told they must have, by unlawful means, often violent or threatening violence. Sometimes they take out the anger of their frustration, at some early opportunity, on anyone unlucky enough to cross their paths at the wrong time. Alternatively, they seek escape from their frustration with the help of drugs or alcohol and often crime then becomes a secondary result.

I do not condone the crimes. I do mean to point out that as long as so many people with power in the business establishment and the government actively exemplify and promote the ideals of America B, the rate of crime will continue to be excessively high. People with respected positions cannot place their own selfish interests above the needs of the community and use dishonest short cuts to gain competitive or other advantages and then expect the poor and disadvantaged to play by the rules enacted for the public good.

Organized crime, too, rises naturally from the cultural matrix of America B. From the ruthless economic methods of the "robber barons," the contemporary deliberate overruns of multimillion dollar corporation contracts with the Pentagon, the false advertising of worthless or injurious medicines, and "the game plan" of the Nixon White House to the organized gangsters of Appalachia and the Mafia there is only a continuous gradation of antisocial violence. All alike have made wealth and power the supreme goods and all obscure moral protests under a haze of deception and smooth public relations.[5]

D. The Paradox in Criminal Justice

The contradictions in American society appear in criminal justice as well as in other aspects of our national life. On the whole, as compared with practices in advanced democratic societies elsewhere, it is the vindictive, self-righteous, harsh qualities of America B which characterize our treatment of convicted criminals. But that is not the whole story.

Not infrequently an American judge or jury, faced with a defendant apparently guilty of an offense for which the legally prescribed penalties were dictated by waves of panic and anger in the public, finds him not guilty rather than subjecting him to penalties disproportionately severe. Much more frequently still, the police do not vigorously pursue such people or the prosecutor does not prosecute.

When, as is usual, a judge or parole board has wide latitude, not only are some convicted persons punished with unusual severity, but others are handled with astonishing leniency. Sometimes this is due to corruption. On other occasions it is simply because something in the demeanor of the offender or the persuasive approach of his lawyer touches a responsive chord in the more benevolent—America A—side of the official's disposition. Often it is an aspect of the convicted person which in some way identifies him with the socioeconomic class of the official and so stirs sympathetic understanding.

Such manifestations of our national self-contradiction weaken the positive effect of the criminal justice system. Neither the prisoner who is punished with unusual severity nor the one who "gets off easy" has much respect for the law. Both kinds have often told me in prison conversations that they regarded the law as "just a lottery" or as "a game the lawyers play."*

All this adds up to a significant part of our confused and ineffective "nonsystem."

E. New Pressures for Taming America B

Our ideals which constitute America A constantly exert pressure on us to reduce the force of America B among us or at least to curb its excesses. We should be further moved in this direction by the serious proportions of violent crime. Unfortunately, a rise in the crime rate more often elicits vindictive calls for harsher penalties and in general accentuates the power of America B among us. Serious studies of the problem, such as those of the President's Commission published in 1967 and that of the National Advisory Commission on Criminal Justice Standards and Goals published in 1973, point toward more efficient but more moderate law enforcement and toward the need for more social justice in the whole community. Such recommendations and the people who support them may counter the waves of vindictive passion and make some positive headway, but the progress, if any, is slow.

---

* Cf. above, Chap. 5, A.

Today we are pressed by other forces which may strengthen America A and lead to a higher quality of community life, with similar effects in the system of criminal justice.

One of these new forces is the increasing evidence that we are fast approaching serious ecological trouble. We are crowding some areas of the globe by the rapid expansion of population. The supporting life chain which leads from water, minerals, and air, largely through plants and animals, to our food, drink, clothing, and other things we use is becoming so hard-pressed that it is threatened with disastrous breakdown.[6] This is due, not only to growing population, but also to our multiplying per capita demands. Through advertising, example, and the America B drive to get ahead we feel imperative need to have more and more manufactured things.

The profit-motivated industrial system requires constant expansion in order to avoid depression. When our Gross National Product fails to increase by 4% or more per year, buying power becomes unable to buy all that has been made at a price sufficient to pay all the costs plus a profit.[7] As buying power fails, industries begin to close down, unemployment grows, at further cost to buying power, and we are in a depression.

The growing population, the insatiable demand of the system for expansion, and the desire of individuals for more things are rapidly exhausting our natural resources. To be sure, a Gross National Product could expand in services as well as in goods, but we have been acculturated to demand more and more *things* as visible evidence of our success. The economy has been developed in such a way as to depend also on the rapid obsolescence or breakdown and discarding of innumerable products, from automobiles to home thermostats. Hence we have become accustomed to continual replacement of our possessions, as well as the addition of new kinds of things.[8]

Another means on which we depend to dispose of our industrial products and maintain a demand for more, to keep the industrial production growing, is military activity. Actual war accomplishes this quite thoroughly, with the need to replace shells, missiles, and smaller ammunition used on a large scale along with the aircraft, artillery, vehicles, and other equipment destroyed by enemy fire. Hence wars produce upsurges in the economy, especially in the industrial sector. When we are not in a war much of similar effect can be produced, without loss of American lives, by supplying the war machines of other countries. Thus, even while Americans were complaining of the energy shortage in early 1974 and the prices of fuel were skyrocketing, with manufactured goods following the inflationary spiral, fuel, armaments, and other military assistance were going from the United States to South Vietnam at an annual rate of over $2.9 billion and over twice that amount of military assistance was going to other countries abroad.[9] Budgetary demands of the military have actually gone higher than they were during active participation of American armed forces in Southeast Asia. As Congress debates yet higher askings for subsequent years, one argument used is that these great expenditures are needed to stimulate the American economy. This emphasis on the military component in the expanding Gross National Product is obviously directed toward potential for international violence, even as America B also develops domestic violence.

We enjoy having new possessions and new kinds of luxuries. But we do not enjoy living in smog, seeing pure, running streams polluted by sewage and garbage, or finding that once beautifully flowering glades are covered with rusting remains of discarded automobiles. Prospects are that such unattractive conditions will become worse until human life itself is seriously threatened, unless there is a radical reversal of the trend. To be sure, the problem is worldwide, but the United States, with less than 6% of the world population, uses and discards about 40% of the material resources thus exhausted each year.[10]

The sudden awareness of limitations in energy—brought to abrupt crisis by the Arab oil embargo in late 1973 and early 1974—heightened the realization that our industrial growth was on collision course with diminishing reserves of earth's resources. We may make the mistake of easing the new restrictions on pollution and waste of material things in order to whip up a beleaguered economy and obtain more energy. But if we do, it will be apparent before long that shortages of clean air and water are even more serious than shortages of fuel.

We shall soon be compelled to realize—and many are now aware—that the limited resources of earth require us to change radically our typical American objectives. Possibly, in the process, we may learn to give higher priority to quality of community life and a lower place to individual, aggressive competition for more material articles.[11] Such a change would bring us into a more gentle and benevolent society and a consequent decrease of crime. In such a society we should also predictably change our objectives in criminal justice from so much of anger and vindictiveness against past offenders to more concern for aid to victims and prevention of future crime.

In short, as we meet newly urgent problems of ecology, limited materials, and shortages of energy we may turn gradually from the goals of America B to those of America A. If we do not, we may expect, particularly in our crowded cities, further increases in violent crime. At the same time we shall be increasing pollution, further acute shortages and inflation, frustration, deterioration of our national life, and critical threats to world peace. Nationally and internationally the American Dream will become a nightmare.

At such a time we need to ask what are the goals which ought to guide our national aspirations and our specific programs of official and unofficial action.[12] The tradition of America B has betrayed us into more crime, an ominous depletion and pollution of natural resources, and kinds of criminal justice which are destructive, costly, and ineffective. Our question of basic purpose cannot be answered by America B. It is a question in ethics, and for an answer we must look to the more seriously constructed and responsible major ethical resources of the American people. As we do so our main interest for the present study is the discovery of goals and norms for criminal justice. We shall see, however, that our great ethical traditions have much wider implications, affecting all institutions in the nation.

PART IV

AN ETHICAL PHILOSOPHY OF

CRIMINAL JUSTICE

An Emerging Ethical Consensus

> It is not that Christians should suspend their faith that they may learn to speak well and learnedly with Jews or that Jews should inhibit their eccentric singularity that they may learn to identify the better with Christians. . . .
>
> Upon one thing Jews and Christians agree: the magnitude of creation and the grandeur and misery of man. Out of such agreement an authentic community, a viable consensus, a meaningful cooperation can emerge—the Judeo-Christian humanism.[1]

It should be evident that the tradition of America B cannot guide the people of the United States out of the present morass of high crime and confused, emotionally reactive, ineffective criminal justice. A person who studies recent literature of avowed ethics will also find that American writers in this field give little support to the aggressive, self-righteous individualism of America B and even less to its violence and vindictiveness.

We have three major traditions of serious quest for ethical truth in this country: the Jewish, Christian, and secular philosophical. Within each there are numerous differences. Surely no one who has attended professional meetings of the American Philosophical Association or the American Society of Christian Ethics will be tempted to think that the Christian ethicists are all saying the same thing or that the moral philosophers are all in agreement. The major disagreements among scholars of each tradition and the differences which divide religious from secular ethical presuppositions might appear to make any effort to find a common core of norms for guidance of public policy utterly impossible.

Yet I believe that in relation to those issues which most concern the system of criminal justice there is a remarkably broad and useful consensus. I do not claim that all moral philosophers or all Christian and Jewish ethicists can be included in such a consensus at every point. It is my thesis, however, that there has been a distinct trend toward convergence and that ideals embodied in it have been implanted deeply in the American conscience.

Many Americans try to be faithful to these ideals for whatever reasons their own religious or secular traditions provide. Many others do not take them seriously in most of their personal and political decisions, but when the ideals are voiced do readily subscribe to them and acknowledge that they ought to be more faithful to them. I believe that these two classes of people together constitute a large majority of the adult population. If this is true, it is very important for all who are concerned about criminal justice to know it, for two reasons. If a criminal justice system is to be effective in a country with civil liberties, that system must cohere with, if not express, the deeper moral convictions of the people. In a pluralistic society such as that of the United States the system must not be formed by reference to the norms of one religious or philosophical heritage alone, but must be recognized by people of different religions and those of no formal religion as expressive of their own ideals as well as those of other traditions. We must pause to emphasize these two points.

The President's Commission on Law Enforcement and Administration of Justice, reporting in 1967, said, "Finally, no system however well staffed or organized, no level of material well-being for all, will rid a society of crime if there is not a widespread ethical motivation, and a widespread belief that by and large the government and the social order deserve credence, respect and loyalty."[2] This truth is peculiarly pertinent to those parts of government embraced in the system of criminal justice.

"To separate ethics from the judicial process is to pervert the latter," wrote Jerome Frank. Accordingly, he added, "We must ethicize the work of the courts."[3] But the courts cannot be ethical if the laws which they administer and the corrections to which they sentence convicted persons are unethical. Jerome G. Miller has spoken pointedly concerning the internal inequities and self-contradictions of the correctional system, and he traces them to their ethical presuppositions. "It is crucial," he says, "that correctional reform hit, head on, the moral and ideological contradictions upon which the system rests."[4]

Neither I nor any writer cited is contending that morality should be enforced by criminal law. The extent to which it should and should not be so enforced is another subject much discussed.* My contention here is that the criminal law and the processes connected with it should not violate prevailing ethical convictions and that if the system is to be effective it must be perceived by the leaders of ethical opinion as being morally defensible.[5]

---

* See below, Chap. 20.

Justice Oliver Wendell Holmes said that law was "the witness and external deposit of our moral life," and hence that the history of law "is the history of the moral development of man."[6] If Holmes was right and I think he was, then our American system of criminal law shouts eloquently that the American people have long been morally confused and self-contradictory. As a people we have long been radically uncertain about what it means to be just to accused or convicted persons. If our system of criminal justice is to be made whole and reasonably effective, we shall need to decide what we want with it, and that means principally that we must decide what is truly just—an ethical question.

Some important ethical norms are enshrined in the United States Constitution, for example the guarantees of equal rights and due process. Through many decisions of the Supreme Court, especially during the Warren years, these and other provisions have been incorporated in the scope of Amendment XIV and so made applicable to the states. Yet, despite these highly significant facts, the basic meaning and purpose of justice to the violator of criminal law remains uncertain and the actual working of the system is very far from providing even-handed treatment of rich and poor, powerful and weak. The system still stands in radical need of ethicizing.

On some issues of specific proposed legal prohibitions—of abortion, for example—we do tend to divide along religious lines. When, as in this instance, many citizens feel morally obligated to do under certain conditions what others, principally of one religious tradition, consider a murderous violation of human rights so as to require criminalization as a felony, we have a serious political problem. But such issues do not basically concern the system of criminal justice as a whole or the kinds of problems with that system which constitute the main subject of this book. The presence of such issues does, however, emphasize the need to found criminal law on a consensus of the main ethical traditions and not on beliefs which divide some religious traditions from others.

We propose to search, then, for common ground in the three main types of professed ethical ideals in America. We must limit ourselves to those Jewish, Christian, and philosophical teachings which have explicit or implicit bearing upon the main purposes and principles of criminal justice. In covering such broad areas we can present only brief summaries, but with references for further study.

A. Jewish Ethics

People outside the Jewish community often suppose that the laws stated in the ancient books of Exodus, Leviticus, and Deuteronomy are still regarded, in their literal, unmodified form, as authoritative for Jewish conduct. Actually, the Jewish scholars have long taught that the ancient "written Torah" must be understood in the *halakah* or oral tradition of the learned in successive generations. The latter is a living, growing body of interpretation in the light of reason, experience, and continued enlightenment by the spirit of God.[7] When the new interpretations have become *Minhag,* that is accepted by the learned rabbinical scholars, they hold an authority equal to that of the original Torah and are deemed to have been given with it at the revelation on Mount Sinai.[8]

What, then, are some relevant ideals and principles which modern American Judaism, drawing on deeper Halakic traditions, offers to the consensus of conscience proposed as basis for a reformed system of criminal justice?

1. Chesed (or ḥesed): lovingkindness.

Chesed is the steadfast, reliable love which God has for the people in covenant with him and which they are called upon to hold toward him and toward each other.[9]

"You shall love your neighbor as yourself" is from the Hebrew Torah (Lev. 19:18). Originally the context made it clearly intend application only to fellow Israelites although "the stranger within the gates" was sometimes included in the neighborly duties. But even as Jesus universalized it to include all human beings, so did the ancient Midrash explicitly extend the obligations of neighborliness to all the Gentiles.[10] The contemporary Jewish legal philosopher Julius Stone declares that "undoubtedly the most important contribution of the Jewish tradition was the overriding concept of love. . . ." As Stone points out, this was present in the Pentateuch and elaborated by the great post-exilic prophets and rabbis.[11]

Love, on this view, does not stand over against justice, but must enter into it and even, ideally, control it. Hence, Andrew Sharf says, human justice is obliged to intimate God's own "compassionate equity (Micah 6:8; Mishnah Makkot 24b . . .), and—at the final consummation of history—justice and mercy become identical."[12]

So strong became the motif of love and mercy that, despite the repeated *lex talionis* in the Bible, the whole idea of retribution was repudiated and "replaced fairly early in Jewish thought by the notions of correction of the offender and social protection against the incorrigible."[13] "An eye for an eye" came to be regarded as what it was in historical fact, a stage in the erection of barriers against the barbarous law of unlimited vengeance. It thus pointed the direction to moderation, equity, and mercy. The rabbis then prescribed in place of punishment various monetary forms of restitution for injury.[14]

2. Respect for inherent human dignity.

Closely related to *chesed* is the principle that respect must be shown for all persons, Jewish or heathen, righteous or evil in conduct. This principle is based on belief in God as Creator of all human beings in his own image.

Leviticus 19:17–18 explicitly forbids taking vengeance or holding a grudge and commands the love of neighbor. Commenting on this passage, Rabbi Akiba declares, "You must not say, since I have been put to shame (by a fellow man), let him be put to shame; since I have been slighted, let him be slighted. . . . If you do so, know whom ye put to shame, for in the likeness of God made He him."[15]

The doctrine of human dignity requires measures to safeguard every accused person against false conviction, but also protection of the rights of every convicted person. Some Talmudists therefore, two thousand years ago, favored abolition of capital punishment. Others regarded it as necessary in a few extreme cases to protect the community. But "it was agreed that any court that inflicts capital punishment once every seven years had exhibited brutality."[16] "The execution even of the most violent criminal," writes Ben Zion Bokser, "is a cosmic tragedy. For he, too, was formed in the divine image and had been endowed with infinite possibilities for good."[17]

What of the incorrigible recidivist? Does the community have a responsibility to support and treat with decency even such a rascal? Richard G. Hirsch replies, in Talmudic interpretation, "No man is beyond human concern. No man is beyond repentance and rehabilitation. No man is so bad that the community may be absolved of responsibility."[18]

Judaism has not always spoken with one voice concerning the universality of human claims to lovingkindness and respect for human dignity. The Reform Jewish scholar Michael A. Meyer documents the ambiguity and inconsistency of historical, authoritative Jewish writings on the subject, coming down to the recent past. He advocates loosening the claim of traditional authority in ethics, while selectively drawing on the messianic tradition for a contemporary "moral ideal: the genuine community of mankind." "Such an ethic," he says, "is both flexible in detail and uncompromising in demand."[19]

It is especially significant that, even with varying presuppositions and methods, the leading expositions of Jewish thought, particularly in the United States, are supporting universal lovingkindness, respect for human dignity, and quest for inclusive community.[20]*

---

* One tragic result of the intermittent Israeli-Arab warfare is that it has tended, like war everywhere, to obscure these qualities. However, even in these violent times, the handling of domestic criminals, Arab and Israeli alike, within Israel, has been remarkably humane.

3. Community of mutual dependence.

Presupposed in the idea of *chesed* is a network of close personal interrelationships.[21] Beginning with family obligations, it was extended to embrace the tribe, the people Israel, and finally, in the tradition now dominant in Western Jewish thought, all humankind.

As early as the second century the strong sense of mutual obligation of all for all in the Jewish community was so strong that the poverty of any members was accepted as a responsibility of all and hence systems of social welfare were established. This principle extended to concern for all kinds of needs. The work of caring for all these needs, by various special agencies, centered upon the synagogue and in the Middle Ages became a source of special pride. "A community was judged by the extent to which it became the agent for guaranteeing just treatment to all its inhabitants."[22]

In the United States today the rabbis teach a special obligation of all Jews to their own community and to the nation Israel. Hence the special funds in every synagogue and the United Jewish Appeal. These efforts are assuredly divisive. But the rabbis teach also the obligation to give generous support of public benevolence for other causes in the pluralistic American community.

In addition, they affirm that there is an even wider community of all God's creatures to which man has obligations, embracing the animals and the whole ecological network.[23]

4. Special responsibility to guard the poor and weak from injustice.

As we have seen, the very exposition of the teaching concerning interdependence in the community requires special mention of the poor. The obligations are to all, whether poor or rich, and they are also to be borne by all, so that even the person who receives the aid of public welfare must also give out of his meager means. But the poor will bear an inequitably heavy burden unless special means are taken by others and by the community as a whole to relieve the poverty and share the burdensome disabilities which accompany it.

Both in the written Torah and in the *halakah* there are special provisions to prevent the law from falling too heavily on the poor. For example, it is forbidden to "take a widow's garment in pledge" (Deut. 24:17), and even if a poor man owes you money, you may not keep his cloak in pledge after sundown, for he may need it to protect him at night (Deut. 24:12–13).

5. Requirement of precise, publicized laws.

Judaic ethics stresses the need for the community to have a system of laws carefully and explicitly defining prescribed and forbidden conduct in advance. This tradition is rooted, of course, in the laws of the ancient Pentateuch. Those laws often go into considerable detail, specifying prohibited conduct, prescribing penalties, and distinguishing between different circumstances of the alleged offenses.[24]

Although the prophets and rabbis of ancient times sometimes spoke for love and mercy as opposed to legalism,[25] one important means of giving reality to the prophetic call for freedom and mercy was the elaboration of casuistry—that is, more law. Freedom from an enslaving legalism may be gained by laws which limit the operation of the more severe and exacting laws. Freedom may also be gained by appeal from present unjust laws of the state to a higher order of laws. Both ways have been taken in classical and modern Jewish tradition.[26]

6. Avoidance of overburdensome laws.

It has been affirmed that "it cannot be just to penalize disobedience to a norm which commands what is in fact impossible."[27] Such a doctrine has obvious relevance to laws prohibiting the drunkenness of a chronic alcoholic or the use of heroin by a confirmed heroin addict. In such cases the principle would leave open the question whether an alcoholic or drug addict should be held criminally responsible for the abuses which occurred before he became addicted but which led to the addiction. Yet the principle would, at the least, alter the focus of criminalization.

Haim H. Cohn, a Justice of the Supreme Court of Israel, writes concerning legislation in that country, "While the scope of rule-making authority is virtually unlimited, there is one restriction, already laid down in the Talmud, that is worthy of note. It is that no regulation might be imposed on the community unless the majority 'could stand it'—that is, unless the regulation was reasonable and not too onerous."[28] The Talmudic reference cited by Cohn is Tosefta Sota XV, 10, which invalidated a law prohibiting the eating of meat and drinking of wine after destruction of the Temple because "the majority of the people could not be expected" to abide by such a rule.[29]

7. Presumption of innocence.

In both written and oral Torah there is an emphatic presumption of innocence favoring anyone charged with a crime. The more serious the crime the stronger the presumption. In various ways obstacles are placed in the way of conviction in capital cases.[30] Moreover, in such cases a conviction can be reversed, but an acquittal cannot be reversed. The most impressive support for the presumption of innocence, however, appears in the strict rules of evidence for guilt in criminal cases, the rules occurring both in the biblical Torah and in later interpretations.

8. Strict rules of evidence.

In Deuteronomy 17:6 we read, "On the evidence of two witnesses or of three witnesses he that is to die shall be put to death; a person shall not be put to death on the evidence of one witness." Deuteronomy 19:15 broadens the scope of this requirement far beyond capital offenses, to include "any crime or . . . any wrong in connection with any offense. . . ." Anyone convicted of maliciously bringing false testimony against another is to receive the same punishment as he tried to bring on the falsely accused person (Deut. 19:16–19).

According to the Mishnah, several classes of people were not valid witnesses in court. Those whose testimony was not admitted included imbeciles, minors, blind men, deaf-mutes, non-Jews, professional gamblers, usurers, and persons under sentence for crimes.[31] It is well known that confessions under duress are not acceptable as evidence in American criminal trials. The Talmud goes much further, barring even voluntary confessions. Although Talmudic provision for exceptions leaves a considerable area of ambiguity, there is a clear initial presumption against the acceptance of any confession as evidence.[32]

9. Reinstatement of punished offenders.

When a person has been convicted of crime, with rare exceptions amounting to dangerous treason, he is still regarded as a member of the community. Although a judge must invoke the sentence on a convicted offender which the law specifies, he must still regard the convicted man as his neighbor.[33]

Ex-convicts often complain that as long as they live they cannot escape the opprobrium, disabilities, and reputation of being criminals, regardless of their later good citizenship. In contrast, the Mishnah declares, "If a man is a repentant sinner, one must not say to him, 'Remember your past deeds.' "[34]

10. Restitution to victims.

Restitution by offenders to the victims of their crimes was commonplace in ancient times. In the ancient legal code of the Hebrews there are many examples of restitution as sole punishment. For example, in Exodus 22 restitution, ranging from full value to five times that amount, is specified for stealing cattle or sheep, for grazing another man's fields, for arson or destructive carelessness with fire, and in monetary terms for seducing an unmarried woman (Ex. 22:1–17; cf. Lev. 24:18). A combination of restitution with added penalty, to the victim, plus a guilt offering in the temple is commanded in Leviticus 6:1–7.

The Mishnah further specifies the kinds of injury and loss for which

victims are to be compensated. "A man who injures another person becomes liable to him on five counts: for damages, for pain, for healing, for
loss of time, and for indignity."[35] In the passage which follows, rules are
given for determining the amount due the victims on each of these counts.

B. Christian Ethics

Law has no such prominence in Christian ethics as in Judaism. The opposition of love to law in the Gospels and of grace to law in the Letters of
Paul have even tended to produce an estrangement between Christian
ethics and law.

In Roman Catholicism the issue was met long ago by setting natural
law ethics over secular positive law and adding an ecclesiastical legal order
for governance in the church.[36] More exacting than these are the counsels
of perfection to guide the religious in their aspirations to true holiness. The
Protestant Reformation rejected this structure of law and supererogatory
effort on the grounds that no human being could go beyond nor even
completely fulfill the mandate of God, that salvation is by grace through
faith alone, and that all Christians, not only members of special orders, are
called to seek perfection of life by the help of God.

Modern Protestant scholars who have written books on Christian ethics have rarely had much, if anything, to say about criminal justice and
when they have included chapters on it they have usually done little more
than echo the cultures in which they have lived.[37] Pope Pius XII and the
popular English Protestant lay author C. S. Lewis both defended sheer
retribution. But they represented a rear guard action soon to be overtaken
by Vatican Council II and other modern expressions of more humane
views.[38] When retributive views appear in the United States at present,
they occur as part of that self-righteous, hard aggressiveness of America
B which is itself a primary source of the high rate of violent crime here.

Many Americans have read some works of the French Protestant lay
theologian Jacques Ellul. He wrote *The Theological Foundation of Law*[39]
and the title looks promising. However, the book is exclusively devoted to
effort to refute belief in natural law ethics for any Christian. The refutation
is vitiated by his false assumption throughout that to believe that the
principles of natural law are to be discovered in human experience or
practice (*in ordo cognoscendi*) is to believe that they have their being and
source in human experience or nature (*in ordo essendi*).[40] He does not
try to establish any theological or other norms for an actual system of criminal justice.[41]

There is a little more relevance to this task in his later book, *Violence:
Reflections from a Christian Perspective*.[42] Most of the book is devoted to
arguing that the Christian may find it necessary as a human being to use

violence against violence but is forbidden to do it as a Christian. However, his unstinted praise for Martin Luther King, Jr., and for the actual effectiveness of nonviolence as a social strategy has somewhat indirect relevance. Perhaps he comes nearest to criminal justice when he says, "Neither exaltation of power nor the search for vengeance will ever solve any human situation."[43]

An explicit effort to relate Protestant theology to just law is the work of a conference reported to the World Council of Churches in a book entitled *The Biblical Doctrine of Justice and Law*.[44] There was agreement in the conference that "the manner in which the Christian strives to establish and administer human justice is conditioned by his membership in the body of Christ, and should therefore manifest the influence of Christ's love upon him."[45] One group in the conference stated further that in some countries of live Christian tradition "it is possible for the Church to exercise a strong influence on public life, e.g. Christian love for each individual, even the sinner and the enemy, can humanize the harshness and impersonality of law."[46] But even here there are not offered any explicit guidelines toward an ethically acceptable system of criminal justice.

In 1970 the World Council of Churches sponsored a Consultation on Penal Policies, with over 50 participants, seven of them from the United States. Fourteen countries were represented. Besides theologians there were lawyers, prison administrators, social workers, and prison chaplains, all united in Christian concern about questions of penal policy. The report includes some of the most responsible and clear statements on criminal justice to come from any Christian church source in this century.

According to the report, it was agreed that "it must not be assumed that all the changes must be made by the offender: society itself also needs to change."[47] "It seemed to be accepted unanimously that the primary aim of prisons is to help the offender to integrate himself into the community as well as possible on release. It was also widely agreed that present prison systems do not do this."[48] Questions were raised whether imprisonment can serve such an end. Other ideas emphatically sounded were the need to limit narrowly the scope of criminal law,[49] the obligation of Christians to assist prisoners and ex-prisoners, and to distinguish between moral condemnation of persons and the punishment of acts, only the latter being acceptable in Christian faith.[50]

In the United States an Interreligious Task Force on Criminal Justice was established in 1973, representing nearly all the larger Christian churches and some others, and also the Jewish community. The Task Force is mainly action oriented. However, early in 1974 it was decided that an attempt should be made to draw up a basic statement of Philosophical and Theological Foundations which should undergird and provide ethical guidance of proposals on criminal justice in the United States. A committee of five was appointed to prepare such a statement. I was named chairman and prepared a preliminary proposal. After thorough discussion the committee adopted the proposal with minor changes, it was submitted to the entire Task Force, and, after careful consideration and two slight further changes, was unanimously adopted. That statement is, so far as I know, the first for this purpose in this country. The principles which it states are in complete accord with those which I am stating in sections A, B, and D of the present chapter, indeed are principally identical in substance. The fact of their adoption by a group representing 23 bodies—from Friends to Roman Catholics, American Baptists to Unitarians, Lutherans to Methodists, and Jews as well as Christians—confirmed my belief that I was accurately representing the better informed religious conscience of America in the present account of an emerging ethical consensus.

These expressions of religious views and concerns regarding criminal justice are impressive as representing the kinds of outlook which informed and responsible Christian clergy and laypersons are reaching when they seriously study the issues together. However, few have engaged in such study and thus far their work is not widely known in the United States.

Authentic Christian teachings affecting the American conscience today must be sought principally in the literature of Christian ethics not dealing explicitly with criminal law. Frequent reference has also to be made to the New Testament. Roman Catholics are now more often seeking guidance directly from the New Testament and giving to it an emphasis unmatched in many previous centuries. Among Protestants, lay people and pastors of local churches are more amenable to appeal to the New Testament than to the authority of scholars or of church agencies.

The literal and legalistic reading of the Pentateuch by the Puritans, it will be remembered, exercised an influence on criminal law far beyond the stress on mercy and love in the later prophets and the New Testament. Excepting some elements of the extreme conservative movements, most contemporary American Christians acknowledge a superior claim of the teachings of Jesus over the more ancient Books of Law. As a result, I believe that an effective appeal can now be made to a Christian conscience in America to apply specifically Christian principles to criminal justice in place of the old retributive notions which, from Puritan days, have played such a dominant role in popular views of criminal law. Most Christians will, I believe, recognize the principles below as making authentic Christian contributions to the wider American conscience.

1. Love and respect for all persons.

Nearly all writers on Christian ethics have acknowledged love (or charity or agape) as the first principle properly governing the relations

among human beings. When Jesus was asked "the great commandment,"
he replied, much as did some rabbis of his day, "You shall love the Lord
your God with all your heart, and with all your soul, and with all your
mind. This is the great and first commandment. And a second is like it,
You shall love your neighbor as yourself. On these two commandments
depend all the law and the prophets" (Mt. 22:37–40). Jesus made it
clear that every person is to be treated as a neighbor (Luke 10:29–37).
In designating the three supreme Christian virtues, the church has traditionally followed the Apostle Paul in naming faith, hope, and love, and
making love supreme (1 Cor. 13:13). In some writings faith has been
made all-embracing, while more often love has been so regarded. In any
case, as descriptive of authentically Christian human relations, love has
been and is the virtually universal choice.

Among contemporary American writers on Christian ethics Paul Ramsey champions an ethics of rules against the situationist Joseph Fletcher,
but is nevertheless in hearty agreement about the starting point. "Christian
ethics," says Ramsey, "finds its basis in *agape*."[51] Fletcher affirms, *"The
ultimate norm of Christian decisions is love: nothing else."*[52] Fletcher's
exclusion of all intrinsic values excepting love and Ramsey's advocacy of
generalized rules as well as specific decisions in applying love, although
raising important issues, do not contradict their agreement on the supreme
place of love.

Charles E. Curran represents well the contemporary movement of
American Roman Catholic ethics as he wrestles with the problem of relating natural law ethics to specifically Christian norms. While he insists on
the validity of both, as far as the explicitly Christian norms are concerned,
he assumes that the "distinctively Christian aspect found in the Scriptures"
may be referred to as "agape or *koinonia*," two terms representing human
relations governed by love, the first stressing the individual motive, the
second the communal relationship.[53]

Even Reinhold Niebuhr, with all his "realistic" warnings about the
"impossible possibility" of love in the social order, assumes it as the
Christian ideal. He says too that "the law of love is involved in all approx-
imations of justice, not only as the source of the norms of justice, but as an
ultimate perspective by which their limitations are discovered."[54]

Two men recently touched the American conscience deeply by appeal
to the spirit of Christian love. One was Pope John XXIII who, at the end
of his last encyclical, *Pacem in Terris*, said, "May Christ inflame the
desires of all men to break through the barriers which divide them, to
strengthen the bonds of mutual love, to learn to understand one another,
and to pardon those who have done them wrong." The other was Martin
Luther King, Jr., who, in his nonviolent crusade for civil rights constantly
stressed love as central. He said truly, in the Preface of *Stride Toward*

Freedom, that the book was "the chronicle of 50,000 Negroes"—in Montgomery—"who learned to fight for their rights with the weapon of love." At the end of the same book, he made the following memorable appeal:

> Arnold Toynbee says in *A Study of History* that it may be the Negro who will give the new spiritual dynamic to Western civilization that it so desperately needs to survive. I hope this is possible. The spiritual power that the Negro can radiate to the world comes from love, understanding, good will, and nonviolence. It may even be possible for the Negro, through adherence to nonviolence, so to challenge the nations of the world that they will seriously seek an alternative to war and destruction. In a day when Sputniks and Explorers dash through outer space and guided ballistic missiles are carving highways of death through the stratosphere, nobody can win a war. Today the choice is no longer between violence and nonviolence. It is either nonviolence or nonexistence. The Negro may be God's appeal to this age—an age drifting rapidly to its doom. The eternal appeal takes the form of a warning: "All who take the sword will perish by the sword."[55]

Love in the New Testament sense always embraces within it respect for the dignity of the other person. Without such respect there may be lust or other kinds of personal attraction or exploitation, but not love.

2. Seeking to nurture and maintain community.

The church itself was from its beginning the product of a generous sharing, motivated by love awakened by the power of God's Spirit, as related in the second chapter of Acts. In the last verses of the chapter we read that those who believed shared gladly food, possessions, homes, teachings, prayers, praise to God, and joy. In short, they shared themselves. So, in the Gospel of John, Jesus is represented as praying for his disciples and all who in the future learn his faith, "that they may be one, even as we are one," and again "that they may all be one; even as thou, Father, art in me, and I in thee, that they also may be in us" (17:11, 21).[56]

The *koinonia*, or community of Christian love, has often been sought within the bounds of a sect, a monastic order, or, more broadly, a church with a common body of dogma. James Sellers properly argues that such a limited scope of love and community is inadequate both to the outreaching love demonstrated in the deeds described in the New Testament and also to the urgent requirements of the present day. "*Koinonia,* the gathering of men into commonness under God, must take a radically new form in today's pluralistic world." There must be a coalition of human purpose, even while different people in it have their own various presuppositions.[57] Such a coalition was formed in the civil rights movement of the 1960s, particularly at Washington and on the Selma march. Although most of the organizing meetings were held in Protestant churches, many thousands of

Roman Catholics, Jews, and others took active part, many within the circles of leadership.

3. Due humility and restraint.

"Judge not, that you be not judged. . . . Why do you see the speck that is in your brother's eye, but do not notice the log that is in your own eye?" (Mt. 7:1, 3). These familiar words of Jesus are among various biblical warnings against self-righteous pride and moral condemnation of others.[58] According to the Gospels, one of the charges made against Jesus, from time to time, was that he associated with known sinners.[59]

God alone is to be our judge, for only he knows the secret motives and purposes of human beings. "For the word of God is living and active, sharper than any two-edged sword, piercing to the division of soul and spirit, of joints and marrow, and discerning the thoughts and intentions of the heart. And before him no creature is hidden, but all are open and laid bare to the eyes of him with whom we have to do" (Heb. 4:12–13).

As we have seen, Christian churchmen in America have frequently been self-righteous and censorious. However, in recent decades there has been a strong reaction in the churches against all this. The heavy emphasis of Reinhold Niebuhr and the New Reformation theologians on the sin of pride and the illusions of respected people about their own goodness has helped to create a more chastened and humble mood. Even when such theologies as those of Niebuhr and Karl Barth were rejected and where they have been supplanted, there is a more sensitive awareness that self-righteousness and the spirit of Christ are incompatible. Anyone who reads the documents of Vatican Council II will be impressed with a similarly chastened and humble mood in the Roman Catholic Church. The change has been enthusiastically welcomed in the United States.

4. Special care for the poor and weak.

Throughout the history of Christianity the churches have been much involved in works of charity for the handicapped, the powerless, and the poor. Christians who have engaged in such activity have been seeking to follow Jesus' example and his many admonitions.[60] In the present century, while work of relief to the needy has continued, many Christians have given greater attention to ameliorating the causes of poverty, public financing of social security and social welfare, and reducing the injustice which falls heavily on the handicapped and other poor.

In 1908 The Methodist Episcopal Church officially adopted a statement on the Church and Social Problems, later known as "The Social Creed." With little change it was soon adopted by the Federal Council of Churches. In its original and later revised forms The Social Creed has not only expressed but also influenced the concern of the churches with the policies of business and political institutions on human lives, especially those with little power. The statement adopted in 1908 included, among other items, reference to protection of workers from occupational hazards, abolition of child labor, "suppression of the 'sweating system' " of production, reducing hours of labor, and eliminating unemployment.

The revision of such statements to apply to current issues has continued to the present time. For example, in 1972 the General Conference of The United Methodist Church officially adopted a statement of Social Principles which included the following: "In order to provide basic needs such as food, clothing, shelter, education, health care, and other necessities, ways must be found to share more equitably the wealth of the world." The statement goes on to specify public policies to "begin to alleviate poverty."[61] Many other church bodies subscribe to similar programs.

5. Forgiveness and mercy.

Millions of Christians pray, "Forgive us our trespasses as we forgive those who trespass against us." In all the churches they read and hear the story of Jesus' refusal to condemn the woman taken in adultery although he did condemn the adulterous act when he said, "Go, and do not sin again" (John 8:3–11). Both by preaching and example he stressed again and again that all human salvation rested on God's forgiving mercy and that with such forgiveness must inevitably go our forgiving of wrongs done to us. According to this teaching, the Father's household is, in its very nature, a community of forgiveness and it is impossible to belong to it while maintaining an unforgiving attitude. Thus the unforgiving and jealous elder brother remains outside his rightful home where his father is feasting the return of the forgiven prodigal son (Luke 15:11–30). Jesus taught emphatically that those persons cannot be forgiven by God who are unforgiving toward other human beings (Mt. 6:14–15 and Mt. 18:23–35).

That many people sense, at least dimly, the relation between Christian teaching and the forgiveness of a criminal offender is indicated by the custom in many states of dispensing pardons from the governor or executive council at Christmas time.

6. Community of responsibility for sin and righteousness.

Despite the extraordinary individualism of American culture, some Christian doctrines affirm a deeply communal understanding of human life. The traditional doctrine of original sin has often been taught as if it meant a biological inheritance of sin and guilt by every baby born. That interpretation is not explicitly taught in the Bible (e.g., in the often cited Rom. 5:12–14). In recent generations there has been a growing inclination to understand it as signifying the network of responsibility and influence which relates every generation to succeeding generations and contemporaries to one another. Children grow up with anxieties and hostilities which their parents unwittingly passed on to them by the influence of their own failings. The hostilities of any individual tend to stir hostilities in others. Similarly, we have observed earlier the transmission of a traditional aggressive selfishness as a part of our American culture.

Whether the doctrine of original sin is understood in one of these ways or another, it always signifies a human solidarity in sin from which no person can truly claim to be free. Christians today marvel that so many of the Puritans, who taught and heard of original sin frequently and spoke much of their own sins, could have been so oblivious to their own self-righteous and harsh judgments of others.

As we are bound up in a community of sin, Christian teaching affirms, we are called to a community of righteousness. As all have sinned, so all are called to enter the stream of righteousness flowing down through the centuries from Christ (Rom. 5:15–21).

The Alcoholics Anonymous, outside the organized churches and including many persons not professed Christians, have caught and used particularly well the understanding of temptation and fall, on the one hand, and forgiving acceptance and moral victory, on the other, as communal, not isolated individual events. They know that we are responsible for our brothers and sisters.

7. Law for persons, not persons for law.

When a law has been enacted it tends to develop a kind of independent existence all its own. Many laws remain on the books years, and even generations, after the occasion has passed which made them useful or which once made legislators think they would be useful. Even laws generally useful may, when rigidly applied, sometimes do more harm than good. Jesus spoke to this issue when, confronted with a strict-construction application of the sabbath laws, he said, "The sabbath was made for man, not man for the sabbath" (Mk. 2:27; cf. Luke 6:6–10; 14:1–4).

Again and again, especially in the Letters of Paul, law is recognized as serving a useful purpose, but as powerless to create new good life (e.g., Gal. 3:23–26). Too much stress on knowing and keeping all the requirements of law can lead to arrogance. Love is better. Thus, speaking about knowledge of the dietary laws, Paul writes, " 'Knowledge' puffs up, but love builds up" (1 Cor. 8:1).

We have seen that the frequent opposition of faith and grace to law, in Christian literature, sometimes produces a regrettable division which leaves legal affairs beyond the pale of religious concern. It is ironical that in America church people often have been among the first to respond to some new kind of evil conduct or even of annoying or unpopular behavior with a demand for a new criminal law. We should have learned from the New Testament not to expect law to create the good community, but rather to employ works of love and faith. In short, we ought to place less reliance on criminal law and more on other modes of social influence. We should resort to criminal law only when searching, wide-ranging consideration indicates that criminal law can effectively deal with a particular destructive evil and that nothing else can do so.

C. American Secular Ethics

Outside the appeals to religious principles among Jewish and Christian believers there are other forms of ethical teaching which have both reflected and influenced the humane conscience of America. Among philosophical writers who have carefully delineated such teaching, several themes recur so frequently as to constitute a wide range of ethical consensus, though with varying proportional emphasis and differing rationales.

1. Consistency and coherence with empirical data.

Brand Blanshard's ethical viewpoint is set forth in a book with the significant title *Reason and Goodness*.[62] *"The Good,"* says Blanshard, *"in the sense of the ethical end, is the most comprehensive possible fulfillment and satisfaction of impulse-desire."*[63] Similar commitments to comprehensive coherence are to be found in the ethical writing of John Dewey,[64] William K. Frankena,[65] Peter A. Bertocci and Richard M. Millard, and many others. Bertocci and Millard are particularly explicit and clear as they affirm that "the *criterion of value* . . . is experiential, growing coherence within the total life of value experience in self and others and all the factors relevant to the creation of value experience. This means that the dependability test of any value claim is its capacity to 'live with' other value claims in a supportive relation."[66] Even when this principle is not stated the philosophical moralist nearly always assumes it because the very nature of philosophy is usually understood to involve a rational defense of ideas held to be true, taking experience into account.[67] This is true even when the place of intuition in ethics is especially emphasized.

Moreover, philosophical moralists, like thoughtful people generally, place a high premium on such related qualities as honesty, sincerity, integrity, and dependability. If a person or a government acts inconsistently or in ways not coherent with the facts, such action is undependable and throws the person's or government's integrity into doubt. Certainly when the system of criminal justice acts in inconsistent and undependable ways it seriously violates the most basic rational notions of justice.

2. Respect for all persons.

May and Abraham Edel, writing explicitly about criminal sanctions in the many societies studied by anthropologists, say, ". . . a given sanction is better because it involves *less violence*; violence against humans should be a last resort because it is contrary to *the ideal of the dignity or worth of every man*."[68] The philosophical sociologist Pitirim A. Sorokin maintained that if human civilization was to survive the perils on the horizon, then the elements in our social order which produce selfishness, hate, and war must be eliminated and we must promote altruism. Hence the ideal persons whom we should emulate are those "the scope of whose love is widest, being coterminous with the whole universe and God; the intensity of whose love is highest; whose love is wisest and most creative, and whose acts are motivated only by love itself, continuous and durable."[69]

As Alan Gewirth points out, "The western liberal democratic tradition of justice differs from other traditions on both the formal and the substantive components of justice. It holds that certain basic rights must be distributed equally, and that they must be consonant with the dignity of human personality."[70]

Few writers on ethics in this century have had so much influence on the ethical ideals of nonchurchgoing Americans as John Dewey. In the ethical work which he shared with James H. Tufts is a significant paragraph about criminal justice. The authors begin by seeming to give support to retribution when they say, "What erring human nature deserves or merits, it is just it should have." However, they go on to say that "a moral agent deserves to *be* a moral agent; and hence deserves that punishments inflicted shall be *corrective*, not merely retributive." Moreover, they condemn the effort to excuse punishment devoid of reformative influence "under the plea that it vindicates law." "Such failure," they write, "comes rather from thoughtless custom; from a lazy unwillingness to find better means; from an admixture of pride with lack of sympathy for others; from a desire to maintain things as they are rather than go to the causes which generate criminals."[71]

Gregory Vlastos defines the very meaning of justice in terms of personal respect. He writes, "I offer the following definition: An action is *just* if, and only if it is prescribed exclusively by regard for the rights of all whom it affects substantially."[72] William K. Frankena supports the principle of love, understood as meaning benevolence, and "the principle of distributive justice or equality" as the two basic principles of ethics and of justice.[73] Speaking of criminal sanctions, Frankena declares, "Society is morally justified in requiring . . . at least a certain minimal subscription to the moral institution of life. . . . But . . . society must be careful here. For it is itself morally required to respect the individual's autonomy and liberty, and in general to treat him justly."[74]

William Ernest Hocking acknowledges that a wrongdoer may be in such a mood of violence that before he can perceive a loving word or act we may need first "to induce a quiescent frame of mind." But justice requires a way of love in dealing with him and in the end it is only by love that the evil will is to be overcome.[75]

When we remember how harshly Americans are accustomed to punishing criminal offenders, as compared with the laws and practices of other developed democratic peoples, and how much emphasis is placed on retribution here, we see that the teachings of universal benevolence and invariable respect for human dignity pronounce a serious judgment upon us. For the sake of integrity we must choose between those teachings and our vindictive practices.

3. Equality.

When our founding fathers declared that "all men are created equal" they implied a serious demand on our system of criminal justice, as well as on our other political and social institutions. Even though they conveniently sidestepped questions about slavery and were probably not at all aware of the inequities suffered by women, they declared an ideal norm which in time would be seen to reach far beyond the boundaries which they saw. Alan Gewirth observes that this tradition "puts human equality into the very rules or principles of human treatment."[76]

People frequently complain that by any standard of value which we may reasonably adopt, people are *not* all of equal worth. It may even be asked, if my life as a criminally selfish and undisciplined person is worth as much as it would be if I were a wise and saintly benefactor of mankind, what is the point of my trying to improve my character? Frankena speaks to this point when he asserts his firm belief in "the equal intrinsic value of every human being as such," but goes on to say that this idea "is valid only as a principle of what is right or obligatory. It is not valid as a value-judgment about the intrinsic worthwhileness of different good lives"[77]— let alone, we must suppose, good lives and wickedly destructive ones.

Paul A. Freund believes that social justice, and not only criminal justice, requires "*Equality*: the measure of equivalence or proportionality." He adds, "The problem is to determine the relevant peer group . . . and the criteria of equivalence or proportionality."[78] This is not an easy task. Sentencing, regardless of the purpose or goal adopted, is therefore a difficult art and not an exact science. On the other hand, as we observed in

Chapters 4, 5, and 6, there are many present practices which are obvious violations of the principle and therefore so unjust as to cry out for reform.

4. Minimal interference with personal freedom.

A Polish criminologist remarked that crime can be brought to a low level if the law-abiding citizens are willing to pay a sufficiently heavy price in loss of freedom.[79] If our uniformed and secret police were to be multiplied; if every person in the country were required to carry an official identity card at all times and to keep a police office constantly notified of his employment and all his movements outside a limited district; if the police were free to seize and search any person or building at will, and summary court procedures were used; and if such drastic measures were generally acceptable to the populace—then "crime" could be reduced drastically. But many activities of the police and other government officials would be of such character that we would now regard them as criminal invasions of our rights. From such invasions citizens would, of course, have no protection. When the police are the criminals, with official government authority, there may be a high degree of public *order*, but *freedom under law* has been lost. So have been many values invaded by such activities of public officials, values which our present laws protect.

The obligation to respect every person's freedom is rooted in the fact that "persons, and only persons, are 'ends in themselves,' " whether so valued by others or not.[80] So writes Gregory Vlastos, following a well-worn trail of thought first blazed by Immanuel Kant. Because of this intrinsic worth or dignity of every person, Vlastos argues *"one man's well-being is as valuable as any other's"* and *"one man's freedom is as valuable as any other's."*[81]

Speaking of restrictions imposed by law, Frankena concedes restrictions, but says law must respect "the individual's autonomy and liberty." Society "must remember that morality is made to minister to the good lives of individuals and not to interfere with them any more than is necessary."[82]

Americans have always been a freedom-loving people. Among the "unalienable Rights" by which "all men" are "endowed by their Creator," the Declaration of Independence proclaims, are "Life, Liberty and the pursuit of Happiness."[83] If these rights are "unalienable," then even for cause such as the commission of crime they must be infringed as little as possible and only so far as necessary to protect the rights of others.

As we observed earlier, Americans have deliberately and flagrantly violated these most basic human rights by the practice of slavery, by many dealings with the American Indians, and by oppressing some other minorities.* It would seem that some of our practices in criminal justice have institutionalized such violations.

5. *Responsibility of the whole community for opportunities of all persons.*

Going beyond "respect for all persons" many philosophers believe in the ethical obligation to seek the well-being of all. Bertocci and Millard do not include love among the virtues. They write, "The main reason for this is our conviction that love is not one virtue among others, but the *style of life* that is willed in and through each of the virtues. *Love is the total orientation of a person's thinking, feeling, and willing insofar as his controlling commitment is the ideal growth of personality in himself and in all other persons.*"[84] Similarly, Blanshard explains that the "*most comprehensive possible fulfilment and satisfaction of impulse-desire*" which is "the ethical end" of all moral conduct "takes account . . . not only of this man's desires, but of all men's."[85]

Sorokin contends, as we have seen, that only a large-scale turning from selfishness to altruism can save the future of humankind. Present quantities of selfish, heedless, pathological, and frustrated attitudes will continue to produce ever more crime and more destructive wars.[86] Speaking of the great creators of altruism who point the way out of our present disastrous trends, Sorokin makes a statement highly relevant to policies of criminal justice. Says he, "In this point their main technical rule is: *only love and kindness generate love and kindness; hatred and enmity produce only hatred and enmity; selfishness breeds only selfishness.*"[87]

John Dewey, in the closing appeal of his book *A Common Faith*, says, "Ours is the responsibility of conserving, transmitting, rectifying and expanding the heritage of values we have received that those who come after us may receive it more solid and secure, more widely accessible and more generously shared than we have received it."[88]

The inclusiveness of obligatory concern for all persons is emphasized by Edel and Edel. As anthropologists these authors speak about the wide variety of mores and customs in different societies. This variety does not lead them, however, to reject the quest for objective ethical standards. Among the "common goals" which they believe "would survive the most critical evaluation" and receive substantial reflective acceptance would be the active belief "that the widening of the moral community, at least in the sense of treating all people however different or alien as human individuals who count, is a human good."[89]

Paul A. Freund argues that justice must move beyond the consideration of individuals to concern for the larger community. One constituent of

* See especially Chap. 12, above.

social justice, he contends, is "*Community*: the interrelation of individual justice and social justice. . . ." Accordingly, it is "artificial and unsatisfactory to consider individual justice apart from the interests of larger groups, and the most relevant groupings."[90]

When we observe how narrowly criminal justice commonly focuses on the individual defendant alone, we can glimpse some far-reaching implications of Freund's teaching. Yet many moralists and probably most thoughtful Americans would agree with him.

In this chapter, to the present point, we have been concerned with religious and secular ethicists and their teachings which have important implications for criminal justice. Of course there are also important philosophers of jurisprudence who have written extensively on the law in general and criminal law in particular. Some of them will be considered in the next chapter as we seek to construct the basic outlines of an American philosophy of criminal justice.

D. Ethical Norms of Criminal Justice

After this rapid survey of converging relevant teachings from the three great ethical traditions in the United States, we must now move to formulate some ethical norms of criminal justice. If we are to ask meaningfully whether any law, sentence, policy, or practice is just, or whether a proposed philosophy of criminal justice is ethically acceptable, we must have at hand ethical norms to be used as criteria.

The norms which follow are all, I believe, supported by the three traditions we have examined as related to empirical realities of American society. I believe that few Americans would deny that they represent valid moral standards.

1. Consistency and coherence with realities.

Consistency in the substance and procedures of the law is required by the very idea of government by law and not by persons. The principle is explicit in much philosophical ethics. It is also required to conform with the second norm, which is supported by all three traditions. As indicated earlier, consistency in practice requires coherence with factual realities.*

2. Benevolent good will and respect toward all persons.

The Torah teaches steadfast love, the New Testament makes lovingkindness toward every person central in human relations, and a dominant teaching of secular American philosophy is the moral obligation of universal benevolent good will, with respect for human dignity.

---

* See above, C, 1.

Hate, vindictive anger, and demeaning personal indifference are destructive of human values and exacerbate alienation, a prime cause of crime.

This norm and the requirement of consistent practice form the basis of the others. *A consistent, hence dependable, respectful, benevolent good will toward all persons is the fundamental requirement of ethically defensible criminal justice.*

3. Equal rights for all persons.

Respect and good will toward all persons and the principle of equality require that in the enactment and enforcement of criminal law all shall have equal rights. This norm, as we have observed, is included in the Constitution, Amendment XIV.

4. Presumption of innocence.

The written and oral Torah, as we have seen, both include strict rules for safeguarding the rights of accused people against their accusers, placing a clear and emphatic burden of proof upon the latter. The Christian injunctions against judgmental attitudes and for love and respect give strong support, as does the principle of mutuality expressed in the Golden Rule and similar formulas of various religious and secular traditions. The presumption of innocence until guilt is proved beyond reasonable doubt is strongly affirmed in Supreme Court decisions, especially *In Re Winship* (1970).

5. Special care to protect the poor, weak, and unpopular from unfair treatment.

Experience among all peoples reveals strong tendencies to provide less than fair treatment to persons ill-equipped to cope with the forces of organized society. Our religious traditions, as we have seen, make emphatic special provisions to compensate for such handicaps. The ethical principle of equity as generally supported by secular moralists implies the need for such provisions when related to the realities which empirical observation discloses. The handicaps of poverty, ignorance, membership in an ethnic minority, and unpopular life-style all pose threats to fair treatment by the lawmakers, the police, judges and juries, correctional officials, parole boards and parole officers, as well as by common citizens involved in reporting offenses, testifying in court, employing ex-offenders, or receiving them back into the open community after incarceration. The treatment of Mr. Nixon and Mr. Agnew, contrasted with official actions at Kent State, Jackson State, Wounded Knee, and daily in court, come to mind. If equal rights are to be more than a mockery, special arrangements must be made to overcome the handicaps of poverty, youth, and minority status.

6. Restoration of community when disrupted.

Both Jewish and Christian ethics stress the importance of community. Some secular moral philosophers do also. The personal values affirmed by all ethicists are threatened or destroyed when the community is disrupted. Division, hostility, and alienation in the community increase the rate of criminal homicides and suicides, thus threatening the lives of residents in the community. Property crimes, family dissolution, and infant mortality are all high where community is fragmented and hostilities are unresolved. Every crime of one person against another arouses feelings of insecurity, hostility, and alienation in both victim and offender and often in narrow or wide circles of other people.

An important goal of criminal justice ought, therefore, to be to restore community at a level no lower and preferably higher than that existing prior to the crime.

7. Responsibility of all individuals for the community.

Neither social justice nor criminal justice is confined to the responsibility of public officials. All citizens share responsibility for the health of the community in proportion to their ability to influence it. A person who has good will toward other persons must, in view of the realities, be concerned that true justice be done, for in the long run injustice is injurious to all. Justice is everybody's business.

17

A Basic Philosophy of Criminal Justice

Now that we have established some ethical norms for critical evaluation we must face the constructive task of proposing a single coherent philosophy of criminal justice in accord with those norms. This philosophy should define the basic purpose of the whole criminal justice system, including all its parts.* When the legislator is considering a proposed change in the criminal law, what should be his controlling aim? When the citizen is deciding what to do about a criminal violation he has observed, what should be his dominant purpose? What should determine the structure and

---

* For discussion of *methods* and of specific *reforms*, see below, Chaps. 18–24.

program of a police department? When a judge is trying to determine a just sentence for the convicted person before him, how should he define a "just" sentence? Similar questions need to be faced by correctional officials of all kinds, parole board members, potential employers of ex-offenders, and others.

Different people and even the same people at different times are giving radically different answers. That is the main reason for the gross disparities in our legislation, in sentences, in police conduct, in parole actions, and in the pressures exerted by citizens.*

The National Advisory Commission on Criminal Justice Standards and Goals, in its discussion of needed legislation on corrections, declares, "State and Federal correctional and penal codes are a hodgepodge enacted over the generations and follow no consistent pattern or philosophy." The Commission recommends that the reform legislation should be done by any state through adoption of a single inclusive penal code. The changes should be "guided by a single philosophy and legislative policy. . . ."[1]

But what should the single philosophy be? This is the question with which we propose to grapple in the present chapter.

A. John Rawls' General Theory of Justice

The most discussed book on the basic philosophy of justice in recent years is undoubtedly John Rawls' *A Theory of Justice*.[2] The book is not on *criminal* justice and devotes explicitly to that subject very few pages. Rawls is concerned with the abstract definition of a just society. He acknowledges that he is leaving to the side various important questions of justice. In his task he will be "satisfied if it is possible to formulate a reasonable conception of justice for the basic structure of society conceived for the time being as a closed system isolated from other societies."[3] However, his work is relevant to more concrete issues like our question concerning the goals of criminal justice. As he says, a sound theory of the just society would render other problems of justice more tractable.

Rawls represents justice as "fairness." Justice as fairness is constituted by "the principles that free and rational persons concerned to further their own interests would accept in an initial position of equality as defining the fundamental terms of their association."[4] The acceptance must be such as would be made "under a veil of ignorance," that is, without knowing what their own roles, abilities, positions, or time spans would be in the society, nor whether the society would have abundant or limited resources.[5] It will be seen that Rawls' method is a precise and abstract development from the

---

* Such disparity must, of course, be distinguished from differences due to principled individualization of cases.

theory of the social contract, especially as formulated by Immanuel Kant.[6]

What are the general principles of a just society which rational persons would accept under the veil of ignorance? Rawls believes there are two such principles:

> *First Principle*
> Each person is to have an equal right to the most extensive total system of equal basic liberties compatible with a similar system of liberty for all.
> *Second Principle*
> Social and economic inequalities are to be arranged so that they are both:
>> (a) to the greatest benefit of the least advantaged, consistent with the just savings principle, and
>> (b) attached to offices and positions open to all under conditions of fair equality of opportunity.[7]

The First Principle seems clear enough without elaboration. Concerning the Second Principle it must be explained that "the just savings principle" is the requirement that one generation is not to squander resources to the detriment of later generations so far as the conditions of the latter can be foreseen. Rather, the present generation must so save that a rational person not knowing whether he or she was destined to live in this generation or a future generation would approve the arrangement.[8]

It seems evident that the values which are the subject of the First Principle are incommensurate with those of the Second Principle. Liberties are different from economic resources and social status. Rawls believes that rational persons in the conditions he has specified would place so high a value on liberties that no restriction could be placed upon them for the sake of economic benefits or social status. Hence "liberty can be restricted only for the sake of liberty."[9]

Anyone who wishes to gain the full force of Rawls' argument must, of course, read the nearly 600 pages of his book. Some readers, including me, would quarrel with his placing an absolute priority on liberties above economic goods. It is often argued by champions of Marxian socialism that economic goods are more basic than political liberties and it must seem so to many persons who are on the verge of starvation. Some other specifics of his argument are open to question, such as his contention that striving for status will no longer be a serious problem in a society of equal liberties.[10] However, none of these more specific points nor even the absolute priority of liberties is essential to Rawls' most general theory of justice nor to seeing some implications of that theory for *criminal* justice.

Rawls affirms that all members of a society would benefit by the establishment and maintenance of a society which all rational members would see to be fair. If some members violated the liberties, persons, or property of others, thus disturbing the just structures of society, all would have a stake in stopping such violations and restoring the just arrangements. Since "the principles of right and justice are collectively rational . . . it is in the interest of each that everyone else should comply with just arrangements. . . . It is also the case that the general affirmation of the sense of justice is a great social asset, establishing the basis for mutual trust and confidence from which all normally benefit. Thus, in agreeing to penalties that stabilize a scheme of cooperation the parties accept the same kind of constraint on self-interest that they acknowledge in choosing the principles of justice in the first place."[11]

It is not claimed that offenders against the social order will be happy with the penalties constraining their misguided activities in pursuit of self-interest. But since the arrangements and the penalties used to stabilize them are actually for the collective best interests of all, the complaints of the aberrant members are ill-founded and it is just to override them. So far as possible the social order will be maintained by general consent, but "under normal conditions public knowledge and confidence are always imperfect. So even in a just society it is reasonable to admit certain constraining arrangements to insure compliance, but their main purpose is to underwrite citizens' trust in one another."[12]

According to Rawls' doctrine that "liberty can be restricted only for the sake of liberty," it would appear that those penalties of criminal justice which involve incarceration or even the lesser restrictions of probation should never be used for property crimes, leaving only restitution and fines as proper penalties for such offenses. He has not discussed this matter explicitly and has left the issue in doubt. It is in doubt because many property crimes have the effect of invading liberty. If my car is stolen, my liberty of movement is restricted. If I am defrauded of my savings, the effect may be to take from me the liberty to travel, to live in a neighborhood of my choosing, and to do what I have by hard work prepared the means to do.

In fact, does not the pressing of this question cast further doubt on the sharp distinction between liberty and all other values and even more on the absolute priority he has given to liberty?

Be that as it may, Rawls' basic theory of justice as fairness, with its First and Second Principles, but leaving aside his more questionable statements on priorities and other matters, should, I think, be accepted. It appears to accord with the enlightened American conscience. However, when limited thus, the theory is too abstract to take us very far. What does the theory suggest concerning criminal justice? I propose the following inferences:

(1) The sanctions of criminal justice may be ethically invoked as penalties to assist in securing or safeguarding a structure of society which is basically fair in the opportunities for life, liberty, and other values which it affords to all its members.

(2) The penalties invoked must be employed solely against persons whose acts disrupt or weaken that structure and so deprive other members of liberties or other rights and opportunities afforded by the social structure. The penalties are justified to protect the community, not as moral retribution somehow restoring an ethical balance between subjective moral culpability and punishing pain suffered. They are not morally indifferent like the penalties for "offside" in football, or for failing to make a bid in a game of bridge, or for hitting a golf ball into a pond. Such penalties as these mentioned, in our games, are parts of the structures of the games themselves and the incurring of them by no means implies a willful disruption of the structure which makes the games possible for all the participants to enjoy.

Some penalties in sports are for actions which go beyond this description. For example, when a hockey player seriously threatens or attacks an official and is given a "game misconduct," his expulsion from the game is not for a mere infraction of a rule but for a violation which threatens the game itself.

A criminal sanction is a much more serious penalty for it is directed against a violation, not merely disrupting a game but attacking the orderly social structure on which the personal security, liberty, and opportunity for other values of all members depend. Criminal justice is, or ought to be, a social defense against disruption of the social order.[13]

It may be protested that even without defending retribution we should grant that to express sufficiently emphatic social disapproval of some acts the state must punish them. Reprobation should be supported even though retribution or retaliation is not. I agree, provided that the purpose of the penalty as reproof is to make repetition of such acts by the same offender or others less likely. But in that case reprobation is subsumed under the heading of deterrence and is directed to the future, not the past. It must then take such forms and be used in such cases as experience indicates will be likely to make it useful as a preventive measure. In some instances the embarrassment of incurring solemnly formal public disapproval will exert more deterrent influence than the fear of physical discomfort and temporary deprivation of liberty.

(3) The justice of a criminal sanction is tainted so far as the social order itself is lacking in justice as fairness. The moral right of the society to enforce conformity to its regulations is limited to the degree to which the regulations are fair to all the people involved. This is a restatement of

Augustine's rhetorical question, "Justice being taken away, then, what are kingdoms but great robberies?"[14]

Does this mean, then, that it is unethical to enforce any law until the state has become perfectly just? Emphatically not! Perfection of social justice is not attained anywhere in this world. But if *no* laws were enforced there would be far less opportunity for life and liberty than there is now, even among the most deprived minorities in the seriously imperfect and often unjust states of the United States. Moreover, ethical distinctions may be made between some laws and others. Enforcement of laws against burglary, aggravated assault, forcible rape, robbery, criminal homicide, fraud, and violations of safety regulations in the housing codes is as useful in protecting the poor and friendless as the affluent and popular. In fact as we observed earlier, one of the most frequent complaints of ghetto residents has been the *lack* of adequate police protection.* Enforcement of laws depriving Indians of their treaty rights or supporting the exclusion of black people from some housing or full suffrage is unjust, while enforcement of various other laws, even against Indian or black violators, is just. The actual effect of the use of a given criminal law must be taken carefully into account. A law against trespass in privately possessed buildings, for example, is needed by nearly everyone. However, when it has been used to subject black people to criminal penalties because they entered restaurants and sat at tables or counters awaiting service, like the white customers, it was obviously unfair, unethical, and unjust.

The best criminal laws are tainted by the social injustice of the order which they protect, but often it is far more damaging, even to the poorest victims of the social inequities, to fail to enforce them than to enforce them. Enforce them we must, but with special care when victims of social injustice are involved, lest the social injustice be compounded by inequities in the criminal court.

Rawls has not been mainly concerned with criminal justice and some of our most urgent questions concerning it remain unanswered. Especially basic and important is the question, What is just enforcement of criminal law? Closely akin are questions concerning the morally acceptable scope of criminal law and principles for determining ethically appropriate penalties for its infraction. Finally, when the judge is seeking to determine the just sentence which he should pronounce upon the convicted person before him, what ought he to mean by a just sentence?

Pursuing these questions further, we turn to a writer treating the philosophy of jurisprudence explicitly and at length. Among writers on this subject the preeminent figure in the history of American law is Roscoe Pound (1870–1964).[15]

---

* See above, Chap. 3, A.

B. Roscoe Pound's Theory of Interests

Pound set forth his basic philosophy of law as follows: "A legal system attains its end by recognizing certain interests, individual, public and social; by defining the limits within which these interests shall be recognized legally and given effect through the force of the state, and by endeavoring to secure the interests so recognized within the defined limits."[16] What is meant by interests? As subject of law, "an interest may be defined initially as a demand or desire or expectation which human beings, either individually or in groups or associations or relations, seek to satisfy, of which, therefore, the adjustment of human relations and ordering of human behavior through the force of a politically organized society must take into account."[17]

How is the legislator, judge, or legal philosopher to know what interests are present in the jurisdiction with which he is concerned? Pound was not quite clear on this point. In general, he classified and enumerated interests in the societies governed basically by common law, especially the United States, by referring to interests actually asserted and claiming notice in existing law.[18] Yet he was not fully satisfied by a definition limited to such legally articulated claims. His definitions speak of "desires," "needs," and "expectations," as well as of "demands" and "claims."[19]

Julius Stone, present Australian legal philosopher friendly to Pound's approach but one of his most exacting critics, observes Pound's apparent uncertainty about the precise definition of interests. Stone wants none of the subjectivity of judgment to which the psychological definitions would open the way. He insists on "attention to *de facto* 'demands' as such, to 'interests' in *that* sense; and also on the importance of avoiding language which secretly embraces 'desires' or 'needs' as well."[20] At the same time he seeks to guard Pound's legitimate concerns by insisting on a diligent "openness towards new evidence" and claims which may not be sufficiently heeded in the legal order.[21]

The issues involved are not easily settled. The law should not be expected to probe every recess of the citizens' minds to make sure that every secret desire or every need—even if not recognized by the conscious self—is taken into legal account. On the other hand, there are persons having a right to legal protection who are not capable of making demands on the legal order. Such persons would include some seriously handicapped children with special needs for their full development, some elderly patients in infirmary wards, and some people long imprisoned and forgotten in correctional and psychiatric institutions. Many other people need protection against dangerous drugs, even prescription drugs, but do not know of the dangers and so make no demands. Fortunately for all of us, a few interested citizens and lawyers, not content with letting the law wait to hear demands, have, by persistent investigation, discovered many needs and brought a measure of legal assistance.[22]

A possible solution, not far from a direction now under way in some quarters, would be to define interests in the broad manner of Pound, then to specify that they are ordinarily to be identified by the articulated demands, as Stone contends, but that special measures must be taken to discover the needs of certain "voiceless" members of society and others unaware of dangers to which they are being subjected. Special provision must accordingly be made for several kinds of ombudsmen and public advocacy lawyers to discover such needs and to voice them in appropriate demands upon the legal and political order.

Pound, following Rudolf von Jhering, classifies interests as (1) individual, (2) public, and (3) social. The relations between public and social interests are somewhat ambiguous and Stone proposes reducing the three classes to two: individual and social.[23] Pound himself agrees that the two classes may well be understood to include all, but includes public interests only as a matter of convenience, apparently in deference to certain customary, though by no means universal, usages.[24] Here I agree with Stone and observe that for our purposes, at least, the threefold classification would even entail a loss of convenience while the inclusion of public interests as a separate classification incurs the risk of being thought to imply distinct and perhaps superior interests of the state over against those of its own citizens.

Under individual interests we include such individual rights[25] as inviolability of the physical person; freedom of will against coercive force, threat, or pressure; honor and reputation against wanton insult or defamation; privacy and sensibilities against invasion or affront; and belief and opinion, including free speech, against needless restraint. Included also are domestic relations and various economic rights. Social interests include interests of the state against treason, interference with the machinery of government, and foreign violation or invasion. Social interests include also all interests of the people generally. Thus when larceny is committed against one person, not only does that person suffer a violation of his own right, but the community suffers a violation of security for all members. Social interests, in a different aspect, appear also as individual interests. Among social interests Pound lists security of social institutions, such as family, church, and political and economic institutions; the general morals; conservation of natural resources—including human resources; general progress; and the individual life—especially its fair opportunity for developing full potential.[26] All these are of value because they are of interest to individual persons.

According to this theory, it is the business of law to secure the interests selected within the proper limits. But how ought the law to select the interests to be protected or promoted and how determine their proper limits? We have seen that Rawls advocated restraining liberty by law, only to protect liberty. In this his view is similar to some jurists of the 19th century.[27] As Pound observes, this has proved to be impossible. Liberty is too closely bound up with other social interests which a civilized society must take into serious account.[28]

Clearly, not all interests deserve protection. Some persons demand the right to defraud the poor and the gullible, others to spread heroin addiction among youth for their own profit. Should the law defend such interests of people in exploiting other members of society?

Evidently, criteria must be adopted to distinguish between valid and invalid interests. Moral philosophers devote much attention to the distinguishing between true values and spurious value claims. The most useful method, widely adopted in various forms, implicit or avowed, is to recognize as genuine values the desired or appreciated experiences which tend to reinforce other such experiences so as to help produce a whole life which is appreciated by that life itself. At the same time desired or enjoyed experiences which have the net effect of diminishing for the subject more appreciated experiences than they themselves constitute, or of undermining his efforts to develop a coherently meaningful and appreciated life, are rejected as false value claims.[29]

As stated thus far, the norm is purely individualistic. This will not do for the law of a society, however, and the moral philosophers have not stopped at that level. True values and the interests to be protected by law must also be at least consistent with the similarly coherent and socially acceptable interests of other persons. The cultivation and pursuit of individual interests is primarily the business of individuals. It is the business of law to protect and encourage a kind of social matrix in which such pursuit of individual values by all the people can take place with greatest likelihood of success. Other social institutions share this responsibility. Individual interests which undermine efforts by the law, the family, religious and educational institutions, and various voluntary associations to cultivate such a social matrix do not merit legal support. Laws and legal actions which undermine such efforts are unjust.

Pound himself puts the ruling principle of law as follows: "Secure all interests so far as possible with the least sacrifice of the totality of interests or the scheme of interests as a whole."[30] To act according to this principle, in legislature, police department, court, or parole board, is not an exact science, but an art. Yet adopting it by no means reduces the meaning of legal justice to sheer relativity. Neither does it depend on mere emotion as Hermann Isay charged.[31] Many claims cannot be reasonably regarded as coherent with the interest in a society fertile for the growing of mutually useful and happy lives. The principle certainly does not dictate a fixed and uniform individual or social life-style. But it does provide a way of judging present laws and procedures and future proposals of change.

Where does Pound see criminal justice in relation to the whole legal system? "The criminal law," he says, "is the chief agency of legal systems for securing social interests as such, i.e. as dissociated from any immediate individual interest which might be subsumed under them."[32] The criminal law is not alone in this task, however. Among the various other means for securing social interests one which is being used "more and more today" is the administrative agency.[33]

Criminal law, Pound tells us, uses four sanctioning devices: Punishment, specific redress, substitutional redress, and prevention. "Of the four . . . punishment and substitutionary redress are the oldest and the least satisfactory."[34] He favors the development of specific redress (included in Chap. 19, below) and prevention as "ordinary legal remedies." He adds that the "prejudice against them in our law is historical and has no sound basis."[35]

Beyond such general statements Pound has little to say about meting out justice to criminal offenders. He describes unjust treatment of the weak and poor by police and by *abuse* of the elaborate individualizing devices which are present and needed through the entire process of criminal justice.[36] He speaks against "the old-time ignominious punishments that treated the human offender like a brute, that did not save his human dignity."[37] He also acknowledges with apparent approval the conservation of human assets by the constructive use of juvenile courts and special provisions for youthful offenders and recent extensions "to the reformation of mature delinquents."[38] He gives us little further direct guidance in the critically important matter of purpose and criteria by which to choose sanctions.

C. A Form and Extension of Pound's Theory Indicated by the Present Study

In 1954 I had a fruitful conference with Stanley E. Qua, then Chief Justice of the Supreme Judicial Court in Massachusetts, on my question about what was meant by a *just* disposition of a criminal case in which the defendant had been found guilty. He said much about the limits set for the sentencing judge by the statutes and judicial precedents. But in the end he came down on a principle which clearly echoes Pound but makes explicit application to the task of sentencing a convicted person. The judge, he pointed out, stands at the intersection of various conflicting interests. The convicted person normally has an obvious interest in a sentence which opens the way to the largest possible degree of liberty and promise of a respected and rewarding life. His dependents, if any, want the restoration of his earning power and loving presence—if he has been giving these. The victim or victims, in a typical case, want to be assured that they will not be victimized again by the same person and that his sentence will make such victimization by others at least less likely. Then there is the whole neighborhood, with its heightened anxieties, and even the larger community, which loses some degree of security with every crime and needs as much restoration of a sense of security as possible. There may be other interests represented also. The judge, said Chief Justice Qua, must pronounce the sentence which, on the whole, will best serve this whole array of interests in conflict. To the extent that he succeeds, the sentence is just.

Is this not the goal which would be required by the ethical norms of justice at which we arrived in the last chapter? Most of those norms rested on the basic principle of benevolent good will toward all persons. When I am dealing only with one good person it is usually not difficult to know how I can express good will toward him. But when I must make a decision which affects two or more persons whose interests are in conflict, then Christian lovingkindness, Jewish steadfast love (*chesed*), or the philosopher's general benevolence must be expressed in the form of justice.

Justice is often assumed to mean retribution in proportion to moral desert and then lovingkindness and mercy are set in opposition to it.[39] This, of course, begs the question. We are here seeking an answer to the question how a people reared in the high religious and secular ethical traditions of the United States ought to define the very meaning of justice. Has not our argument prepared us to answer?

Justice is a rationally coherent expression of love or benevolence distributed fairly in a situation of interests in tension or conflict. This is true, no matter whether a mother is dividing a prized and limited dish of food between two hungry children, the writer of a will is apportioning an estate among persons who have claims upon him, a legislator is writing a tax bill, or a judge is sentencing a serious disturber of social order.

But what is meant by the judge in criminal court distributing his good will *fairly*? We might get a clue by looking again at the mother's division of food. Some wise mothers have asked one of the clamant children to divide the food into two portions, with the proviso that the other will then choose the portion to be his. As nearly as possible, in complex situations of conflicting interests, the legislator, judge, and other officials are to follow the Golden Rule, doing what they would want done if they were in the places of the various persons affected. Obviously, this cannot be done perfectly. Justice is the object of an art of balancing interests in conflict.

The reader acquainted with European legal philosophy will recognize affinity between the view being advocated here and Marc Ancel's philosophy of "the new social defense."[40] Like Ancel, I am advocating that criminal justice have the positive purpose of protecting society for the sake of the people in it. Likewise, I urge the reform of criminal law, the courts and corrections, not the substituting for them of universal therapeutic procedures—which in practice prove to be especially unjust and dehumanizing when legal safeguards are removed or relaxed.[41] Like Ancel, I think punishment should be employed for positive purposes of deterrence and incapacitation (usually for a short period), but not for some kind of "abstract and theoretical satisfaction" for the offense by prescribed suffering.[42] When Ancel accepts "retribution" in some instances,[43] I am puzzled. However, the difference may be only linguistic, in view of the sentence from which I have just quoted. He may simply be insisting on proportionality between offense and punishment, which I too defend.

On the other hand, while Ancel would seek to readapt and even integrate the offender into society and he recommends restitution to victims, he does not go so far as I do, in the pages to follow, in centering attention on the community.

One more requirement must be made of criminal justice. I contend further that if the benevolent intent toward all is to be consistently fulfilled as well as possible, then this goal must be made the central organizing principle, not only of the sentencing but of all that is attempted in the criminal justice system from beginning to end.

D. Social Restoration as Goal of Criminal Justice

We have noted that realization of valid human interests needs a kind of community in which individually and socially coherent interests can be created and prosper. Earlier, among the normative principles we derived from the great American ethical traditions, we included "restoration of community when disrupted." Furthermore, we observed, the more unresolved disruptions of community occur, the more alienation there is, and the more crime.

From ancient times societies have had to employ some means of restoring their own orderly sense of community when social relations have been disrupted by crime. In many societies restitution* and rites of reconciliation have been employed. Some have killed or banished the offending members. Often when this method has been used the family or even clan of the offender has shared the culprit's fate, thus eliminating the people who would otherwise feel most intensely alienated and perhaps vengeful as a result of the punishment meted out to the offender.

From Augustine to Pope Pius XII and from Leviticus to Hegel's *Philosophie des Rechts*, the false claim has been made that retribution restores the holiness or wholeness of the community. The criminal has

---

* Chap. 19, below.

disrupted the social order. It must be restored by his suffering the punishment which he deserves.[44] So the argument goes.

The idea that a community disrupted by crime should be restored to wholeness is sound and important. Innumerable values of all members in a community are heightened when the social bonds of the community are strong, dependable, and all-inclusive. Every disruption of these bonds lowers the general sense of security, the will to cooperation and mutual service, inclinations and opportunities for social enjoyment, and the sense of well-being which accompanies the playing of a significant role in an accepted social order.

Crime against others, and especially violent crime, is itself a symptom of alienation. The alienation may be of an individual only or of a group, temporary or long-lasting, deep and all-pervasive, or relatively superficial and affecting only relations with one individual or a few persons. When one person robs, exploits, or otherwise willfully injures the interests of one or more others, the offender is not feeling bonds of responsible concern with the victim or victims.

Just as crimes are symptoms of alienation they are also aggravations of it. The offender psychologically separates himself even more from the victim. The victim and his friends can hardly escape living under at least a thin cloud of anxiety and of suspicion toward the offender and other possible offenders. When there are many serious crimes, the sense of secure community becomes eroded with numerous divisive cross-currents of suspicion, guilt, estrangement, and fear. The securing and keeping at hand of weapons increases and the climate of crime worsens.

The writers about the need to restore community after a crime are making a point the importance of which can hardly be exaggerated. The retributive method, however, has been discredited by human experience. Private revenge is notorious as an incitement to counterretaliation, often leading to blood feuds. Similarly, retribution visited upon the offender by the state is more likely to aggravate than to relieve his alienation and hostility, even in those cases where fear may deter him from further crime or sharpen his wits so that he is not caught and convicted for any new offense. If there are other persons who feel a sense of identity with him—and there are often many such, especially in youthful gangs, in families, or in ethnic minorities—the punishment of the offender is likely to produce widening circles of disaffection with the order of law and increased estrangement from the larger society.

I see no way to avoid the incarceration of some offenders for the temporary protection of society. Some punishment seems necessary also for deterrence, for example to make acquisitive crimes counterproductive. However, we need to recognize that these measures by themselves, especially when taken against people who already feel frustrated, deprived, and outside of any real participation in the good opportunities of society, are almost certain to aggravate the problem of crime in the community. This is so precisely because punishment itself, even when necessary, does *not* restore the social order but further fragments it.

Every wise parent knows this. If young Jane must be sent to her room or deprived of her dessert because of her persistent annoyance of other family members, the punishment does not make her a cooperative member of the family circle. The parents must be careful not to punish her too much and as soon as the penalty has been completed, warm signals of assured welcome to the family circle of affection must be given. Likewise, a skillful schoolteacher who must discipline a pupil seeks a way to bring that pupil into especially happy cooperative activity soon afterward.

There is a kind of personal bookkeeping required here. If the family, school, or state must debit its account with an individual by causing him the unpleasantness of punishment, care must be taken to enter new deposits on that account soon. Whenever the account is in the red, that is when, *from the individual's point of view*, the social unit is more of a liability than an asset to him, his attitude toward it will be one of hostility or withdrawal. Any additional unpleasantness imposed will simply increase the negative attitude and sooner or later may give rise to further misconduct.

Imprisonment produces such negative effects in a most serious way. Particularly as prisons are usually operated in the United States, they cut off the inmate from most or all meaningful economic activity, and such activity is a large and important part of normal human life. American prisons also sever almost completely the social relations which have had most positive meaning for him. If the inmate is married, the marriage will probably not survive a year of incarceration. Can you wonder? Watch the inmates in many of our jails and prisons trying to carry on one of the strictly limited visits with their wives across tables or even through heavy panes of glass, by means of telephones, all under the scrutiny of guards and the eyes of other inmates and visitors. How well can such visits repair the damage already done to their relationship by the offense and consequent humiliation? How long is a meaningful personal love likely to endure under such strained conditions? This is only one of a whole chain of circumstances cutting such positive ties as the offender may have had with the society outside.

For the incarcerated prisoner the most meaningful social relations usually soon become the relations with other prisoners. Most of them have in common their alienation and bitterness toward the legal order and often the general social order as well. Whatever the official rules which may have to be outwardly obeyed, the internalized ethical standards are likely to be mostly the antiestablishment attitudes of the prison society itself. A few inmates will become involved in Alcoholics Anonymous, the Seventh Step program, or other self-help associations. Even among these, some participants are only trying to make an impression in hope of early parole. Those who genuinely work at self-improvement and assistance to their fellow members frequently report that in order to do so they must brave the taunts and threats of the large majority. It is not hard to understand why our prisons are generally schools of crime.*

The end goal of the whole system of criminal justice ought to be *social restoration*—in a double sense. It should be the restoration of the social order to wholeness from the disruption of which crime is both a symptom and an aggravation. It should also be an effort to restore each offender to an integral place in the society. By this terminology it is not intended to imply that we are merely to return the society or the offender's relation to it to its former state. In most instances the *restoration* must be a renewal or reconstruction genuinely creative of relationships not previously existing. Despite the contrary suggestion of the word, the dictionary meaning permits this understanding and on the whole its connotations are the ones here intended. Especially welcome is the common use of the word for the healing of a sick or handicapped person, so bringing him to a state of health and wholeness. In our present usage it is the social relations of the offender with others in the community which are most in need of healing.

Is social restoration a practicable goal for criminal justice? One requirement of it, restitution to victims, will be considered in the next chapter and others in the succeeding chapters. However, some possibilities may be at least suggested at this point by brief description of the guiding philosophy and some practices of a remarkable prison in Mexico.

The past reports of some United States youth on their experiences in Mexican prisons have not served to develop high expectations of finding desirable models among our neighbors to the south. There have been frequent accounts of corruption, cruelty, degeneracy, and neglect, as well as such poor conditions as might be attributable to the lower economic resources of Mexico.

But under the liberal government of President Luis Echeverría Álvarez, far-reaching penal reforms are well under way.[45] In the forefront of the movement are several able younger officials. An especially impressive one is Antonio Sánchez Galindo, Director of the Penitentiary Center of the State of Mexico, through whose writing I first became acquainted with the work there, and whom I later visited in person.

Mr. Sánchez believes heartily in the idea behind the name of the national department. Not retribution, nor individual therapy of a sick

---

* For more specifics, documentation, and proposals on this subject see above, Chap. 6, B, C, and D, and below, Chap. 23.

personality, nor even individual rehabilitation is the ruling concept, but rather "prevention and social readaptation." If careful examination in the classification center shows that an inmate is physically or emotionally ill, he is treated accordingly by the medical or psychiatric staff. But his illness is not assumed. Indeed, the main cause of the trouble may not be any personal defect in the convicted person even though a criminal action of his was intolerable. The one thing known assuredly is that something has gone wrong in his relations with other persons in the community. Hence there must be social readaptation.

This is not easy. The approximately 600 inmates come from a variety of social contexts—the city of Toluca, predominantly Spanish neighborhoods of city or small town, and Indian farming villages representing different tribal cultures. The majority of offenses have been violent. Some have been episodes in sporadic feuds of long duration.

In general, the inmates are lacking in sufficient sensitivity to other people to restrain them from doing injury to them. As Mr. Sánchez puts it, it is therefore essential to "humanize" them or to develop further their "humanity." Unfortunately, prisons tend to do precisely the opposite. If we set out to devise a system to *de*humanize people we might as well use as ideal model an average prison. Hence the humanistic director at Almoloya de Juárez must do everything possible to reverse the usual trends and make the penitentiary a humane and humanizing environment.

Many of the guards had to be shifted to other kinds of government jobs. Some were given extensive training and new, carefully selected ones were brought into the Center to implement the new policy.[46] New physical designs were adopted, including adequately spacious grounds inside the walls, and the "open prison," an attractive halfway house outside, built by inmates and managed by its occupants, with no locks excepting the bolts inside the private rooms. Within the walls, as a visitor walks through the gardens, workshops, classrooms, kitchens, children's playground, family picnic area and offices, he hears continual beautiful music. Artistic appreciation and expression are encouraged and cultivated. Work is paid at levels very close to those outside.

Instead of the grudging admission of visitors which is the practice at most prisons of the United States, at Almoloya positive and wholesome relationships with people outside are encouraged. Human beings are by nature social and their maturing in personal, sensitive humanity requires active personal relationships with people for whom they care. By mutual choice and after careful medical examination wives of inmates are admitted into a wing of the main dormitory by special entrance, for conjugal visits with their husbands in private bedrooms. Prostitutes and casual girl friends are screened out, but any married man, regardless of his crime, is permitted the conjugal privilege with his wife once a week if both are healthy and both desire it.[47] Toward the end of the preliminary medical examination a nurse offers the wife contraceptive aid if she would like to be freed from fear of an added childbearing burden at this difficult time. She always accepts the offer. In the last month of incarceration the inmate can qualify for week-end home furloughs.

Money earned is divided according to circumstances. Some goes to pay in part for room and board. In suitable cases, some is set aside for restitution to the victim of the crime. A small portion is available for small expenditures within the prison. Some is placed in a savings account in a local bank, which will be the exclusive property of the inmate when he is released. A major part, in many instances, goes to the support of dependents.

While the inmate is being assisted toward a fuller humanity, coordinated teamwork is being done also in his home and neighborhood. Every time parole or work release is being considered by the professional staff, reports are heard on each case from a security officer, educator, psychologist, medical officer, psychiatrist, legal officer, and work supervisor in the prison and a social worker from the home community.[48]

After the nearly complete freedom of residence in the halfway house, the inmate is usually far on his way to adequate social readaptation. However, he is not dropped from concerned interest when he is released and returned home, for there is a continuing program of assistance as long as needed after that.

Hearing of such arrangements, one man exclaimed, "They are rewarding those people for their crimes!" Without doubt, he spoke for many. Such people have not begun to imagine how hard it is to be shut up behind walls, away from home, even under benign conditions. But perhaps the best reply is in words quoted by Sánchez from Cesar Lombroso: "The penalty ought to take into account not so much the suffering of the guilty as the well-being of society, and not so much the crime as the guilty person and above all the victim."[49]

Summing up, let us now define the just disposition of a criminal case. When a crime has been committed, *true justice is action well designed to move toward restoration of community on terms best serving the valid interests of all persons concerned.*

Criminal laws should be formulated and all the processes of criminal justice should be carried out in harmony with this purpose and the ethical norms we have established. The essentials can, I believe, be stated in the following normative proposition.

Criminal justice ought to be designed to protect a community of persons freely seeking fulfillment of their compatible interests against disruption by its own members, and after disruptions nevertheless occur, to restore such community with special concern for the persons most deeply affected. Let me emphasize again that when I speak of restoring community I am *not* speaking of theoretical, retributory negating of negations (Hegel) or expiatory equilibration (Kant), but of actually establishing community of feeling and cooperation. This is *not* accomplished by retribution. Penalizing sanctions must be used in many cases, for preventive purposes, but they must be accompanied and followed by activities of social healing and integration.

We may properly call this conception of criminal justice a philosophy of social defense and restoration.

PART V

SOCIAL DEFENSE AND

RESTORATION IN PRACTICE

18

Fortifying the Community

A philosophy of criminal justice as social defense and restoration requires that we base criminal law and procedures in the community. In fact they cannot be based anywhere else if we are to hope for reasonably effective control of crime in a relatively free society. So far as the community is demoralized and so far as it excludes some classes of people from full participation in its economic, political, and social life it will have a large measure of crime. Crime is committed by persons who feel alienated from the people around them.

The Index types of crime—so-called street crimes—are committed mostly by people who feel that they have been rejected, whether from family, the economic order, the political process, or social acceptance. White collar crime, such as conspiracies in the White House, or in executive offices of banks and other corporations or corrupted local governments, are committed by persons who have set themselves above or apart from the obligatory ties of community. There are many combinations and variations of these two processes. For example, an embezzling banker may have felt unloved as a youth, so that through all the apparently cooperative relations he has subsequently entered he has carried a covert frustration and hostility. He experiences no positive ties with the community strong enough to hold him in honest faithfulness to his trust in times of pressure and temptation. Having been excluded in his youth, he now shuts out the community from his own responsible concerns.

The most important things we can do to reduce crime are the steps we can take to build and fortify a strong, inclusive community. Such actions are outside the formal institutions of criminal justice. But if we take seriously the task of social defense, we must look first of all to the strength and soundness of the society we propose to defend. Even when a nation seeks to defend itself against external enemies it must give careful attention to its internal health. How much more is this true when we are concerned with defending against the internal enemy, crime, which rises in our own streets and households!

A. Social Justice

The President's Commission on Law Enforcement and Administration of Justice reported that it had "no doubt whatever that the most significant action that can be taken against crime is action designed to eliminate slums and ghettos, to improve education, to provide jobs, to make sure that every American is given the opportunities and the freedoms that will enable him to assume his responsibilities."[1] The Commission goes on to say, "To speak of controlling crimes only in terms of the work of the police, the courts and the correctional apparatus, is to refuse to face the fact that widespread crime implies a widespread failure by society as a whole."[2] Six years later (in 1973) the National Advisory Commission on Criminal Justice Standards and Goals pointed out that "The connection between alienation and violence" had been "documented,"[3] and devoted a large volume of its report to *Community Crime Prevention*, dealing mostly with urgently needed social reforms outside the formal system of criminal justice. Yet between 1967 and 1973, and on through 1974, the rich continued to get richer and the poor, in each year, remained at about the same level or became poorer.[4] Inflation and disproportionately high rates of unemployment have struck especially hard at the elderly poor and the young adult members of minorities. It is not surprising that Index crimes have continued to increase.

We should give to social justice our highest national priority if we truly care for fairness and the "unalienable rights" to which we were committed at our nation's birth. We should rededicate ourselves to this national task simply because decent, respectful benevolence (Norm 2, Chap. 16, D, above), caring for equal rights (Norm 3), and special care for the poor, weak, and unpopular (Norm 5) demand it. The more we bring the impoverished and alienated into full participation in our society, however, the more, as a byproduct, we shall also reduce crime. The most basic task in social defense is to strengthen the society we mean to defend. Crime is symptomatic of illness in the social fabric. Anything done to bolster the robust health of the community will reduce the illness and its symptoms.

Because this volume is especially devoted to the criminal justice system, we can here devote only closely limited space to specifics of social justice, even though, in the larger picture, they are of primary importance. We can but suggest briefly some directions we must go.

1. Make social services, especially medical care, available to all.

Many persons who are persistent criminal offenders are so handicapped by early malnutrition, other forms of ill health, low mental ability, limited energy, or lack of home training that they cannot cope with the complex and competitive society in which they live. We can either provide them with medical and dental care, home assistance and guidance, or we can suffer criminal injuries from their dishonest or violent efforts to express or overcome their frustration and then assume support for them and their dependents after their crimes. Helpful clues to effective methods can be found in Great Britain, the Scandinavian countries, and others.

Coherent benevolent response to the realities of our society require adoption of a program of universal health service and other social services where needed.[5]

2. Fund public advocacy for the poor and for consumers.

The defrauding and exploitation of the poor is endemic in every section of the United States, but especially in our large cities, and on farms worked by sharecroppers and migrant labor. Housing codes are flagrantly violated by poor people's landlords, labor laws by their employers, merchandising regulations by those who sell them goods, insurance, loans, and services. All people need to be watchful to avoid being injured by the unscrupulous, but the poor, especially if meagerly educated, are peculiarly vulnerable because they have neither the knowledge needed to defend themselves nor the means to engage legal counsel.

The federally funded Office of Equal Opportunity made a beginning of providing legal services to protect people who could not afford to pay attorneys' fees and some of whom did not even know lawyers could help them. This part of the OEO program was especially strongly attacked by some business interests and was discontinued. It has been reinstituted, under other auspices, but its extent and effectiveness remain in doubt.

Our norms of benevolence, equality, and special need to protect the poor and weak (Chap. 16, D, above) all require that it should be vigorously supported.

3. Enact guaranteed annual income.

At present many people who do not wish to work get welfare checks and manage to scrape along. Many others, some handicapped, some not, work all they can but still receive even less income than welfare would provide. They may get work only seasonally or part time or receive less than the minimum wage. Meanwhile, large numbers of children, through no fault of their own, receive so little protein that they will be physically and mentally handicapped throughout their lives. From such backgrounds a disproportionate number of Index crimes are generated.

The enormous wastefulness and inequities of the present piecemeal ways of dealing with poverty have caused even such a conservative economist as Milton Friedman (in 1964 a principal economic adviser to Senator Barry Goldwater) to espouse a system of guaranteed minimum income by means of a negative income tax, along with such more liberal economists as Leon Keyserling and Robert Theobald. One plan of this kind was even proposed by former President Nixon during his first term.

The subject of choosing the particular economic method of reducing or eliminating poverty, though urgent, is too complex and too marginal to our main subject of criminal justice to permit an ample discussion here. In order to go into it further, the reader is urged to read *Guaranteed Annual Income: The Moral Issues* by Philip Wogaman.[6]

B. Employment and Recreational Activities for Youth

Much criminality begins with vandalism or petty thefts by idle children or youth who can find no jobs and who have not been drawn into any sports or other recreational activities. Some laws intended to prevent the exploitation of child labor need careful changing so that boys and girls can earn for their own recreation, future education, or other purposes. In most localities the will of the community is the principal ingredient required. Have we not enough benevolent concern, even for our children and youth, to take such steps?

C. Making Crime Difficult by Designing and Planning

The National Advisory Commission recommends that building codes include requirements related to security of the property and the people in it. Security against crime is affected by design and placement of doors, windows, locks, and other features.[7] Such things as public lighting, design of automobiles, arrangement of shopping centers, and automatic alarm systems are also important.[8] Measures of this kind cannot prevent all crime. They can, however, make many crimes difficult and assure a higher rate of arrests and convictions when crimes occur.

In New York City many warning and punitive measures failed to halt a high rate of slug use in parking meters which was costing the city millions of dollars annually. In the years of 1968–1970 approximately four million slugs were used each year. Then a change in the design of the meters was tried. The new meters rejected the slugs most commonly used and exposed the last two inserted coins or slugs to plain view under a strong, transparent plastic shield. In areas equipped with the new meters the use of slugs dropped dramatically and continued at rates 30% to 79% below the former rates.[9]

Riders on city buses are generally aware of the many barbarous robberies and murders of bus drivers which the penal system was unable to check. Yet even these grave crimes, many committed by seasoned offenders or drug addicts, were virtually ended by the installation of heavy, locked cash boxes to receive fares and warnings to the public that the drivers carried no change. It is a minor inconvenience to riders to make sure of having tickets, tokens, or exact fares in advance, but the results make such inconvenience seem trifling.

One of the most lucrative and widespread crimes is shoplifting. Measures of wide variety have failed to end the relentless spread of this crime. Yet a department store in Red Bank, New Jersey, has a device which has proved almost perfectly effective. A tiny electric circuit enclosed in a wafer attached to every garment triggers a buzz if taken near the exit. Only special equipment at the cashiers' desks can remove the wafer without damaging the garment. This and other devices are described by the National Advisory Commission.[10]

How much better it is to divert juveniles or adults from careers of delinquency and crime by careful designing than to give them records and perhaps start them on careers of crime by resort to penal devices!

D. Effective Public Oversight and Public Funding of Political Campaigns

Organized crime requires the corruption of some public officials if it is to prosper long. Especially is this true of crime rings based on financing by number games or prostitution which must be publicized to do business. In the wake of the "Watergate" disclosures several states have taken action to lessen the dependence of candidates for public office on campaign financing by private interests. Congress occasionally takes hold of the issue, but it is not likely to do anything very substantial until public demand rises to a higher pitch than has been heard thus far.

In addition to reasons for other preventive measures we must reform political financing to stop the gross inequalities of prosecution and punishment (vs. Norm 3, Chap. 16, D, above) which result from political payoffs.

E. Community Programs of Diversion

The best time to stop a career of crime is at the beginning before the individual is labeled a delinquent or criminal. Much of such work can best be done by volunteers.

One night in a Maryland suburb of Washington two tires were slashed, on each of thirteen cars, each belonging to a different family in the neighborhood. It happened near midnight, but fortunately the two young teenagers were caught as they were leaving one of the cars. Although the boys and their parents were called in by the police, they and the injured neighbors took care of the problem. The boys made full restitution in labor or their own earned cash and no charges were filed. At least one of the boys had better relations with the neighbors than before as a result of the positive experience in working off the claims.

In Amsterdam, Holland, on September 18, 1973, I visited, late at night, *Het Prinsenhof*, a volunteer center. The first floor and basement serve as a refuge for street people, open to anyone who has no place to stay. Almost any kind of conduct may be found there, excepting violence and overt exploitation. The police have agreed not to enter. Some young people are using drugs. Quietly, several resourceful young adults circulate through the building and offer friendly conversation. Frequently they find the street people there desirous of escaping the addiction or purposelessness in which they are caught. The staff members bring them hope. When they discover someone with a genuine practical interest in achieving a lawful and socially useful life-style they invite him or her to move into the second floor dormitory as a resident. Fifteen beds there are always filled. Many such people, with close personal and group support, break drug habits, settle into jobs, and eventually move out into normal, useful life. The residents say that the personal acceptance, respect, and caring by the staff are the principal sources of restorative influence there. Like many other activities in Holland, *Het Prinsenhof* represents a combination of dedicated voluntary initiative and official financial support, in this instance from social service funds of the city.

In the United States prosecutors sometimes agree not to press charges when young adult first offenders have been arrested but agree to place themselves under the guidance of respected mature citizens who have volunteered their services. In other instances, at sentencing, instead of placement under supervision of an official probation officer, a judge may release a convicted person to residence, supervision, and treatment in a facility maintained and staffed by volunteers.[11]

All such diversionary programs are especially important for many weak members of our society who cannot, alone, cope with the pressures and temptations of the present era. (Cf. Norm 5, Chap. 16, D, above.)

Addiction to alcohol and to various drugs is a cause of a large number of crimes, many senselessly violent. Prisons are no help to the addicts beyond possible temporary forced abstinence. Actually there seem to be drugs available to some extent in all large prisons and many small ones. Many addicts say they first became acquainted with drugs or addicted to them in prison.

There are many public treatment centers, though all together would provide for only a small fraction of persons needing treatment. Moreover, results are generally disappointing. There is no single solution.

The National Advisory Commission on Criminal Justice Standards and

Goals devotes much attention to this problem.[12] Because alcohol and the various kinds of drugs have their own characteristics and because addiction results from a wide variety of personal motivations, there must also be many approaches to the treatment of alcoholics and drug addicts. Some of the most successful are those of such voluntary organizations as Alcoholics Anonymous and Teen Challenge. There are many other voluntary and official therapeutic communities, some residential, others nonresidential. None shows great success without the willing cooperation of the addict, although in some instances such cooperation is elicited after the initial use of incentives which amount to coercion or which at least approach it. For example, willing participation in the program of a treatment center is often offered by a judge as alternative to a sentence or as a condition of probation.[13]

There appears to be no more important asset in this work than the personal caring which many volunteer workers exhibit. While other ethical norms are relevant, benevolent good will and personal respect constitute both the main rationale and the most valuable resource for such work.

F. Reducing Violence in the Media, Especially Television

It is frequently argued that violence in drama of the movie screen and of television has no effect on violent action in the real world or even decrease it by the cathartic influence of draining off aggressive emotional energies. Such argument was effectively answered by The National Commission on the Causes and Prevention of Violence in its final report: "Each year advertisers spend $2.5 billion in the belief that television can influence human behavior. The television industry enthusiastically agrees with them, but nonetheless contends that its programs of violence do not have any such influence."[14] After telling about effects of televised violence on young children, the Commission reports on research into the attitudes of teenagers and finds that their social environments deeply influence their response to television. "Of teenagers asked whether they agreed or disagreed with such statements as: 'The programs I see on television tell about life the way it really is' . . . 40 percent of the poor black adolescents and 30 percent of the poor whites strongly believed in the true-to-life nature of television content, as compared with only 15 percent of the middle class white youngsters."[15] In other words, the television drama, with its heavy emphasis on gun play and other violence, is most frequently taken as a realistic view of life in our society by precisely those youth who live in the poor neighborhoods from which a disproportionately large amount of violent delinquency and crime issues. The Commission found also that it was the same low-income teenagers who had especially "strong preference" for "crime, action and adventure stories," who were the least subject to ameliorating influences from parents and community, and spent especially long hours watching television.[16] Their chosen television programs must, therefore, have reinforced heavily the more violent influences of their deteriorated neighborhoods.

Access to television broadcast channels is a privilege. To restrict partisan expression of points of view would raise serious issues of constitutionally protected free speech. But the promotion of violence by use of the limited, privileged commodity of television channels is clearly contrary to all lawful interests in the community. The industry has repeatedly acknowledged its obligations in this connection but its efforts at self-regulation have been fainthearted and inadequate. A combination of federal regulatory pressure, more adequate and permanent financing of Public Broadcasting, and citizen involvement is urgently needed.

Our appeal is based on the same norms which support other efforts at fortifying the community and preventing crime. In addition, we are here concerned with protecting the weaker members of our society from exploitation (Norm 5, Chap. 16, D). Because we love our children (Norm 2), we want to see them grow up in a less violent, more peaceful society.

The police, courts, and correctional procedures must be employed in any society to deal with occasional violations of criminal law. But these specialized agencies cannot bear the principal burden of maintaining an orderly society. Most of that responsibility must be borne by citizens who feel that they have a stake in the social order and voluntarily cooperate in countless ways to sustain its smooth operation. Some of these ways will entail inconvenience, the moderating of personal advantages, and the renouncing of opportunities to exploit weaker persons for gain. There is no cheaper price for the secure, orderly community most people desire.

19

The Victim: Forgotten Person of American Criminal Justice

If our much-publicized American concern about crime is more than self-centered fear and vindictive anger, then there must be increasing evidence of public interest in victims. Certainly if we are to take seriously the task of social restoration after crime, we cannot continue our neglect of those who have suffered most directly and deeply from it.

To study victims of crime is to participate in victimology, a new and rapidly growing branch of criminology and criminal law. Ezzat A. Fattah, in his recent important book on this subject, *la victime, est elle coupable?*[1] traces its development. He says that novelists, as early as Daniel Defoe, have been intrigued by study of the victim, his traits, and his possible guilt. But the term "victimology" dates back only to the psychiatrist F. Wertham who used it in a published book, *The Show of Violence,* in 1941. The scientific study may be dated from the work of Hans von Hentig, beginning about 1940.

Victimology is mainly concerned with three topics.

The first of these is the empirical identification of people most likely to be victimized by crimes, and the conditions under which those crimes take place. Some persons or groups seem particularly susceptible to crimes which injure their bodies or reputations and which cause property damage or loss. It is thought that if we can find out what kinds of people most often become victims of crime and the circumstances of their injuries, then the problem of crime may be attacked obliquely by giving special attention to these types of potential victims and of circumstances conducive to crime, as well as directly by attention to potential and actual offenders.

The second topic is the responsibility of victims for crimes against them. In what ways do victims often, unwittingly or even intentionally, invite crime? What responsibility do they bear and how should such responsibility be assessed and treated?

The third topic, the one to which we must devote most attention, concerns the propriety and means of compensating victims of crime.

A. Segments of the Population Most Often Victimized by Crime

The most careful American study of this question to date is one still in progress when reported by Terence P. Thornberry and Robert M. Figlio to the meeting of the American Society of Criminology in Caracas, Venezuela, in November 1972, in an otherwise unpublished paper. The researchers began with a 10% sample from the nearly 10,000 males born in 1945 and living in Philadelphia between their tenth and eighteenth birthdays. Their research followed the study of delinquency and crime among the nearly 10,000 reported by Wolfgang, Figlio, and Sellin in their instructive volume *Delinquency in a Birth Cohort,* already cited. Of the 10%, or nearly 1,000, Thornberry and Figlio succeeded in interviewing 567.

By the report of the men themselves on a specific list of offenses, not one had reached age 26 without being victimized at least once. Some, however, had been victimized disproportionately often. By far the most significant characteristic of boys and men most commonly victimized by serious crimes included in the study was that they were nonwhite. Of these Philadelphia men, nonwhites (mostly blacks) were precisely twice as likely to have been stabbed and more than five times as likely to have been shot as whites. Blacks also had their pockets picked more than twice as often as whites, and were robbed more frequently.

Women who have been victims of forcible rape have been studied elsewhere by racial classification. The National Opinion Research Center at the University of Chicago reports, from a survey of 10,000 households, that per 100,000 population 22 white women report having been forcibly raped, as compared with 82 women of Negro and other races, implying that a black woman was nearly four times as likely to be forcibly raped as a white woman. The Chicago study showed also that people of the minority races were much more likely to have been victims of robbery, aggravated assault, burglary, and motor vehicle theft. This is probably due to the fact that they are most often alone in areas of high crime rates. Frequently lack of adequate lighting, secure locks, and police protection also are blamed. Only in grand larceny were whites more frequently the victims —about five to three.[2]

If we were to include serious victimization by fraudulent merchandising, we should probably find both blacks and the poor particularly disproportionate among the victims, because of lower educational levels, more limited financial credit, and the less likely legal prosecution by them.

Criminal homicide is often a family affair. The President's National Crime Commission reported "In 1965 killings within the family made up 31 percent of all murders. Over one-half of these involved spouse killing spouse and 16 percent parents killing children. Murder outside the family unit, usually the result of altercations among acquaintances, made up 48 percent of the willful killings. In the latter category romantic triangles or lovers' quarrels comprised 21 percent and killings resulting from drinking situations 17 percent."[3]

If all violent crimes and disorders in and outside the family are considered, the place of alcohol looms much larger. Especially frequent victims of violent crime are the intoxicated. Von Hentig believed, from his studies, that alcohol was the most important of all victimogenic factors[4] and Fattah found considerable evidence of that in his recent studies of murder in the course of robbery in Austria. In the District of Columbia a Presidential Commission found that nearly half the victims and offenders in cases of murder had been drinking prior to the crime.[5] Other kinds of frequently victimized people are the city dwellers, the greedy gamblers who are easy marks for smooth con-men, and the well-to-do but unalert, often elderly, who are similarly vulnerable. People of careless habits, who leave keys in their cars, or let money lie around in plain sight, also invite some kinds of crime. Finally, we must mention people who themselves commit crime.

The relations between committing crime and being victimized by it are complex and in need of much further study. Thornberry and Figlio found evidence that being victimized by crime often leads to crime by the erstwhile victim. On the other hand, a person who has committed a crime is often an inviting target for the blackmailer or he may fall victim to a vicious beating, robbery, or execution by competitors in profitable crime. He is often in high crime areas and since he is afraid of contacts with the police he is especially vulnerable as a person who dares not call for help.

B. Responsibility of Victims for Crimes Against Them

Some of the people already mentioned bear a degree of responsibility for crimes of which they are victims. This is especially obvious in the cases of criminals whose own crimes invite others to victimize them. In varying degrees it is true also of the careless, the greedy gamblers, and the intoxicated. But there are others.

As Fattah points out, some victims of acts legally defined as criminal are themselves the persons inflicting the injuries. This is true, for example, of people who injure themselves attempting to commit suicide, or who mutilate their bodies to escape military service, or who undermine their own health by the use of narcotics.[6]

Great numbers of assaults, aggravated assaults, and homicides are culminations or episodes of quarrels in which the eventual victim has been actively engaged, sometimes with maddening aggressiveness. Before the homicide, the victim in some instances has been mostly to blame for the development of bad feeling.[7]

Rapes and other sexually motivated crimes are sometimes fomented by combinations of sexually suggestive dress and conduct by women. If a woman purposely attracts a man sexually, but finally refuses his advances, then in certain instances she may bear some responsibility for the emotional response she incites and for its tragic consequences.

In this brief discussion of victim responsibility for crime we must include also half-intended and fully intended invitations to crime. For example, if a person owns a well-insured property for which he would like to recover the cost, but which he is unable to sell, he may invite its theft or destruction. His old automobile may be left unlocked with key in the ignition or his vacant house may be left open with paper and matches handy.

C. Compensation to Victims

1. Frequent in other times and places.

During the reign of Alfred the Great (871–899) West Saxon law provided that punishment for some kinds of personal violence should be by *bot*, that is a prescribed payment to the victim. For example, "If the great toe be struck off let twenty shillings be paid him as *bot*. If it be the second toe, fifteen shillings. . . . If the little toe be struck off let five shillings be paid him."[8] An important purpose of such provisions was to prevent private revenge, counterrevenge, and continuing blood feuds.[9]

In African tribal law most convicted criminals and their families are required to make restitution to the victims and their families. As William Clifford reports concerning older tribal laws of Zambia, "Where the safety of the community was involved, . . . death or exile was the usual penalty. In other circumstances, the law was dominated by the idea of compensation to counterbalance loss and restore amity in the local residential group."[10] The same practice was reported to me among the Shona.

A study of criminal law among the most widely distributed African tribes is reported in an unpublished paper by Edward M. DeWolf. Again and again, in far separated regions and in customary law concerning offenses ranging from theft and simple assault to murder, he documents requirements for restitution or compensation to victims or their families. Everywhere, he finds, "The whole system of law was based on the need to bring men and women together again after they had had a disagreement between them."[11] The same principle is emphatically affirmed by President Kenneth Kaunda of Zambia.[12]

Marvin E. Wolfgang mentions other examples of victim compensation from the tribal law of Cheyenne and Comanche Indians and the Ifugao in northern Luzon. He refers also to provision for compensation in lieu of punishment for property damage in the ancient Code of Hammurabi. Exodus 12:18–19 bears witness that the ancient Hebrews permitted and required compensation for loss of working time by a personally injured victim. Wolfgang cites also a reference to compensation for a brother's death in Homer's *Iliad*.[13] Further information about early provisions for restitution in ancient societies is given by Stephen Schafer.[14]

Schafer reports that in the Middle Ages a number of Germanic communities required that a person killing or injuring another must make a prescribed payment to the victim or his family and an additional payment to the king or other authority who exercised oversight over the arrangement and reconciliation between the parties.[15] Gradually the payment to the victim diminished and disappeared altogether as the "feudal barons and ecclesiastical powers" greedily claimed all.[16] Later the law of torts made it possible for some victims to bring civil suit for damages, as today.

In the present day a number of countries in Europe and elsewhere have made provisions for restitution by criminal offenders or compensation by the state. English criminal law makes carefully designed provisions for compensation.[17] Restitution is more often required in England than in America in conjunction with probation and suspended sentence. In Sweden the law makes specific requirements for compensation including even payments to dependents of the victim. Other countries specifying compensation for victims of crime include Norway, the Netherlands, New Zealand, Poland, and the Soviet Union.[18]

At the Penitentiary Center of the State of Mexico arrangements are frequently made for restitution to victims in preparation for convicted offenders to return home on parole. Three values are stated: assistance to the victim, advancement of the offender's sense of responsibility, and placating desires for revenge.[19]

2. Neglect of the victim in American criminal law.

In the criminal laws of the United States there are very few states which make any legal provisions for compensating victims. Attention and great expense are concentrated on the accused. He is provided with transportation, lodging, food, clothing, and legal counsel. He may be found guilty and incarcerated at a continuing cost greater than would be required for all expenses at an Ivy League college. But the victim walks away from the trial empty-handed. He may have been robbed of his life savings or be physically disabled so that he can no longer earn. It will give him little or no satisfaction to know that the person who has done him such grievous injury is now suffering some kind of punishment or receiving treatment. Such knowledge is of no help with his own financial and personal burdens. He is simply left alone with his loss or injury, the forgotten person of American criminal law.[20]

3. Why this neglect?

One reason for this lack of provision is that the law of torts is supposed to meet the need. Criminal prosecution, according to the legal theory, is undertaken in behalf of the society as a whole to maintain a secure public order. For wrong suffered by an individual the proper course is a private lawsuit for damages. So goes the theory, and occasionally it works, but not often.

The victim more often than not lacks the money to engage counsel and file suit. If he can overcome that obstacle, he will probably spend his time and money in vain. Whatever the court may order the offender to pay, it will not be paid. Most people prosecuted under criminal law are poor. If an offender is convicted, his earning power, probably already low, will be further reduced. If he is imprisoned, he can earn nothing of any significance because wages for work in American prisons run at such token levels as 25 cents to one dollar a day.

A second cause for the neglect of the victim in our laws is that the majority of victims are from segments of the population for whom there is little of understanding concern in the dominant, lawmaking sector of the public. There is a strong desire to "crack down on crime" because crime is feared as a threat to everybody. But the majority of individuals actually victimized are people who are poor or of minorities with whom most legislators do not readily identify. Such feeling for them as is experienced is usually a distant pity rather than an urgent, active concern to assist.

A third explanation for our neglect of victims is that even without special knowledge there is frequently a feeling that the victims were partly responsible for the crimes against them. We have observed that this is often true. Besides, it is all too comforting to assume that it is usually true. Such an assumption supports both the feeling that "it will never happen to me" and the sense of proud aloofness with which we keep from getting involved.

A fourth reason for our neglect is that we fear the rise in taxes which might be needed to pay for compensation of the many victims in whose behalf no collection could be made from the offenders.

4. Why there should be compensation.

In order to determine intelligently what should and what should not be included in the criminal justice system we must first remember the meaning of justice. Justice, in any situation, requires doing the best possible for all the persons affected. To ignore the interests of persons vitally affected by an action is to contradict all the major ethical traditions of our people. Certainly the primary victim of crime is deeply affected. To ignore the needs of the victim which result from the crime is contrary to the Christian and Jewish principles of love for the neighbor. In fact it was precisely the care for a victim of crime which Jesus used to illustrate the scope of love to a neighbor in the Parable of the Good Samaritan. It should be noted that in Western countries modern Jewish teaching extends the principles of *chesed* and neighbor love to all members of the community and not to Jews alone. The secular humanism of John Locke and Thomas Jefferson, with all their American successors in the traditions of natural law ethics, utilitarianism, and Kantian doctrines of universalizing autonomy, consistently applied, would likewise require caring for the victim of a crime.

When the issue is raised the need to give special assistance to the victim of a crime strikes most Americans as a matter of basic fairness. After a crime justice has not been done when the larger society has left the victim to bear his injury or loss alone. Arthur Goldberg has written that since society has failed to protect the person who is victim of a crime, "society should assume some responsibility for making him whole."[21]

When victims are left to bear their injuries alone there are bound to be innumerable spreading circles of resentment and bitterness in the population. Such feelings of resentful frustration among victims and their friends add to the irrational angers and hatreds which clamor for vindictive retribution. Victims justly compensated and sustained by offenders or by the community would find it easier to consider rationally policies of criminal justice which would be just, that is, on the whole, best designed for all the persons concerned with their various conflicting interests.

Another value of victim compensation would be improvement of prompt reporting of crime to police. Compensation laws usually do and should require such reporting when possible. Victims would then have an incentive to report, at least offsetting the nuisance of police questioning and possible embarrassment, harassment, danger, and loss of time in court appearances.[22]

A final consideration demanding victim compensation brings us again to the larger purpose of criminal justice. Justice must be directed to establishing the unity and order of the community where it has been broken by commission of a crime. The ways of accomplishing this must be sought with all the empirical aids at our disposal. The wisest teachers have long known that establishing or reestablishing community requires maximum effort to meet the real needs of its members by other members and by the corporate society. In short, caring and lovingkindness build and restore the community.

The implications of this principle for policy concerning the offender are as complex and difficult as they are urgent and compelling. In succeeding chapters detailed proposals for such policy will be presented.

On the other hand, these considerations point unambiguously and simply to the need to compensate the victim of crime. In other fields people of the United States have often put professed ideals of benevolence into impressive practice. It is ironical that from the ancient traditions of criminal justice we Americans have taken seriously the supposed order-restoring notion of retributive punishment for the criminal, while mostly neglecting, in our legal system, the idea of kindness and help for the victim. The angry and vindictive side of ancient custom we take and use literally with a vengeance, while the ancient requirements of lovingkindness our law has with few exceptions omitted, even as they apply to the victim, who should most readily win our sympathetic and active concern.

Suppose we do decide that we ought to compensate the victim of crime. Methods remain to be considered.

5. How should it be done?

When it is practicable the offender should be required or encouraged to make direct or indirect restitution. Some of the juvenile courts in New York have required delinquent youths to clean up graffiti with which they had massively defaced subway cars and public buildings. In many a suburban or rural neighborhood a juvenile case has been continued while youthful offenders have done repair work, made financial compensation from their own earnings, or "worked off" obligations incurred by vandalism, pilfering, or other delinquent acts. When this has been accomplished the judge has simply dismissed the case. In such instances there often occurs a genuine cementing of a positive, friendly relationship between erstwhile victim and offender. Sometimes similar arrangements are made at other stages in the process of youth administration. They should be used much more often, at any suitable point in the legal process, or even in prelegal action, generally the earlier the better.

In cases of adults and of older youth involved in more serious offenses the problem of making compensation is usually much more difficult. Often for crimes of violence against the person no adequate compensation is possible. What price shall be put on a person's life or his eyesight or the ability to walk?

How shall an offender pay if he has never even supported himself by honest labor? If he is sentenced to a correctional institution where it is impossible to earn significant wages, how can he provide even moderate compensation to a person or family to whom he has done injury?

Certain changes in sentencing and correctional policy would greatly broaden the possibilities of restitution by the offender. Ever larger proportions of offenders are being placed on probation or early parole. It is possible and desirable to establish the making of installments of restitution to victims an important evidence of progress toward readiness for final release.

In the new Hawaii Penal Code enacted in 1972 there are explicit provisions for restitution by offenders. According to that Code, probation and other penalties not involving incarceration are regarded as the normal sentences, with "Sentence of imprisonment withheld unless imprisonment is necessary" for definite reasons specified in the Code (Sec. 620). There are eleven conditions which, it is suggested, the judge should consider to be reasons for *not* imposing imprisonment. One of these is that "the defendant has compensated or will compensate the victim of his criminal conduct for the damage or injury that he sustained" (Sec. 621). It is also suggested by the Code that in ordering either a withholding of sentence or probation the judge may "require the defendant . . . to make restitution of the fruits of his crime or to make reparation, in an amount he can afford to pay, for the loss or damage caused thereby" (Sec. 624). The State of New York also has a provision for restitution as a condition of probation.[23]

There are two ways by which prisoners may be enabled to pay restitution and so prepare for early release. One is the work-release program by which inmates leave the prison walls for certain hours of the day to work in a factory, hospital, auto repair shop, or on the farm at regular prevailing wages. The other is by bringing some seriously productive industries inside the walls and paying for work in it wages close to the prevailing rate outside.

When by one means or another the way is opened for the convicted offender to earn, his wages should be divided according to his family responsibilities and present needs, as well as the required restitution to victims.

Even when restitution by offenders is developed to the highest practical limit, there will still remain much which must be done for the victim by the public if he is to receive suitable compensation at all. There are several different methods by which public obligations for compensation are determined. Sometimes it is done by the criminal court itself. However, in the majority of cases the perpetrators of known crimes are not found or are not convicted. Yet the injury to victims is no less real. For this reason several of the better systems of compensation are in the hands of special boards established for the purpose. In such cases it is sometimes wisely provided that the board may then institute action to recover part or all of the funds required from the offender.

So far as restitution can be made by the offender it is highly desirable that this be required. Many people convicted of serious crime think of their offenses as having to do only with their relations with an impersonal law or government. Our dominant practice of omitting any consideration of the victim, excepting as a possible witness, encourages such a rationalization. Schafer has found that nearly all homicide offenders would like to make some kind of reparation but only about 55% of other violent offenders expressed any such desire.[24] The dominant regret or remorse, where such sentiments are present, seems to be a generalized feeling relative to law or the order of society, not in relation to particular human beings.

An important step in social readaptation is the realization that criminal offenses have done serious damage to human beings, damages which are costly to repair even in part. The offender's facing this reality and bearing as much of the practical burden of it as he can may cut through his defensive rationalizations, bring his guilt to the surface of his consciousness, and enable him to come to rational terms with it.

Schafer, who has given much serious attention to this subject, writes, "In terms of correctional benefits of a modern restitution scheme, the offender must be made to understand that he has directly injured the victim as well as the state and law and order. Thought of in this way, restitution would not only redress the injury or loss of the victim, at least in part, but would help in the correctional rehabilitation of the offender at the same time. . . ."[25]

Since 1965 there have been bills before every session of Congress to provide compensation to victims of crime, at least in federal jurisdictions like the District of Columbia and the high seas. In some sessions such a bill has carried in one house of Congress but died in a committee of the other. At least seven states have adopted legal provisions for compensation of victims, first, California, in 1965, and later, New York, Massachusetts, Hawaii, Maryland, Nevada, and New Jersey. Other states are considering such legislation. Glenn E. Floyd reports that the plans adopted in the United Kingdom and various states of the United States "provide for compensation for personal injury and not for property damage."[26] In general, property damage is less devastating, more likely to be partially compensated by insurance, and would be more readily the subject of fraudulent claims.

Some laws of compensation enacted or seriously considered have instructed the courts or compensation boards to exclude victims found not to have been altogether innocent in relation to the crime. In Massachusetts and Maryland there is a more flexible requirement that decisions regarding awards of compensation to victims should be made after considering the conduct of the victim. The award may be reduced or denied altogether if the conduct of the victim contributed to the inflicting of the injury. The reduction or denial is not to be made, however, when the victim was aiding another victim, trying to prevent a crime, or attempting to apprehend a criminal. New York excludes compensation if the victim was "criminally responsible for the crime." Nevada simply requires that the board "consider the provocation, consent or any other behavior of the victim." California, New York, and Maryland provide no compensation if the victim is not in serious financial need. Massachusetts does not take into account the financial needs of the victim.[27]

The largest-scale experience with victim compensation in this country is in New York, where the first four and one-half years of a compensation program cost the state in total awards approximately $3,500,000. This does not appear to be excessive expense when compared, for example, with New York's payment of workmen's compensation of $236 million in 1968 alone or 67 times as much as paid for compensation of crime victims in four and one-half years. Workmen and their employers pay into an insurance fund for this, to be sure. But so do citizens pay into the state very substantial funds for protection against crime. Should not there be included in appropriations for public safety funds to insure that when the state or other jurisdiction fails to protect a citizen, that citizen will be compensated, at least in part?

Marvin E. Wolfgang, an able advocate of victim compensation, maintains that merely "paying bills for hospital and physician care, or even for wages lost during recovery from an injury is not compensation. Payments to cover these losses produce a kind of financial equilibrium but do not compensate or make amends for the crime which caused the victim to suffer."[28]

It seems likely that laws providing compensation to victims of crime will increase in the years just ahead. It is to be hoped that such laws will not be regarded as only additional welfare provisions, diverting attention from the need for a basic, unified antipoverty program. Rather they should be framed as part of the effort to do justice when a crime has occurred as a symptom of social disunity and a further disruption of the social order.

If we are to regard justice after a crime as social restoration on terms serving the needs of all persons affected, then victims must be compensated. In this context tests of the victims' financial means are inappropriate. Neither do we need to stress compensation as a kind of penalty which the state pays for its failure to protect some of its citizens from crime, although Wolfgang and others have a point of some validity in urging this rationale. Rather we should simply emphasize that when a community has been wounded by a crime, the community has not been made whole while its living members who have most grievously suffered from the crime are uncompensated.

Criminal justice is not even formally complete until serious effort has been made to compensate the victims of crime.

20

Criminal Law: Its Scope and Penalties

When, despite efforts to strengthen an inclusive community, crimes occur there are both victims and offenders needing attention. We have discussed our strange and scandalous neglect of victims and needed changes of policy affecting them. We now turn attention to the offenders. If we are to take seriously an ethically defensible philosophy of criminal justice as social defense and restoration, what changes in criminal law and procedures affecting offenders are demanded?[1]

The criminal justice system must include such elements of prevention as incapacitation, deterrence, and rehabilitation. But all means must be adapted to the purpose of protecting and restoring the community of free persons. Such a task is bound to include elements of tension. Measures of deterrence and of incapacitation are especially apt to cause resentment, division, and alienation, thus further disrupting community and generating more crime. Incarceration in particular, by its very nature, disrupts community by putting a wall through it. The more impervious is the wall the more radical is the disruption and the more serious are the likely psychosocial aftereffects. Nevertheless, both deterrent penalties and incapacitation are necessary in many cases to defend the community against even more serious and destructive disruptions and sometimes these penalties include incarceration. Hence there is a continual problem of balancing the protective and disruptive effects to be expected from different sanctions under consideration. It is also required that whenever disruptive sanctions have been used, especially incarceration, restorative measures must be taken, both to heal the original disruption caused by the criminal act and to heal the further wound in the community made by the exacting of the penalty.

In recommending changes five segments of the criminal justice system will be distinguished. They are (1) the scope and penalties of the laws; (2) the police; (3) the courts; (4) corrections; and (5) public responsibilities in criminal justice. However, all of these overlap and interact, so that to find all the proposed reforms affecting one segment, for example the courts, it will be necessary to read the recommendations labeled with the names of all the segments.

A. New and Informed Penal Codes

As we have seen, many traditions have affected the development of our criminal laws. Since different laws, even in the same state, have been passed under different conditions, often in response to outbursts of feeling after certain highly publicized crimes or judicial decisions, some represent points of view radically different from those which shaped others. Less dangerous and less injurious acts may be subject to penalties more severe than the maximum permitted in sentencing more serious offenders.

Social and economic conditions, too, have changed radically. To take a small and simple example, grand larceny was defined many decades ago in terms of quantities of money now worth only a fraction of the value at that time. Yet in most states the legal definition stands unchanged. Thanks to inflation, much petty larceny has thus become grand larceny.

The National Advisory Commission recommends that every state adopt a whole new penal code unless it has done so in the last decade.[2] Only so can the state laws be in accord with our Norm of consistency and coherence with realities (Norm 1, Chap. 16, D, above).

In the rapidly changing societies of the present era laws and procedures are rapidly outmoded. If the system is to serve the needs of the present age, it must be changed in systematic, orderly response to carefully organized facts. In the process correlation of efforts by different states should be assisted by federal agencies and such organizations as the American Bar Association and the National Council on Crime and Delinquency in order to remove extreme disparities.

There have been a number of excellent studies made of our problems with crime and of methods successfully used in some times and places, in our states or abroad, to cope with them. But little legislation has been affected by these studies. Indeed, American studies appear to have made a greater impact on practice in some countries of Western Europe than here because of the higher official regard for scholarship and rational planning there. The National Advisory Commission strongly recommends such planning here and the development of information systems to support it.[3] If we are to have laws and procedures consistent and coherent with known realities (Norm 1), this must be done.

B. Decriminalization

Many acts which most citizens regard as immoral and habits which are damaging to the doer himself are demonstrably uncontrollable by criminal law. Trying to treat them as crimes has the effect of overburdening the police, the courts, and the jails, so that they cannot properly handle seriously destructive or dangerous offenders who must be restrained to protect the community. Some acts have been legislated into crimes even though neither ethically evil nor self-damaging.

We must remember that the capacity of the criminal justice system is limited. Processes of education, organized religion, and informal social opinion have their own work to do in the community. When we feel inclined to say "there ought to be a law," especially a criminal law, we need to stop and ask whether there may not be a better way to handle the matter at hand.[4]

We should generally prefer alternatives to criminal justice in order to protect the community without further disrupting it and often also in benevolent good will and respect and with special care to protect the poor, weak, and unpopular. When unenforceable laws are on the books they invite corruption of the police and also the use of these laws for discriminatory prosecution and harassment. We ought to decriminalize the kinds of behavior discussed below.

1. Juvenile status offenses.

Activities of a child or youth which would not be regarded as criminal if performed by an adult should not be subject to prosecution in court. Examples are unexcused absence from school, running away from home, and stubborn disobedience to parents. The young members of society engaged in such conduct may be having trouble, but, if so, neither police, criminal court, nor juvenile court is equipped to handle it. Many a child has been officially labeled "delinquent," packed off to a "training school" or other institution, and there developed for the first time into the criminal offender he understands society to have called him.[5] Marvin E. Wolfgang reports that the United States is the only country in which juvenile status offenders are arrested and put into the system of criminal justice, adding that in neither Western nor Eastern European countries is this done. Yet, he says, about one-third of all juveniles in the juvenile justice system in the United States are status offenders.[6]

2. Vagrancy.

Rich people are not subject to arrest for unproductive idleness or lack of fixed, permanent address. Vagrancy laws are a device for punishing people unpopular and poor, or subject to suspicions too vague to provide proper grounds for arrest. Such laws are expressions of prejudice and general hostility which have no proper place in a decent society.[7]

3. Drunkenness.

People who are committing no offenses other than being intoxicated in public or endangering themselves by their intoxicated condition must often receive concerned attention. However, in such cases the processes of arrest, appearance in court, and sentencing to jail have long been shown to be unhelpful to anyone. Yet more people are arrested for drunkenness than for any other non-motor-vehicle offense. Many alcoholics become familiarly known to the judges as leaving and reentering jail in such rapid succession that they are dubbed "revolving door" cases. The FBI estimated that in 1971 there were 1,235,761 arrests for public drunkenness.[8] The cluttering of the courts and the expense of maintaining these people in jail seem a pointless burden, since large numbers of them are intelligent, good-natured people, holding jobs and supporting themselves and their families while they are sober. But worse, by far, is the demeaning of persons and the abusive injustices which commonly arise in the selective arrests and discrepant sentencing of drunks. The National Advisory Commission "recommends that drunkenness in and of itself should not continue to be treated as a crime."[9] The Commission reports experiences in better ways of handling the problem.[10] In addition to the recommendations of detoxification centers and referral for special treatment by civilian organizations such as Alcoholics Anonymous, I add one comment of my own.

Let the reader consider the question of an alcoholic whom I transported several times from the Montgomery County (Maryland) Pre-Release Center to a County treatment center. He said he could not understand why the law permits advertisers to use every imaginable device to persuade people to drink alcoholic beverages and always to drink more, then arrests the people who are most completely persuaded and pays out big money trying, usually unsuccessfully, to persuade them in the treatment center not to drink anymore. He wanted to know why. What is the answer? Is there any good reason why alcoholic beverages should be allowed to be advertised outside the places of business where they are sold?

4. Drug use.

The use of marijuana, the narcotics, hallucinogens, amphetamines, and other drugs frequently subject to criminal law is probably not reduced and may be increased by being labeled a crime.

The legal handling of marijuana as if equivalent to the opiates is especially damaging. In most places marijuana is not hard to obtain. Its use has not been reduced by draconian measures. Even while Texas was punishing first offenders in simple possession of it with sentences up to life imprisonment, half the students in the state university at Austin reported having tried it.[11] Youth who try it quickly discover that it does not have the awesome effects widely publicized and the great majority find it simply depressing and boring. Because it has been officially classed with the opiates, those who do want to go on with their adventure move easily to heroin, which has the special advantage of being used in minute quantities easily concealed.

In general the drugs are less prone to cause criminal acts than alcohol, excepting as the law makes their use a crime and by making them hard to get induces the addict to commit crimes in order to support the addiction. The *use* of them should be regarded as a medical problem. Importation and traffic in the drugs should be subject to criminal penalties, but with care to distinguish sharply between different kinds of substances.[12] The 1972 Penal Code of Hawaii is a useful model in this respect.

5. Gambling.

Many Americans, including me, regard gambling as unethical because it is an effort to gain for oneself at the expense of others, with no service in return. Moreover, some people become psychologically so addicted to gambling that they deprive themselves and their families of decent livelihood and become dependent on public assistance. But there are many other forms of selfishness, some of them more flagrantly immoral, which we do not even consider subjecting to criminal law.

Making gambling or the operation of gambling a crime has not prevented many millions of Americans from engaging in it every week. It has delivered the business of catering to people's gambling desires to the criminal underworld where it is reputed to be the single greatest source of steady illegal income. It has thus become a mainstay of organized crime.

The popular numbers game could not operate on its huge scale without its local operators being widely known. It is evident, therefore, that they carry on their business with the bought indulgence of the police. The illegal gambling rackets are corrupting law enforcement on a large scale.

The operators often become channels for paying off the police, not only to protect gambling, but also much more serious organized crime.

Several states have attempted to cut off this base of organized crime by operating under state auspices lotteries of which the profits go into the state treasuries. They have not produced nearly so much revenue as hoped and have not appeared to cut deeply into the illicit operations. One important reason is that they have required too big an outlay and too long a wait for payoffs to compete with the daily nickel-and-dime numbers games. A serious objection to state-operated lotteries is that they put the state into the business of persuading people to gamble.

The National Advisory Commission recommends that incarceration not be employed to enforce laws against gambling.[13] We should go further than that. Gambling itself should be decriminalized. Police have more important jobs to do than breaking up crap games in doorways or on vacant lots of the inner city or arresting a tiny sampling from the millions who gamble in other ways.

As for the operation of betting establishments, let the state license and tax off-track betting for everybody so inclined as it now permits on-track betting for the more affluent, but with limits on places and methods of advertising. Let administrative control take the place of the present self-defeating prohibition by criminal law. Like all administrative law this would depend on criminal law to back it up when violated.

6. Sex between consenting adults.

Christian and Jewish ethics, along with much of secular ethics, have, through the centuries, opposed sexual intercourse between men and women not married partners. Large numbers of people who practice fornication or adultery still believe both to be wrong. It does not follow that criminal law should forbid such ethically illicit unions. Religion and public opinion must do their own work of promoting standards of morality in personal life. Neither the churches and synagogues nor the moral standards which they have traditionally taught gain in strength when religious institutions underestimate their own power and responsibility by calling on the state to do their work by unenforceable criminal law.[14]

Sexual relations are usually so personal and private that criminal law is powerless to control them. When it attempts to do so it intolerably invades privacy and still falls on its face.

Decriminalizing sex between consenting adults does not imply that faithful marriage is a matter of public indifference. It means a recognition that criminal law has not been effective in preventing or substantially controlling either premarital or extramarital sex and that it is unwise to attempt using criminal sanctions for this purpose.[15]

7. Minor traffic offenses.

To label as criminal a person who fails to see or heed a red light or road sign or who exceeds a speed limit by five or ten miles per hour when no danger results drains the word of proper meaning and overloads police and courts. Such offenses should be handled administratively by payment of scaled fines, and when persistent, or when fines go unpaid, by required attendance at traffic schools or by suspension of licenses without court procedure unless the motorist initiates a court appeal. This recommendation does not apply to driving to endanger or without being licensed and certainly not to driving while drunk, about which more is to be said below.[16]

C. New Moves Against the Deadliest Crimes

1. Ban private ownership of operable handguns; license other guns.

About 65% of all murders in the United States are accomplished by means of guns,[17] 51% by handguns.[18] This compares with less than 10% in the United Kingdom. Someone will ask what difference it makes whether he is killed by gun, knife, or bare hands? The main difference is that in the United States ten to twenty times as many people are murdered per 100,000 population as in the United Kingdom and other countries with strict gun controls. Most murders are emotional attacks. When means used are not very deadly the result is injury and a charge of aggravated assault. Thus, "on the basis of the UCR figures we find that whereas 13 percent of assaults with firearms were fatal, only 3 percent of knife assaults resulted in the death of the victim."[19]

It is commonly argued that if handguns were forbidden, the criminal use of them would go unchecked because outlaws would not obey the gun laws any better than they obey other laws. Meanwhile, respectable people would be disarmed and helpless. This argument is refuted by the facts. The guns which people buy only to protect their homes are precisely the ones used most often to kill—for the majority of homicides are of family members, relatives, neighbors, or acquaintances and result from quarrels, mistaken identity, love triangles, and the like. The most frequent locale of murder is the bedroom at home.[20]

Probably most guns used by outlaws are illegally acquired even now, so some people say that a ban would not affect them. But it is one thing for the would-be robber or killer-for-hire to steal a handgun when there are millions of such guns in households and business places throughout the country; it would be much harder if there were only a few.

The National Advisory Commission seems to have lacked the political courage to recommend the present banning of private handguns and licensing of other guns to which their facts clearly point. The best they could do regarding even machine guns was to recommend their federal registration![21] The Commission does, however, recommend that by the end of 1982 (!) each state should prohibit private civilian possession of handguns and the manufacture, importation, and sale of such weapons. Further, it recommends that states should acquire all existing handguns.[22] Good! But why wait until 1982? We should go further and require also the licensing of all firearms. Privately owned guns in the United States have killed 30% more Americans since 1900 than have been killed in all wars since the birth of the nation two centuries ago.[23] It is about time this was stopped. Benevolent good will (Norm 2, chap. 16, D) toward the potential victims requires the measures recommended.

The polls indicate that more than 70% of the people want gun control by law. But the politicians think that most people do not care enough to let the issue influence their votes. Until people who care about checking violent crime and saving life match the lobbying of the gun industry and the National Rifle Association, this carnage will probably continue.[24]

2. Effectively ban drunken driving.

One instrument kills more Americans than the gun. This is the automobile in the hands of an intoxicated driver. According to the President's Crime Commission report of 1967, intoxicated drivers were killing about twice as many people as were slain by *all* willful homicides. When so many people are fearful of "crime on the streets" why are so few incensed about these deaths at the hands of drinking drivers? Probably because so many can identify with the drivers. Drinking drivers kill about 25,000 persons per year and injure 266,000 others, according to the National Safety Bureau of the U.S. Department of Transportation and the National Safety Council. Yet the FBI does not even count fatal drunken driving an Index crime. Only about one out of eight of these drunken killers is arrested for negligent manslaughter.[25]

Most European countries have expressed a higher valuation of life on the streets and highways by enforcing serious sanctions against driving while intoxicated. With the privilege of driving goes the legal obligation to cooperate with the police in a breath-balloon test. If the test gives evidence of considerable alcohol in the breath, then the motorist is taken to a laboratory for a blood test. The limits for acceptable levels of alcohol in the blood vary, country by country, from 30 to 80 milligrams (mg) to the milliliter (ml). In Norway and Sweden the alcoholic driver is subject to loss of license for a year and nearly always a short prison sentence as well. In Denmark the usual punishment on first offense is two weeks in jail. In Holland loss of license and also short-term imprisonment are almost invariable. Prison sentences are often served in weekend installments. Arrests for the offense are still frequent in the Scandinavian countries, but accidents from drunken driving are infrequent and fatalities rare. These laws have resulted in sharp drops in motor vehicle fatalities in all the countries concerned.

Morris and Hawkins recommend with exemplary moderation a maximum tolerance of 80 mg per ml, and propose a mandatory one-year suspension of driving license for first offense, with five years for each subsequent offense.[26]

D. Repealing Death Penalty Legislation

On June 29, 1972, the United States Supreme Court ruled that capital punishment as practiced in the United States was unconstitutional. The five justices who voted with the majority wrote separate opinions and gave differing reasons. William J. Brennan, Jr., and Thurgood Marshall believed that the execution of any individual was degrading or barbaric by its very nature. The votes of the other three were to some degree based on its comparative rarity and hence the obviously discriminatory way in which the legal provisions for the death penalty were brought into actual use.

Within less than two years 28 of the 50 states had enacted new death penalty laws by which legislators sought to avoid the objections of one to three of the justices on the Supreme Court bench and so escape a new adverse court decision. The most important device intended to accomplish this is to make the capital sentence mandatory following all convictions of certain crimes, usually murders under certain specified conditions. Debates on these bills have disclosed a difficult dilemma facing politicians who want to respond to popular anger against convicted criminals, especially murderers. If the categories of mandatory capital crimes are made broad enough to conform to the popular anger, past experience with prosecutors, juries, and judges shows that the laws will not stand a chance of being uniformly enforced, for many persons committing the crimes will be convicted of lesser ones when prosecutors, juries, and judges believe that under all the given circumstances the offenders ought not to be executed. On the other hand, if the crimes are narrow in definition—for example specifying only murder of a law enforcement official during an attempt to escape—then they cannot be expected, as one legislator protested, to protect farmers and their families, or for that matter any other civilians.

Actually, the idea that the death penalty decreases the number of murders is only an airy theory which the facts of the real world do not support.

There is a fairly large body of information on the consequences of instituting and using the death penalty on the one hand, and of eliminating it on the other. Four of our states repealed their laws providing for capital punishment more than 85 years ago, namely Michigan (1846), Rhode Island (1852), Wisconsin (1853), and Maine (1887). Nine other states subsequently abolished the death penalty. Thorsten Sellin made comparisons of paired states with similar economic conditions and population distributions, one of each pair using capital punishment, the other not. He compared also years with and without capital punishment in the same state in cases of repeal and later reinstatement. Reviewing his tables and graphs, any realistic and fair-minded person would seem bound to come to his conclusion. He says, "The inevitable conclusion is that executions have no discernible effect on homicide death rates which . . . are regarded as adequate indicators of capital murder rates."[27] In the same article he analyzes the facts regarding the hazards of police work in states with and without the death penalty for the killing of policemen, again showing no discernible deterrent effect of that penalty. The international picture is similar. "A comprehensive United Nations report found that abolition of the death penalty has no effect on murder rates. With or without capital punishment, murder rates are about the same."[28] Twenty-eight countries have abolished capital punishment completely (9), or with exceptions for rare, extraordinary crimes (16), or, with legal provision for it still on the books, have not used it for 40 years or more (3).[29]

Why is the death penalty not an effective general deterrent? Criminal homicide is an act involving violent passion. Those who commit it are usually so desperate, so emotionally disturbed, or such reckless gamblers that they are not deterred by the considering of a possible sentence if caught and convicted. Probably a few are deterred. But apparently as many or more are incited to kill by their own suicidal "death wish," increased hostility stirred by the execution of a fellow convict or member of the same class or minority, or by the lurid imagining of the legal killing. In Pennsylvania and California studies showed increases of homicides up to 25% on days close to execution dates, increases unexplainable by other factors.[30]

Capital punishment on the books seriously overburdens the courts and decreases convictions of persons guilty of serious crimes. Capital cases receive disproportionate space and time in the media, in investigation, in jury selection, and in appeals. So long as there is the slightest doubt (not only the "reasonable doubt" required by law) that the defendant is guilty and deserving of death there will be great reluctance to have him executed. Jurors, judges, and governors are properly anxious about incurring guilt themselves for sending to death persons who ought not to be executed. Death is irretrievable. Hence a legal provision for it is extremely costly and self-defeating.

Capital punishment itself is the killing of a human being. By that act the state expresses its own belief in solving its problems by violence against life. It thus cheapens life and adds to the social climate productive of violent crime. Its degrading effect is especially serious in the lives of people involved in administering it.

Finally, passing death penalty laws diverts attention from measures which experience shows actually do reduce crime. Legislators now voting to restore the death penalty lead some of their constituents to think they have done something to make life more secure. Actually, they have done nothing of the kind, while other proposals which, when adopted, do make life safer, are swept under the rug.[31]

Benevolent good will and respect toward all persons (Norm 2, Chap. 16, D), related coherently to the known facts (Norm 1), requires elimination of the death penalty. Furthermore, the death penalty is always applied by selection based on poverty, race, unpopularity, or the like, in violation of equal rights (Norm 3).[32]

21

The Police

The police have an exceedingly important part in the system of criminal justice. They constitute the visible presence of criminal law on the street and the part of the system with which the most citizens have contact. It is their action, usually in response to civilian complaint, which starts the procedures of criminal justice in any given case. They have wide latitude of discretion whether to act or not to act and to decide what kind of action to take in response to many a situation. Thus a patrolman may decide whether to give some friendly counsel to a boisterous group of young men crowding a street corner, to bark a command that the group scatter, to issue warnings to certain leaders, to issue summonses, or to make arrests. On the highway the policeman may signal a motorist driving above the speed limit to slow down, stop him and warn him to "take it easy," check his license and hand him a formal warning slip, give him a warrant to appear in traffic court, or arrest him. A great deal of what may happen afterward depends on the policeman's first move. While the law and the orders of his superiors affect his action, much depends also on his own personal judgment.

Several policies concerning the police are indicated by our basic philosophy of social defense and restoration and our ethical norms.

A. Enhancing Roles of Crime Prevention and Diversion

In other connections we have noted how far better it is to prevent crime than to charge an offender after a crime has been committed. This needs to be emphasized in every police force. Too often police persons are judged by their aggressiveness in law enforcement and receive little credit from superiors or public for preventing crime, whether by their visible presence, work in boys' clubs, educational activity in the schools, informal helpfulness to youth, or other means. When a police officer proves especially effective in order-maintaining activities and so deserves promotion it should not be necessary to remove that officer from such work in order to provide proper rewards in promotion and pay increases.[1]

The National Advisory Commission observes that efforts of police for diversion of many minor offenders from the criminal justice system "have two main advantages: relieving the burden on the courts and on corrections, thus freeing valuable criminal justice resources, and providing more help to the individual."[2]

Disorderly juveniles, drunks, drug addicts, and mental patients frequently require attention from the police because of citizens' complaints or to prevent injury. Yet all are especially likely themselves to be injured by the processes of criminal justice rather than assisted to avoid further trouble. The juveniles may need nothing more than a few words of friendly advice or a vigorous warning from a policeman, especially if he is well known to them as understanding and fair. The drunks need to be taken home or to a detoxification center and when sober encouraged to join Alcoholics Anonymous or enter a therapy program.[3] The drug addicts and mental patients may need hospitalization. For problems of all such persons arrest, prosecution, and sentence seem peculiarly unfitting means of remedy.

Benevolent purpose, both for the individuals and for others in the community, applied realistically (Norms 1, 2, and 4), dictates that, so far as the law and circumstances permit, police use diversion with all such persons, in preference to arrest.

B. Improving Personnel Policies

1. Raise standards of selection, training, and pay.

A police person needs to be equipped with a wide range of knowledge and skills. If he is to enforce the laws in a lawful manner, he must know the statutes and court decisions most directly affecting his own work. He must have a high degree of self-discipline and be able to use quickly his body and instruments of control with both due restraint and effectiveness. He needs the understanding of practical social psychology and the wisdom to intervene in situations of emotional crisis in such a way as to moderate passions rather than intensifying them. A good policeman has also the comprehensive grasp and sense of proportion necessary to use wisely his wide discretionary powers. Every sizable police force requires also specialists of various kinds with qualifications additional to some or all of the above.

These are exacting requirements, demanding quite special kinds of persons. To have such persons in police service requires both careful selection and appropriate training. But selection at suitable level is possible only if positions are sufficiently attractive to draw applicants in adequate numbers and quality. That requires levels of pay considerably above those now prevailing in most jurisdictions.

The Advisory Commission on Criminal Justice Standards and Goals quotes James Q. Wilson as saying that low rates of pay and allowances "are interpreted by policemen as palpable evidence of the contempt in which the police are held by the public and the politicians."[4] Wilson found that innumerable cities, towns, and counties paid so little that even a high school education could not be required, no one bothered to take the civil service examinations, and the senior officers minimized the new state requirement of six weeks' police training.[5]

The National Advisory Commission reports that in 1971 the median starting salary for the police in cities of less than 100,000 was "around $7,500" and the maximum salaries "only $8,750."[6] The recommended standard is relative to prevailing incomes of other people in the various communities possessing qualifications of level similar to those needed by police officers. One test is the number and caliber of people applying for police work.[7] The Commission believes it to be important also that maximum salaries be enough higher to offer incentive for officers to continue in police work and seek constant improvement in preparation and performance.[8]

Our conception of criminal justice as serving the purposes of crime prevention so far as possible and social restoration when crime has nevertheless occurred requires such upgrading of police service as the Advisory Commission recommends. Only so can we hope to have police agencies effectively devoted to such demanding ends.

2. Increase employment of minorities and women.

When a neighborhood is predominantly black or Spanish-speaking and the police force nearly all white and English-speaking, the wide tendency to view the police as a hostile occupying force is encouraged. The ability of the police to make arrests is diminished in such a situation. Even more are the police handicapped for prevention and for diversionary alternatives.

The National Advisory Commission recommends "Every police agency should engage in positive efforts to employ ethnic minority group members," and when there are substantial numbers of such people in the jurisdiction, effort should be made to recruit from them police personnel "in approximate proportion to the makeup of the population."[9]

Certainly this is necessary if we are to achieve a high level of cooperation between police and community for the purpose of crime prevention and social restoration. Because with such minority representation higher levels of information and understanding can be achieved, movement toward justice as fairness and the norm of equity can also be strengthened.

Women ought to be increasingly employed in a wide variety of police work. This is essential, not only as part of the general effort for equitable employment opportunities, but also for the effectiveness of police work itself. As long ago as 1922 the International Association of Chiefs of Police said that women were essential, especially in preventive work. Women were believed to be particularly important in "the areas of juvenile delinquency, female criminality, family crises, runaways, missing persons and sex offenses."[10] At that time the IACP thought that women should not be expected to serve in police units which must make arrests. Now the National Advisory Commission recommends their employment for every kind of police work for which individual women can meet the essential requirements. A further recommendation is that there should be no separate classification or paths of promotion for women. This accords with our ethical Norm 3 (Chap. 16, D). The Commission reports that some cities are now acting in accordance with these recommendations.[11]

3. Establish and publicize appropriate norms for promotions.

Police officers were cited earlier as saying that there were serious differences between the actual roles predominating in police work and the kinds of records weighted in promotions. In the former, prevention of crime and services to persons in need occupied the most time. On the other hand, it was believed that a reputation for aggressiveness and the making of many arrests was the important criterion of promotion.

If prevention and social restoration are to be the purposes of the criminal justice system, then it is especially important that the more benign, cooperative, and serving functions should not only be clearly recognized in promotional policy but that they should be understood to be so recognized throughout the agency and community. It is therefore important that the various roles and qualities required should be publicly adopted, after open hearings and participation of both civilians and police officers, and continually publicized. Not only will such policy put expectations in proper perspective for ambitious police personnel, but, by drawing the public into the process, will lead to more understanding cooperation between police and citizenry.[12]

C. Increasing Use of the Summons; Less Use of Arrest

An arrest is an experience which is calculated to demean and alienate. It is therefore to be avoided when the principal ends of justice can be achieved without it. It has the additional disadvantage of using valuable time of policemen. If the arrestee is held after arrest there are added human and financial costs to both the community and the person arrested.

The National Advisory Commission wisely recommends as follows: "Every police agency immediately should make maximum effective use of state statutes permitting police agencies to issue written summonses and citations in lieu of physical arrest or prearraignment confinement."[13] Policies for doing so should be adopted by police agencies and guidelines should be provided to all police officers, not to eliminate their own discretion, but to support and limit it and to provide equitable treatment throughout the jurisdiction. Most misdemeanants apart from offenders who are under the influence of drugs or alcohol or are bent on continuing illegal acts can be advantageously handled without arrest. Where the law does not permit this it should be changed.[14]

22

The Courts

A committee chaired by Justice Robert Jackson reported in 1953, "There is widespread doubt that existing criminal procedures can be relied upon either adequately to protect society or to protect the individual accused."[1] Lewis R. Katz and two coauthors of *Justice is the Crime*, published nineteen years later, quote that statement, then add, "The widespread doubt has not been eliminated; in fact it has now reached epidemic proportions."[2]

The courts are the very heart of the criminal justice system. To a considerable extent abuses by the police, the legislatures, and the correctional institutions can be checked and rectified by the courts. But when justice is not done in the courts injustice has the last word. Radical changes in the courts are long overdue.

A. Streamlining and Relief

Roscoe Pound told the American Bar Association in 1906 that the work of our courts in this century could not be done by methods and procedures of the 19th century. Sixty-four years later Chief Justice Warren E. Burger noted that the inadequate mechanism and procedures of 1906 remained basically unchanged. The Chief Justice added, "In the supermarket age we are trying to operate the courts with cracker-barrel corner grocer methods and equipment—vintage 1900."[3]

The changes to be recommended here are not novel suggestions. Some have already been made in certain places. But together they would bring about a radically renovated court system. Most would require new legislation in most states, while some could be put into effect by concerted effort of the courts within a state. All require leadership from judges, law scholars and practitioners and state executives.

1. Relieve courts of most traffic cases and many others.

The courts are burdened and clogged by much business for which such complex and expensive procedures are not needed. They cannot perform their essential tasks unless relieved.

As previously observed, when minor traffic violations are formally described as "criminal" and the violators summoned to "criminal court" to answer, the very word "criminal" is downgraded and the court is needlessly burdened. Such matters should be handled by a traffic bureau, with monetary penalties to be returned by mail. When the citizen fails to respond with the prescribed fine, the amount due should be increased with each succeeding notice until, after persistent failure, the driver's license is suspended by the registrar. Other penalties may be handled similarly. For example, compulsive speeders may be required to attend traffic school, for which they must pay. A system of "points" for moving violations substantially increasing insurance costs, and, after a prescribed number of points, incurring suspension of license, can also serve as an effective deterrent in most cases. None of such procedures should require a court unless the citizen chooses to take the registrar or director of the bureau to court on his own initiative.

Chief Justice Burger calls attention to the fact that at present "automobile cases are the largest single category of civil cases in the courts."[4] Since civil cases, as well as criminal, burden the courts, a high degree of relief can be gained by removing most of this load. Massachusetts and some other states have demonstrated that this can be accomplished by means of "no-fault" motor vehicle insurance. Besides unburdening the courts for more important tasks and reducing insurance costs, this change eliminates much conflict between rival claimants, with consequent marring of personal relations, and many unhappy experiences of witnesses losing much time awaiting their turns to testify and chafing under rough cross-examination.

2. *Improve the efficiency of administration.*

Judges in lightly loaded rural jurisdictions may be able to maintain the organization of their own courts satisfactorily. But in urban areas administrators chosen for their preparation and skill in personnel management should be appointed to take over this nonjudicial function. It is not a simple matter to have the necessary records, prosecutors, defendant, defense attorneys, witnesses for both sides, clerk, and panel of prospective jurors in the courtroom at one scheduled time. If one essential individual is not there, many persons are losing time, and some witnesses, on their third or fourth wasted day, may be vowing never again to report having witnessed a crime.

Many judges, clerks, and bailiffs insist that there is no better way matters could be handled. Chief Justice Burger, the experienced members of the National Advisory Commission, and countless expert coordinators of complex industrial operations know that is not so.[5]

3. *Reduce the role of the grand jury.*

Among the cumbersome, time-consuming, and delaying devices in criminal procedures, an important one is the grand jury as regularly required for criminal indictment. As the National Advisory Commission recommends, "Grand jury indictment should not be required for any criminal prosecution, but the grand jury should be retained for its investigative functions."[6] Various concomitant recommendations by the Commission should, however, be carefully observed.

4. *Sharply reduce delays.*

"In all criminal prosecutions, the accused shall enjoy the right to a speedy and public trial. . . ." So says the United States Constitution, Amendment VI. How speedy are criminal trials today? Most cases are disposed of without trial, but studies of timing begun in 1968 showed that the *average* felony case required from arrest to disposition (whether by conviction, dismissal, or not-guilty verdict) from 245 days (Cleveland, 1968) to 170 days (Philadelphia, December 1970).[7]

Such delay keeps many defendants presumed innocent, and sometimes adjudged later to be in fact innocent, incarcerated for long periods. At the same time in case of later conviction and sentence it robs the penalty of nearly all deterrent effect. Especially is this true of general deterrence. When conviction and sentence occur six months or even years after arrest most citizens who heard about the robbery or other crime do not learn of the resulting sentence or do not associate it with the now long-forgotten crime.

Delays have other evil results. Witnesses forget details or become unavailable so that the court becomes less likely to learn the truth. When the delay results in part from postponements this often means that witnesses have lost time waiting in court to be called, with consequent lowered opinion of the law.

Delays of justice have the effect of denying justice both to defendants and to the community. While deeply respecting judges who work long days in perpetual struggle with the present anachronistic system, we must insist that current practice is actually a flagrant violation of Amendment VI and of reason. Many experienced judges, as well as others, agree that such delays as are common in our urban courts today are unnecessary.

Chief Justice Burger would like to see the provision of necessary personnel, especially trained administrative managers, "to try criminal cases within 60 days after indictment."[8] The National Advisory Commission proposes as a standard that "The period from arrest to the beginning of trial of a felony prosecution generally should not be longer than 60 days. In a misdemeanor prosecution, the period from arrest to trial generally should be 30 days or less."[9] The Commission presents further standards concerning intermediate procedures to make the 30-day and 60-day periods realistic in most cases. Schedules should be established with the aim of disposition or trial of as many cases as possible within half the maximum periods, i.e., 15 days for misdemeanors and 30 days for felonies.

B. Eliminating Plea Bargaining

The National Advisory Commission, under Standard 3:1, declares, "As soon as possible, but in no event later than 1978, negotiations between prosecutors and defendants—either personally or through their attorneys—concerning concessions to be made in return for guilty pleas should be prohibited."[10] The Commission details safeguards which should be employed until the early date when all plea negotiations are abolished.

Since we have already observed in previous passages typical injustices which commonly result from plea bargaining, we need not spell them out now. So long as the negotiation of pleas is permitted, it will continue, in actual effect, to deprive great numbers of persons of their right to trial, to hide corruption of public officials by wealthy and powerful kingpins of organized crime, and to serve as an escape hatch for the affluent or politically powerful violators of our criminal laws.

Many pleas of guilty will be made without bargaining. Not anticipating bargaining sessions, prosecutors will not be so inclined to inflate charges. When defendants and their counsel know that the prosecutor has the evidence to convict and there will be no delays in the process they will enter pleas of guilty. When they believe the charges unprovable they have a right to go to trial.

The Commission says that this recommendation "may be the most far-reaching in the entire Courts Report." It recognizes that many critics of plea bargaining still think it a necessity. Nevertheless, quite rightly, the Commission "totally condemns plea bargaining as an institution and recommends that within five years no such bargaining take place."[11] If we are to have equal justice (Norm 3), this is imperative and should not wait until 1978.

C. Rationality and Equity in Sentencing

"Consider that a civil judgment for $2,000 is reviewable in every state at least once. . . . Then consider the unreviewability of a sentence of twenty years in prison and a fine of $10,000." So writes the distinguished judge Marvin E. Frankel.[12] The resulting disparities between practices of different judges are among the more scandalous realities in American criminal justice.* In 1968 the American Bar Association urged appellate review of sentences.[13]

Every conviction and sentence should be subject to one review. A special panel of judges, with a staff, should be established for this purpose. Ordinarily, cases of misdemeanors would be covered in rapid, routine fashion. Now and then an unusual misdemeanor sentence or a conviction under strange conditions may require a second look. Usually, in both misdemeanor and felony cases, the very existence of the panel and procedure will prevent judges from indulging such eccentric fancies and prejudices as occasionally come to light.

Because the review will be automatic in all cases it can move much more quickly than in present procedures of appeal. The Advisory Commission emphasizes the saving of time and money which should result from the simplified procedures. These savings would depend, however, on certain restrictions of the *appeal* process. I concur in supporting generally the restrictions proposed, but would note one reservation. It must always remain possible for an appeal to be made to a state supreme court on a question of violation of the state constitution or to the United States Supreme Court on a question of violation of the federal Constitution.[14]

In sentencing, every judge should be required to state pointedly the reason why, within the limits provided by legislation, he is choosing the sentence he is pronouncing. This statement would be part of the record going to the review panel. The practice would (1) increase the systematic

---

* Cf. above, Chap. 5, A.

thought of those many judges who now depend on hunches in the mood of the moment, (2) assist the review panel, and (3) impress the convicted offender with the reasonableness of the sentence.[15]

D. Safeguarding Rights of the Young and the Poor

It is important to protect juveniles from the trauma, role-typing, and public record of open court procedures. For this purpose the states have established juvenile courts to handle cases of defendants under a prescribed age, varying in different states from age 16 to 21.

In theory juvenile courts do not punish, but seek to rehabilitate and assist. Hence there is no adversarial proceeding, but instead a private informal discussion with the judge, usually attended by principal witnesses, the juvenile, and the parents. There may be a prosecutor and a defense counsel.

Unfortunately, the judge and other adults present often assume the truth of the accusation and devote all their attention to seeking the most promising assignment of the boy or girl for rehabilitation. The 1967 Gault decision of the United States Supreme Court guarantees the right to defense counsel, and this has brought much improvement. However, the adults concerned sometimes display a misguided paternalism which denies the theoretical presumption of innocence until proof of guilt.

We have advocated, in Chapter 20, that all juvenile status offenses be removed from criminal law. Such problems, along with all other noncriminal matters relating to marriage and family life, when they require court action, should go to special family courts, as recommended by the National Advisory Commission.[16]

Serious felony charges against juveniles should be tried *in camera*, but with all the rights of due process accorded adult defendants. The defendant should have the right to public trial on demand by defense counsel. "A determination of delinquency should require a finding that the State has proven that the juvenile has committed an act that, if committed by an adult, would constitute a criminal offense."[17]

While the Commission recognizes that institutionalization of juveniles is undesirable when not necessary,[18] there is not in the recommended standards a basic critique of institutionalization and no such emphatic recommendation of alternatives in most cases as will be presented in the next chapter.

As pointed out earlier,* despite the Gideon decision of 1963 many poor defendants are still denied legal counsel worthy of the name. Often the public defender has so many cases that he does not have time to study

---

* See above, Chap. 5, B.

an individual's story or, indeed, even to hear it. If the judge assigns a case to an attorney of private practice, he is often a man who has little business of his own and so attends criminal trials in hope of being assigned cases for which he will be paid from public funds. Besides being frequently lawyers of poor quality, such persons sometimes take on more cases than they can properly handle.

In pursuance of that benevolent justice which requires special care to protect the poor and weak (Ethical Norm No. 5, Chap. 16, D) it is imperative that counsel provided a defendant unable to pay must not be a mere warm body designated as a defense counsel, but an able lawyer with the time and will to protect the defendant's rights.

One way to provide such defense at reasonable cost is to assign seniors in law school to public defense staffs. There is a present movement to requiring clinical experience of this kind for graduation for the law schools and, encouraged by the American Bar Association, most legislatures are cooperating. Even where permissive legislation has not been enacted law students can assist lawyers, although care will be needed to know and observe the law regarding privileged information and confidentiality.[19] Besides helping to provide adequate counsel, such clinical programs aid greatly in the education of lawyers for their careers and especially in broadening their social perspectives.

E. Better Selection and Training of Judges

Many American judges represent the finest traditions of the law. At the opposite extreme are some without even law education, and others with flagrant prejudices, uncontrolled tempers, or lazy habits which mark them as conspicuously ill-equipped for their grave and exacting responsibilities. Even when distinguished attorneys are appointed they have usually studied little of criminal law. A highly successful counsel of corporations or insurance companies may have made no serious study of *criminal* law since his first year in law school and he may have little understanding of people outside the circles in which his professional and personal life moves.

The National Advisory Commission recommends a number of standards on the selection and training of the judiciary. Selection of a panel should be by a special commission in each state, representing the judges, the bar, and the public, with final appointment by the governor. Subsequently, sitting judges should be subject to unopposed reelection by popular vote.[20] Every state should fund a program for judicial education of all judges, in courses at both state and national levels, and the training should be mandatory for every new judge. The training should include a visit by every judge in every institution to which he may sentence any criminal offender.[21] As Roscoe Pound wrote over 60 years ago, the training of judges for work in the city should include sociological instruction on urban conditions.[22] Similar training adapted to rural conditions is needed also for judges who are to serve in small town and countryside, for rural areas present their own serious problems of social division and tension. The courses offered at The National College of the State Judiciary in Reno, Nevada, are especially valuable for the broadening of outlook, the cultivation of human understanding, and the sharing of new information and ideas by the distinguished staff members and the participating judges.

The discussion of corrections, below, will be deeply related to sentencing in the courts.

23

Corrections

The very word "corrections," as commonly used, carries connotations with which a philosophy of justice as social defense and restoration cannot be satisfied. We commonly call the whole aggregation of prisons and other institutions to which adult and juvenile offenders are sentenced, together with the agencies controlling probation and parole, "corrections" or "correctional," and we use the words in this broad sense here.

The usual implication of the terms is that all these institutions and agencies exist to *correct* the individuals who have offended against the law. This idea is an improvement on the vindictive notion conveyed by the phrase "penal institution." Unfortunately, much that occurs in "corrections" is actually vindictive in spirit, retributive in purpose, and has little or nothing to do with correction of anyone. When prison officials are not vindictive most of their effort is usually expended on custody, with correction receiving little attention. Even if everything included under "corrections" were truly intended to change the offenders, however, we would consider this purpose inadequate. As we have pointed out, a crime is both a symptom and a further aggravation of a socially intolerable relationship between one or more individuals and the surrounding society. Acts worthy of being legally defined as crimes do injury to people and further break the fabric of social order. What is needed is to make the society whole, with victims, offenders, and others affected by the crimes brought into reasonably acceptable mutual relationships.

Although we are using the term "corrections," we will be proposing changes to make the institutions and processes included serve the larger purpose of social restoration. We will include also other agencies and procedures to be employed for this purpose. We are concerned with the purpose of correction, but correction of social relationships as well as of individual attitudes and behavior. We shall also be concerned with trying to avoid as far as possible the further disruption of society which is produced by the very processes of criminal justice and especially by incarceration.

A. Reducing Incarceration

1. Sharply reduce jailing before trial.

In legal theory and according to our ethical Norm 2, a defendant is presumed innocent until proved guilty. Often he is actually innocent of the charges made against him. The most obvious demands of justice, then, dictate that defendants not be incarcerated before trial unless urgently required to assure presence at trial or to protect the public against continuing or repeated injurious acts. Avoidance of the further individual and social damage inevitably caused by incarceration dictates the same requirement.

Experiments of the Vera Institute in cooperation with the courts of New York show that large numbers of defendants ordinarily detained for trial or released only on bail can be released on their own recognizance or under personal supervision of responsible citizens without social injury and with even higher likelihood of appearance for trial than defendants released on bail.[1] Such release of similarly screened persons, together with the speedy trial and larger use of the summons in lieu of arrest, advocated in our sections on Police and Courts, would reduce incarceration before trial to a fraction of its present level.[2]

2. In sentencing, incarcerate only as a last resort.

Since incarceration exacerbates alienation and hostility, thus tending to incite further crimes, it should be used as little as possible consistent with no greater risks involved in alternatives. The pain and injury inflicted by imprisonment, not only on convicted persons but also on their families and friends, are additional reasons why it should be used only as a last resort. This recommendation is in accord with our ethical requirement of general benevolence (Norm 2, Chap. 16, D, above), the National Advisory Commission's Standard 7.1,[3] and recommendations of other groups and individuals who have studied the effects of incarceration.[4]

If the reader envisages an increase of crime as the predictable effect of using alternatives to prison, let him consider the results of a mass release of convicts which occurred, without any alternative supervision, in 1963.

As a result of the Gideon decision in that year, more than 1,000 prison inmates were suddenly released in Florida alone. To observe the effect on crime many of those releasees were matched by individual characteristics against another group released at the same time on completion of their sentences. "Over a period of 2½ years, the *Gideon* group had a recidivism rate of 13.6 percent, and the other group had almost twice that rate, 25.4 percent."[5]

Of course I do not advocate general unsupervised release, but the use of alternatives. Some of these will be mentioned. Others in effective use are described by the National Advisory Commission and yet more in Benedict S. Alper's book, *Prisons Inside-Out*, and in other literature.

Where there is a jail or prison there is an invitation to judges and parole boards to fill it and there are vested interests favoring incarceration. We must establish a moratorium on building prisons and jails, excepting highly unusual circumstances. The National Advisory Commission makes this recommendation and lays down strict guidelines for such construction as seems unavoidable.[6]

3. Reduce the number of long sentences.

Crime for crime, Americans use the longest prison sentences in the world.[7] Long institutionalization tends to make inmates more unfit for life outside and increases the likelihood of further offenses.

The National Advisory Commission recommends that no sentences be longer than five years maximum, with no minimum standard, excepting persistent (three or more convictions), professional, and dangerous offenders. In the Netherlands few sentences are as long as three years maximum and the results are good. That country, however, has a special power of "Detention at the Government's Pleasure." Designed for criminal psychopaths posing special danger of violent injuries, the use of this power requires suitable treatment and a renewal of the order by the court every two years on convincing evidence that the extension is required.[8]

4. Use fines scaled to ability to pay or earn and to the profits of crime.

When fines are scaled solely to the seriousness of the crime they are usually inequitable and flagrantly unjust. A fine of $1,000 for a rich man is a light tap on the wrist; for a poor man it may be impossible. Because of such injustice the use of fines beyond $5 to $25 has fallen out of favor. Yet one still sees cases of people who have committed property crimes netting many thousands being fined much smaller amounts. Under such circumstances, unless restitution is also required, the fine is comparable to a minor tax on the criminal business. In other cases poor people are fined sums of money as alternatives to incarceration, when actually the fines are impossible to pay, and hence no alternatives at all.

The fine is a useful device in certain kinds of cases as a means of taking the profit out of property crime. To serve this purpose it must be large enough to make the crime not only unprofitable but seriously counterproductive. If the offender lacks means to pay, then arrangement must be made for withholding of installments from his wages or other income for this purpose. The State of Hawaii includes provision for fines scaled to profits of crime and ability to pay by installments in its Penal Code of 1972.

When by such devices the fine can be used as a deterrent it serves as a means of reducing incarceration in accord with the need already described.

5. *Require restitution when appropriate.*

Restitution by the offender to the victim(s) of his crime is highly desirable as a partial or total alternative to imprisonment in many cases, as explained in Chapter 19.

6. *Use work-release and part-time incarceration when appropriate.*

In the United States work-release programs have been spreading since the 1950s and are now widely used, not only with misdemeanants but also with serious youthful offenders and adult felons.[9] Usually in such programs prisoners are released only during the hours of work and necessary travel time. Weekend home furloughs are also granted to selected inmates throughout the federal system and in many states.

A natural development from both work-release and home furloughs is the use of part-time incarceration. In Great Britain some of the younger offenders are sentenced to weekends and some additional evenings in prison. Since they are free for the remainder of each week employment or education can be maintained and there is not a complete disruption of normal relationships in the community.[10] In the Netherlands adult men serving sentences of one month or less may apply to the Public Prosecutor for the serving of their sentences in short installments. When approved some of them spend only weekends in a nearby remand house.[11]

The National Advisory Commission reports some similar arrangements, apparently in the United States.[12] The Commission comments that in view of the fact that most misdemeanants are not regarded as dangerous, "it is astonishing how little use has been made of work release, study release, 'weekender' sentences, and similar programs that take advantage of community resources." The Commission is convinced that "weekender" programs ought to be "used much more extensively" and points out that they can be used without statutory change.[13]

Weekend serving of sentences seems especially appropriate in cases of misdemeanant conduct occurring exclusively during the days off from work. It should be employed also in some other cases when the judge wishes to express hearty disapproval by society and provide a deterrent, but sees little likelihood of injurious misconduct resulting from permitting a large measure of freedom to the offender.

7. Close most juvenile institutions.

Most career criminals began their arrests by the police in their early teens or younger. Among criminological studies, Daniel Glaser's findings are typical. He reports that "the younger a prisoner is when first arrested, convicted, or confined for any crime, the more likely he is to continue in crime." He adds, "For those under 14 when first arrested, nearly half cling to a criminal path after imprisonment, compared with only one in ten of those arrested for the first time over the age of 35."[14] Many criminologists have found evidence that the high correlation between early age of first arrest and later recidivism in serious crime was in considerable part due to the bad influences of institutions for delinquent children.[15]

Jerome G. Miller, as Commissioner of Youth Services in Massachusetts, acted on this theory by closing the five residential institutions for juvenile delinquents in the state. After partial measures beginning in 1969, the closing was dramatically completed in 1972. About one-third of the juvenile delinquents were placed in their own homes, provided with new social assistance and supervision. Many went to approved foster homes. Others were placed in therapeutic community homes in residential areas. Only a very few were held in locked quarters, most of them as psychologically disturbed. The policy has been continued, with revision of details, by Miller's successor, Joseph Leavy. On an ordinary day in December 1974, 2,030 juveniles were under the supervision of the Department of Youth Services. Of these, 835 were under traditional probation or parole. Of the remaining 1,195, 48% (590) were in their own homes with special supervision and care or in boarding schools or elsewhere with nondelinquents. In group homes were 28% (334) and 15% (178) were in foster care. Only 9% (113) were in intensive and secure care. It is not true as rumored that many juveniles are now being transferred to adult institutions. Actually, in late 1974 fewer than 11% as many juveniles were in pre-trial detention in adult quarters as in 1968, and only 12 as compared with 39 children in post-trial detention in adult facilities. Similar programs are being introduced in California and elsewhere and, under Miller's direction, in Illinois.

The monetary costs of nonresidential or foster-care programs per youth are only about one-third the cost of traditional institutional programs.[16] The recidivism rate under the traditional programs ranged from 40% to 70%. It is too early for reliable data on eventual recidivism of youth passing through the new programs though early statistics are favorable by nearly one-half. The recorded attitudes of the youth themselves, as compared with those of youth in the old programs responding to the same questions, offer further ground for expectation of substantial lasting improvement.[17]

Clearly, the old severe, custodial reform schools are thoroughly discredited. Most juvenile offenders do not need to be locked up under guard. A few do require such custody, but most will respond favorably to much more benign and free conditions with adults who care and seek to help them with their problems.[18] Unnecessary institutionalization serves to cultivate hostilities and to apply labels of "bad" or "tough guy" which youth tend to act out increasingly in subsequent behavior.

The problem is to classify the youth who will do serious injury if not strictly guarded, in distinction from those who will not. However, in Massachusetts the Department of Youth Services has found that in most cases this is not so difficult as generally expected, though there are always the marginal cases.

The arguments for minimal use of institutional commitment are especially strong concerning juvenile offenders. As compared with adults, the juveniles are more readily damaged by intensive labeling, are more impressionable in the presence of bad company, and suffer more ill effects from being deprived of the character-building influences of church, school, and, in many instances, home. There is sufficiently wide appreciation of these facts so that in all states the great majority of juvenile court cases result in probation rather than commitment to institutions. It is imperative that this trend be pressed much further, that innovative alternatives be increased, and that in the cases of youth who must be kept in custody maximal effort be made to enhance the caring, therapeutic, and educational programs, with much assistance from the free community.

Students in our colleges and universities are in some places giving remarkably helpful leadership in diverting youth from the criminal justice system, in caring for many committed to them by the courts, or in rendering voluntary service in institutions.[19] There is large room for helpful expansion of such work.

B. Means of Social Readaptation

1. Employ inmates usefully at prevailing wage levels.

Most work in prison is compensated at such uniformly low levels as to increase distaste for labor. In order to accomplish punitive purposes and to avoid competition with labor and industry in the free market most prison industries have, since the late 1920s and early 1930s, produced only for the state itself and by means of inefficient routine toil. Neither the skills nor the attitudes learned in prison could be usefully transferred into modern industry outside.

Many unions and employers have ceased to oppose the modernizing of prison industries and some are even ready to assist in installation and job training. If inmates are to be prepared for crime-free lives in open society, then either inside or on work-release outside they must have access to job training and equipment which offer openings to employment after release.

The National Advisory Commission recommends such access. The Commission recognizes also that normal incentives must be provided by financial compensation and adds, "As a long-range objective to be implemented by 1978, such compensation should be at rates representing the prevailing wage for work of the same type in the vicinity of the correctional facility."[20]

Such a policy is in effect in some countries and in certain industries of some federal and state institutions of the United States. Where there are work-release programs normal wages are usually paid. Inmates should not, however, receive and keep money from such work in prison, since the presence of so much cash would inevitably fuel drug rackets, the corruption of staff members, and endless robberies. Usually wages are deposited in a prison account from which the inmate may draw scrip to be used for approved purposes inside. Highly desirable also is the allocation of portions of the earnings to support of dependents, to restitution in suitable cases, to payment for board in the institution, and to a savings bank account for the future—all as part of social restoration. (Cf. also Norm 2, Chap. 16, D, above.)

2. Encourage wholesome contacts with relatives, friends, and community representatives from outside.

In most American prisons administrative officers give such high priority to security that relatives, friends, and volunteers find it difficult to visit inmates. They commonly limit visits from members of the immediate family to one or two per month and often prohibit all other visits excepting those by attorneys, required by court orders. Such policies severely punish innocent people outside as well as convicted persons inside the institutions.

If a person is to overcome alienation and hostility, gain humane sensitivity and social responsibility, and prepare for a law-abiding life in open society, he must have personal relationships with individuals for whom he cares or can learn to care. To attempt social restoration or even individual rehabilitation while permitting only a minimum of meaningful personal relations is to be self-contradictory.

The Advisory Commission "recommends that institutions plan for programs that bridge the gap between institutions and community residents. Institutions should actively develop maximum interaction between the community and the institution, involving citizens in planning and activities."[21] The Commission advocates as well that there be no limitation on frequency of mail, no reading of letters—though opening and search for articles threatening security is approved—and no glass partitions or other barriers to easy personal contacts. The Commission further recommends "provisions for family visits in private surroundings conducive to maintaining and strengthening family ties."[22]

3. Arrange for conjugal visits of married inmates.

On this matter the National Advisory Commission says only that "the so-called conjugal visit is controversial, partly because the concept seems to focus entirely on sexual activity."[23]

I agree with the many humane correctional officials in this and other countries who contend that home furloughs are better than conjugal visits of wives or husbands in prison. Where nearly all sentences are of short duration and furlough policies are liberal, as in Holland, the need for conjugal visiting is not urgent. But nowhere in the United States are these conditions met. At most institutions home furloughs are permitted only in the last months of incarceration, if at all, and then only to selected inmates regarded as most trustworthy. Everywhere in the United States sentences are longer than in other developed countries.

In one American prison conjugal visiting has been a regular practice at least since 1918, probably much longer. The Mississippi State Penitentiary (Parchman) embraces nearly 33 square miles in an isolated area and is operated as a penal plantation. The 1,500 to 2,000 inmates are housed in widely scattered camps of 50 to 200 persons each and there is little contact between the residents of the different camps. Formerly the camps were racially segregated and conjugal visits began informally in the living quarters of the black inmates but soon spread to the white camps. The sergeants in charge of the different camps were mainly concerned with making the farming profitable and avoiding trouble. Under very loose administration they permitted the visits to develop without giving them much attention. Today, however, the Penitentiary is integrated and conjugal visiting takes place in special houses provided at every camp, including the women's, excepting only the maximum security facility.

The administration of Parchman has been notoriously inept, with a history of frequent corruption and brutality. When I visited there in November 1973 it still held this reputation and the governor was temporarily unable to secure a professionally trained superintendent. Like everything else there, the conjugal visiting was reported to vary greatly in the different camps, depending on the sergeants and the types of inmates. In some it was said to be a corrupt racket run by sergeants who did not care whether visitors were wives or prostitutes so long as they (the sergeants) received their payoffs.

Yet on one thing the reports were all in agreement: on balance the conjugal visiting was a good thing. This evaluation was made by inmates, members of the administrative staff, a federal LEAA investigator, and knowledgeable citizens. My own opportunities were limited to one day at Parchman and eight days in the state, but the near-unanimity of opinions encountered was impressive. Fortunately, careful research on the matter has been done by Columbus B. Hopper, Professor of Sociology at the University of Mississippi. A wealth of data and an emphatic positive evaluation are reported in his book, *Sex in Prison*.[24]

Many countries, like the State of Mississippi, grant both conjugal visits and home furloughs. Included are Canada, Sweden, India, and several Latin-American nations. Conjugal visits but not home furloughs are permitted in others, including Japan and the Soviet Union. Puerto Rico grants both, and California, which uses home furloughs, is cautiously experimenting with conjugal visits for inmates near the time of release.[25]

The values of the practice include reduction of general emotional tension and unrest among inmates, lessening of homosexuality, and above all, saving many marriages which would otherwise be doomed. Few single men resent the privilege of the married men. It should be made a part of family visiting, with the children of inmates playing together while the parents retire to private quarters for times sufficient to permit extended conversation as well as intercourse. Participants stress the value of intimate private talk. The significance of conjugal visiting is not primarily biological, but psychological and social. It is commonly charged that the practice is degrading to the wives. Hopper found that most of the wives involved in Mississippi did not so regard it, but favored it.[26]

Many studies have indicated that when released inmates have wives and homes to which to return their chances of going straight are far better than otherwise. Keeping marital relationships alive is important for the minimizing of alienation and for the future of social restoration.

Prison inmates have won many recent lawsuits demanding their rights as human beings.[27] In one such lawsuit an inmate demanded his right to conjugal visits. The judge ruled against him, and said he knew of no such practices being permitted "in United States institutions."[28] That may be true of *federal* prisons, but the judge should be informed about the half century of experience in Mississippi.

Church people and all others who believe in basic human dignity and the sacredness of marriage should support elemental human rights of prisoners, including the right of private visits with their wives in surroundings making sexual expression possible if desired.

C. Coordinating for Social Restoration

Only social restoration accomplishes the true ethical ends of criminal justice. For this purpose our states and federal government must bridge the present nearly absolute division between neighborhood social work and correctional work with individual offenders. The one place where I have observed a systematic coordination of the two is the State of Mexico. A brief account of the program there was given earlier.* However, such coordination is official policy throughout all of the Netherlands. There much of the social work is certified by the government but done by approved volunteers.[29]

Probably the skilled coordination with social work at home is one of the principal reasons for the "reported recidivism rate of only 2.08 percent among those released from confinement" in the Penitentiary Center of the State of Mexico.[30]

The Advisory Commission favors making "both the offender and the community . . . the focus of correctional activity."[31] Unfortunately, it does not follow through with any recommendations for the coordination of such activity. The task is made especially difficult by the usual departmental organization which places social work and corrections in different governmental agencies.

The Massachusetts Department of Youth Services achieves such coordination in many juvenile cases by contracting out the assistance for both the youth and his home to a single organization or individual.

D. Community-Based Residential Centers

Even a man who has developed sound motivation and wholesome purposes in prison finds it difficult to move into the confusing complexity and competition of the outside world. To help in this transition many states have set up halfway houses. There a prison inmate approaching the time of release on parole or final release may live for a few months with less strict regimen than in prison but with more supervision and structured life than he will have after release. In a halfway house or prerelease center he goes out at stated times to work or to classes, returns at designated hours, and remains until he has permission for another trip outside. He is not under lock and key, but knows that to violate the regulations there may put him back behind bars and will surely postpone his release. Work-release, home furloughs, and parole itself are other useful transitional measures.

Similar arrangements are often utilized in place of incarceration rather than after it. Sometimes because of the similarity therapeutic communities or other community-based facilities to which convicted persons are directly sentenced by a court are also called halfway houses,[32] much as in common lay parlance probation granted by a court is often confused with parole subsequent to incarceration. When any such arrangements can be

---

* See above, Chap. 17, D.

used as alternatives without undue risk to the community that is to be preferred.

Community-based group centers have multiplied rapidly in recent years, both in the United States and in Canada. There are now hundreds of them in operation under both private and official management. They offer a wide variety of approaches for offenders with differing needs. They are most successful when offenders have taken part in choosing the programs and houses to which they will be assigned and also when they are in houses near their homes. In the large number of cases not seriously endangering anyone community-based centers offer great advantages over traditional prisons. They produce less disruption of the community, large savings in cost, maintaining of economic and personal responsibility by the offender, use of needed therapeutic and other resources in the community, and easier transition to freedom.[33]

E. Selection and Training of Personnel for Social Restoration

The goals of rehabilitation and social restoration are not often achieved in institutions staffed by people most of whom are concerned predominantly with custody. Officers who see themselves principally as guards will not develop the caring and supportive relationships with inmates needed to assist their becoming responsible citizens. In most prisons the majority of guards seek to avoid such relationships for fear they will weaken authority and control or lower themselves.

The National Advisory Commission has devoted considerable attention to the problem of securing and training adequate personnel for correctional work both in institutions and as probation and parole officers. The Commission recommends special care to recruit socially sensitive and capable people including suitable representatives of minority groups, women, ex-offenders, and young adults. Wide use of volunteers is also urged. Preliminary and continuing training for all must be provided.[34] Such selection and training of personnel is needed even more if staff people are to work beyond individual rehabilitation to social restoration, and for this larger purpose volunteers can play invaluable roles.

Excepting judges, parole boards exercise more decisive control over the lives of convicted persons than do any other persons. Yet their members are often appointed for political reasons—whether to reward prior support in an election campaign or to please some portion of the public. For example, when many police officers and other people are irate about some recent crime committed by a person on parole a governor may appoint one or more well-known policemen to the parole board.[35]

The procedures of parole boards are often as erratic and unpredictable as the selection of their members. As a result a gang leader in violent criminal activity and a relatively passive individual convicted of a property crime may come before a board at different times, both with reports of good behavior in prison. The gang leader may be released on parole and the much less dangerous person told to "come back next year." Many such incidents are well known in the prisons and are a source of added bitterness and alienation.[36]

At best, determining when an offender is ready to be free without undue risk to others is a difficult and uncertain art. Yet many sensitive persons who are acquainted with a large mass of data concerning recidivism of different types of offenders and in various life situations can make such judgments with a fair degree of equity and probability of success. It is imperative that governors or other persons selecting parole board members seek out such people, taking care to include women and members of minorities. Suitable procedures must then be established to provide wisest possible consideration of important factors in every case. Parole boards should be required to state reasons for their decisions.[37] These changes are required by our ethical norms of equal rights (Norm 3) and coherence with realities (Norm 1).

24

Citizen Responsibilities in Criminal Justice

A. Cooperating in Law Enforcement

We have already addressed the need for community involvement in crime prevention. Public responsibility does not end there. We like to think of crime as something to be handled by the police, the courts, and the prisons. But without civilian help they can do little.

Most police action occurs in response to calls from citizens. Yet, as pointed out earlier,* only about half the serious crimes are reported even by the victims. If most cases are to be prosecuted successfully, there must be other witnesses. Most people feel reluctant to report having witnessed a crime. Those who cannot overcome this reluctance have no right to complain that the law is not enforced. If we distrust the system, our involvement as witnesses may help us to see it more realistically and to act more effectively in changing it.

---

* Above, Chap. 3, B, 1.

Unless prevented by unusual circumstances a person called for jury duty ought to respond. Some citizens usefully volunteer to serve as marshals for protest parades or to form auxiliary forces available to augment the regular police at times of special stress or in areas of high crime rates. The police of New York City have "recruited 14,000 unarmed 'block watchers'—civilian volunteers who are trained in techniques of observing and reporting crime. The city also has organized 6,000 taxi drivers and a corps of private motorists to report suspicious occurrences on the streets and highways."[1]

The National Advisory Commission reports with implied approval other volunteer programs in which citizens assist in law enforcement in Sacramento, Buffalo, Kalamazoo, Joliet, Battle Creek, St. Paul, Kansas City (Missouri), Boston, other cities, and several counties. The volunteers help staff police offices, distribute information, watch for suspicious evidences of possible criminal behavior and report to headquarters, or patrol stores to watch for shoplifters.[2]

The more citizens are involved in all these nonviolent ways of assisting law enforcement, the more the power of public opinion is brought to bear, both on potential lawbreakers and on the system, the more incipient criminal careers are ended early and the less resort will be needed to force and confinement. Such action is in fulfillment of our ethical Norm 7, the responsibility of all individuals for the community.

B. Voluntary Aid to Victims

The case for required restitution to victims by offenders and for public compensation of victims was presented earlier.* While working for such measures, citizen groups should organize to give voluntary assistance to victims of crime. There are some such organizations now, in widely scattered places.** Some groups of women have joined together in bringing sympathetic support, medical care, and counseling to victims of rape. Such victims are especially likely to need help because police and many others —sometimes including husbands—suspect that the rape victim must have provoked the attack or perhaps was even a willing participant. The need is illustrated by the findings and significant opportunities for important assistance of the professional, county-supported Rape Crisis Center of Jackson Memorial Hospital, Miami, Florida. The Center is itself the result of concerned voluntary action. There are rape crisis centers in widely distributed cities, staffed by volunteers for counseling, referrals to medical cen-

---

* See Chap. 19, above.
** For a channel of information, see under C, below.

ters, and friendly support through legal, medical, and other trying experiences.[3]

Among the victims of crime, poor people and members of disadvantaged minorities are disproportionately represented. Injury by crime is often especially hard for them to bear, with narrowly limited resources. Timely aid to them may both accomplish especially needed, useful service and prevent increased bitterness and alienation which could lead to their own commission of crime.[4]

Citizens' aid to victims is mandated by ethical Norms (Chap. 16, D, above) of benevolent good will (2), special care to protect the poor and weak (5), restoration of community (6), and responsibility of all for the community (7).

C. Voluntary Aid to Convicted Offenders and Their Families

The family of a person convicted of a crime often suffers financial hardship, humiliation, grief, and strained relations with neighbors. Voluntary assistance may take the form of helping to establish and maintain communication with the person incarcerated, to apply for public assistance, to maintain self-respect, and to gain friendly social reinforcement. Voluntary aid may protect the family from permanent disruption and prevent additional members from running afoul of the law. Many organizations which supply voluntary assistance to inmates of correctional institutions try to find ways of helping families also. Whether service begins with the inmate or family, it is most effective when it can include both. This is another approach to social restoration.

Many thousands of volunteers are aiding convicted offenders and persons awaiting trial. Often their efforts make the difference between further crimes and a turn to law-abiding citizenship. A volunteer has two important advantages over an officer of probation, of parole, or of a correctional institution. After some initial skepticism the person in trouble usually recognizes that the volunteer is genuinely concerned and seeking to help him, whereas any official must overcome a formidable barrier of suspicion and often of hostility. Moreover, one official has responsibilities for many people, while the volunteer usually relates to one case or a very few cases at a time and can therefore give much more individualized attention.

The superior results which volunteers and professionals working together can achieve was demonstrated in Royal Oak, Michigan, by Volunteers in Probation led by Judge Keith Leenhouts, working with probation officers and the courts. "When probationers from Royal Oak were compared with probationers from nonvolunteer courts, it was found that not only were those from Royal Oak less hostile, but their recidivism rates were drastically lower—15 percent compared with nearly 50 percent."[5] The "Board of Christian Social Concerns of the Methodist Church . . . provided funds to spread the idea throughout the country. . . . Since 1969, the idea has spread to approximately 2,090 courts, prisons and juvenile institutions."[6]

In a Maryland community one church, Rockville United Methodist, provides voluntary drivers to take inmates from a county prerelease center to a medical center for treatment of alcoholism and drug addiction, collects magazines for the county detention center, recruits volunteers to assist local parole officers, and provides a building for an alcoholic therapy program. Another church, Rockville Unitarian, maintains in the church building a small apartment for short-term occupancy at below-cost rent by parolees and releasees just coming out of jail or prison and solicits additional rooms for this purpose among parishioners. The pastor, Rev. William R. Moors, has also organized and led groups of citizens to testify before committees of the state legislature and national Congress on proposals affecting criminal justice. The churches of Rochester and Buffalo, New York, initiated and provide leadership for broad and impressive citywide programs. They include recruiting and training volunteers for one-to-one work with inmates of several state and local correctional institutions, securing employment and housing for former inmates, and in other ways helping them get reestablished for law-abiding lives in the community.[7]

Other volunteers are sponsoring and advising self-help organizations in prisons, such as prison chapters of Alcoholics Anonymous, Seventh-Step, and the Junior Chamber of Commerce. There are literally hundreds of local organizations engaged in voluntary services of these and other kinds. Yet others are providing foster homes for juvenile delinquents, usually with public subsidies to cover costs.

An interested citizen can often learn about programs near his or her home relating to any particular interest by inquiring of local probation or prison officials or a local church office. However, there is one office which maintains information about all kinds of voluntary organizations concerned with victims, courts, corrections, diversionary programs, and reentry, in every part of the country. That office is happy to provide relevant information about a particular locality to any interested inquirer and also to sell a variety of training materials. It is the National Information Center on Volunteerism, Dr. Ivan Scheier, Director, P. O. Box 4179, Boulder, Colorado 80302.

Voluntary service is in fulfillment of ethical Norms 1, 2, 5, 6, and 7, especially the last. Constructing a sound community is the task of all individuals in it.

D. Economic and Social Opportunities for Releasees and Parolees

A person who has been convicted of crime often finds honest employment refused. He may also be excluded from associations in the community other than those with ex-convicts and the underworld.[8] Unless he can soon find a way through the barriers he will be pushed relentlessly back toward a life of crime.[9]

Rules of the bar associations for disbarment of lawyers who have feloniously violated their positions of trust should be upheld. Likewise, a person convicted of embezzlement should not be permitted to charter a bank or any business corporation entrusting him with other people's money. Employment in subordinate offices of such institutions, in the various crafts, in construction and in industrial labor, however, should be open. Many ex-convicts are usefully employed in roles of crime prevention.

The Chamber of Commerce of the United States urges its members and other business persons to employ ex-offenders. The Chamber adds: "If your company has bonding requirements that make it difficult to hire ex-offenders, the Department of Labor's Bonding Assistance program may be able to help. This strikingly successful program posts fidelity bonds for ex-offenders to protect the employer from loss due to theft or acts of dishonesty. In the five years the program has been in effect, less than 2% have defaulted on their bonds."[10]

The National Advisory Commission on Criminal Justice Standards and Goals makes a number of recommendations to increase employment of ex-offenders.[11]

In order to provide opportunities for wholesome associations in the community, church members, both men and women, in many communities invite inmates of halfway houses to attend sporting events, church services, and social occasions with them and seek to continue such relationships after their release.

All efforts to rehabilitate offenders and restore them to free society involve risks. As one calculates the risks one is willing to take in any given case it should be noted that other personal relationships also involve risks, that most offenses do not involve personal injury or threat of such injury, and that to fail to rehabilitate and restore is to assure further crimes. The danger involved in parole, work release, and other efforts to rehabilitate is exaggerated in the public mind by the fact that there are shrill outcries when persons in such a status commit serious crimes, while these crimes are not publicly compared with those committed by offenders released after completion of their sentences or with those committed by first offenders.

Employment and social opportunities for ex-offenders should be afforded in accord with ethical Norms 1, 2, 5, 6, and 7.

E. Diversionary Programs

One useful device employed by Alcoholics Anonymous is to provide every member with telephone numbers of certain other members he is to call whenever he feels the temptation to drink or even a mood (such as depression, boredom, anxiety, or loneliness) which in the past has driven him to drink. In many cities volunteers staff certain telephones 24 hours a day and advertise that anyone inclined to suicide or feeling depressed or simply needing a friendly ear is welcome to call. Such telephones are much used and many people report that calls to them have saved them from desperate acts.

In England, associated with Grendon Prison there is a special center many miles away, in London, for the use of men who have been released from Grendon. When such men become troubled and see that they are in danger of slipping back into crime they are welcome to come in for friendly counsel. That many do so is a high tribute to the spirit and skill with which the Grendon staff led by Dr. William J. Gray have developed relationships of trust. Such centers could be established and staffed by volunteers in our cities after members have developed supportive one-to-one relations with inmates in prison.

Again in England, a number of churchmen led by John Dodd and supported by both churches and individual benefactors established and operate the Langley House (now actually eleven houses). This is called "a Christian venture in the after care of homeless offenders." The 200 men in the houses range in age from 17 to old age and in numbers from 8 to 23 per house. Each house is managed by a resident couple, usually with children. Without the Langley House most of the men would be either remaining in prison for want of any other place to go or would be wanderers, probably soon getting into trouble and returning to prison. About half of them go out to work daily, some of the younger ones are in school, and many work around the place, on attached farms, or in a home industry. Some of them have never before in their lives experienced a home where a man and wife lived together with their children. Individuals who cannot make it on their own may remain permanently. Others, more confident after the security of acceptance in a well-ordered home, move out into quarters of their own, with or without marrying. Often they come back to visit for counsel and reassurance.[12]

Teen Challenge, an American organization now working also abroad, and about which a short account was given earlier,* operates with many

---

* See above, Chap. 8, B, 4.

volunteers along with paid staff members. Specializing in care of drug addicts, this organization receives the majority of its residents from courts or prisons, but also takes in many who have not been arrested but are addicted and are diverted from the criminal justice system only by turning to Teen Challenge in time.

Of course there are innumerable instances of intervention by friendly neighbors or by teachers or staff members at school to turn troubled boys or girls from delinquency and crime. Much work of police boys' clubs is of this kind. Efforts in crisis intervention and diversion are only limited by the depth of concern and the creative resourcefulness of interested people.

The National Advisory Commission reports an estimate that in all "some 100,000 volunteers" are "affiliated with well over 1,000 courts." They include a wide variety of services from recreation leadership and tutoring to office work and employment counseling.[13]

Voluntary work of all these kinds is supported by ethical Norm 7 and various types of such work by all the other Norms as well.

F. Initiative to Change the System

The need for change in the philosophy and practice of the criminal justice system should be evident to every reader, whether or not all the proposals made here are accepted. The system is hard to change beyond superficial tinkering. Vested interests among correctional officers, some lawyers, and others are formidable. The people who have most incentive to want change, namely the convicted offenders, have very little political influence. Most of them have always been weak and poor. Those who were not so before conviction are now viewed as discredited and so have little influence. It is true that most citizens want to see something done about crime, but most demands are emotional and uninformed. The result of citizen outcries about crime is more likely to be bigger police forces, bigger prisons, and added police hardware than basic change. In other words, there is usually a continuance of the same ineffective system, only more of it.

If there are to be better policies for preventing crime and more just and effective ways of dealing with it when it occurs, citizens without special interests must become informed, organize, and lobby urgently and persistently. In this task the report of the National Advisory Commission on Criminal Justice Standards and Goals is an important resource. But all such resources will have only so much effect as concerned citizens make them have. The new commitments by the Chamber of Commerce of the United States are encouraging. On some matters the American Bar Association reports and offices are helpful. The National Council on Crime and Delinquency can be useful, especially in supplying information.

No citizen is likely to find the proposals he wishes to support backed by all the above organizations and agencies, while other interests will strongly oppose change. He needs to join coalitions to support aims he holds in common with others, then seek support for widened objectives.

In most communities the best first step is group study. After the study of relevant literature the group should get its members to visit criminal courts, jails, prisons, and juvenile institutions on a systematically organized basis. Let them compare what they observe with the Standards and Goals and with aims which seem to them truly just. Then they will be ready to move into action, learning more as they go.

All citizens have responsibility for the kind of community they should have. Few things are so symptomatic of community ill health as crime and few things affect the quality of the community more than its system of criminal justice. Criminal justice is everybody's business.

G. Promoting Benevolent, Responsible, Community-Minded Way of Life

The grave crisis of crime and the irrational, unjust system we have for dealing with it are both deeply rooted in the moral crisis of our culture. If we continue to idealize tough aggressiveness, rugged and selfish individualism, and the quick resort to violent solutions of our problems, while self-righteously blaming others for our social ills, the American future is dim. America B, in this day of urban crowding, limited resources, extremes of wealth and poverty, and alienating divisions, is the way to ruin.

There is a better American tradition which offers hope. This is America A, the way of neighborly helpfulness, community responsibility, rigorous honesty, generous tolerance of others, modest self-appraisal, simplicity of life, and gentle reasonableness. Whoever enlarges the scope of these attitudes and habits in criminal justice and in all things is striking at the root of crime and promoting the kind of nation which the better American conscience demands.

Notes

Chapter 1. Present Crisis of Freedom Under Law, *pages 3–10*

1. Abraham Lincoln, "Gettysburg Address."
2. U. S. Bureau of the Census, *Statistical Abstract of the United States: 1974* (Washington, D. C., 1974), p. 150.
3. "Aggravated assault is assault with intent to kill or for the purpose of inflicting severe bodily injury, whether or not a dangerous weapon is used." *The Challenge of Crime in a Free Society: A Report by the President's Commission on Law Enforcement and Administration of Justice* (Washington, D. C.: Government Printing Office, 1967), p. 19. Hereafter cited as *Challenge of Crime.*
4. Leon Radzinowicz and Marvin E. Wolfgang (eds.), *Crime and Justice* (New York: Basic Books, 1971), Vol. I, p. 229.
5. Ibid., Vol. I, p. 239.
6. Federal Bureau of Investigation, U. S. Department of Justice, *Uniform Crime Reports for the United States*, 1973, p. 1.
7. Ibid., p. 6.
8. Ibid., pp. 11, 13.
9. Ibid., p. 148.
10. *The Washington Post*, Sept. 15, 1974.
11. *Challenge of Crime*, p. 21.
12. *The Washington Post*, Sept. 17, 1972.
13. *The New York Times*, April 15, 1974.
14. *Uniform Crime Reports*, 1973, p. 1.
15. "Uniform Crime Reporting (January–June, 1974)," released Oct. 3, 1974.

Chapter 2. Influence on Crime Outside the Criminal Justice System, *pages 10–16*

1. *Crime in America* (New York: Pocket Books Division of Simon & Schuster, 1971 [Orig. 1970]), p. xi. Cf. similar findings in *Challenge of Crime*, pp. 35–36.
2. Cf. Clark, op. cit., p. 45.

3. See Daniel Glaser, *The Effectiveness of a Prison and Parole System* (Indianapolis: The Bobbs-Merrill Co., 1969), p. 160; Daniel Bell, "Crime as an American Way of Life," in Marvin E. Wolfgang, Leonard Savitz, and Norman Johnston (eds.), *Sociology of Crime and Delinquency*, 2nd Edition (New York: John Wiley & Sons, 1970), pp. 174–178; and National Advisory Commission on Criminal Justice Standards and Goals, *Community Crime Prevention* (1973), pp. 33–50.

4. *Challenge of Crime*, p. 48.

5. For an account see John G. Fuller, *The Gentlemen Conspirators* (New York: Grove Press, 1962).

6. *Challenge of Crime*, pp. 63–65.

7. For a sophisticated argument that " 'the broken home,' no matter how defined or measured, accounts by itself for little of male delinquency," see Lawrence Rosen, "The Broken Home and Male Delinquency," in Wolfgang et al., op. cit., pp. 489–495. But note carefully the limiting phrase "by itself." Cf. Elmer H. Johnson, *Crime, Correction, and Society*, Revised Edition (Homewood, Ill.: Dorsey Press, 1968), pp. 88–89.

8. "Working Mothers and Delinquency," in Wolfgang et al., op. cit., pp. 496–498, from *Mental Hygiene*, July 1957, pp. 329–333. See also Eleanor and Sheldon Glueck, *Unraveling Juvenile Delinquency* (New York: Commonwealth Fund, 1950). Cf. Julius Stone, *Social Dimensions of Law and Justice* (Holmes Beach, Fla.: Wm. W. Gaunt & Sons, 1972), pp. 364–365, n. 414; also Elmer H. Johnson, op. cit., p. 90. On the relation between fathers and sons, see *Challenge of Crime*, pp. 64–65.

9. See TRB from Washington in *The New Republic*, July 12, 1969, p. 8; and cf. *Statistical Abstract of the U. S.: 1974*, pp. 59 and 60.

Chapter 3. Public Disrepute of Criminal Justice, *pages 17–22*

1. *Uniform Crime Reports*, 1973, p. 128.

2. Radzinowicz and Wolfgang, *Crime and Justice*, Vol. II, p. 185, reprinted from U. S. President's Commission on Law Enforcement and Administration of Justice, *Task Force Report: Police*, 1967.

3. Ibid., p. 186.

4. Ibid., p. 182.

5. Ibid., p. 184.

6. Cited in ibid., p. 176.

7. Schrag, *Crime and Justice: American Style*. Rockville, Md.: National Institute of Mental Health: Center for Study of Crime, 1971. Publ. No. HSM-72-9052.

8. See his book, *The Crime of Punishment* (New York: Viking Press, 1971 [orig. 1966]).

Chapter 4. Injustice in Criminal Laws and Agencies of Enforcement, *pages 23–31*

1. John F. Simons, *Nebraska Law Review*, 50 (1971), pp. 567, 573.

2. Ibid.

3. Norval Morris and Gordon Hawkins, *The Honest Politician's Guide to Crime Control* (Chicago: The University of Chicago Press, 1970), p. 16.

4. Ibid., p. 19.

5. July 1972, p. 728.

6. *UCLA Law Review*, 15 (1968), pp. 1508–1509.

7. Nicholas N. Kittrie, in *South Carolina Law Review*, 23, p. 364.

8. Senate Interim Drug Committee, *Marijuana in Texas* (Austin: Senate of the State of Texas, May 1972), p. 9.

9. Ibid., p. 49.

10. *ABA Jour.*, 58 (July 1972), p. 728.

11. ABA, *Standards Relating to Sentencing Alternatives and Procedures*, 1968, pp. 162–167.

12. Ibid., p. 164.

13. Ibid., p. 166.

14. Robert O. Dawson, *Sentencing: The Decision as to Type, Length, and Conditions of Sentence* (Boston: Little, Brown & Co., 1969), p. 215.

15. Leonard Downie, Jr., *Justice Denied* (Baltimore: Penguin Books, 1972 [orig. 1971]), pp. 13, 23.

16. The feeling of many beleaguered policemen is eloquently expressed in utterances of Frank L. Rizzo, former Chief of Police and in November 1971 elected Mayor of Philadelphia. For example, see his statement of April 13, 1972, to the United States Commission on Civil Rights and the report of his press conference in *The Evening Bulletin* of Philadelphia, Jan. 11, 1972.

17. James S. Campbell et al., *Law and Order Reconsidered* (New York: Praeger Publishers, 1971), p. 268.

18. Op. cit., p. 35.

19. Cf. *Challenge of Crime*, p. 157, for further facts and some recommendations; and cf. below, Chaps. 5 and 22.

20. I am grateful to some policemen of Montgomery County, Maryland, and the District of Columbia for helping me to understand these problems of their careers.

21. American Friends Service Committee, *The Struggle for Justice* (New York: Hill & Wang, 1971), p. 130.

22. Cf. Hans von Hentig, *The Criminal and His Victim: Studies in the Sociology of Crime* (New Haven, Conn.: Archon Books, Yale University Press, 1967 [orig. 1948]), p. 126.

23. Quoted from *20,000 Years in Sing Sing* by von Hentig, op. cit., p. 314, n. 70.

24. See *The Washington Post*, Aug. 24, Sept. 3, 13, and 14, 1972.

25. *The Washington Post*, April 30, 1973.

26. New Brunswick, N. J.: Rutgers University Press, 1959.

Chapter **5. Injustice in the Courts,** *pages 31–37*

1. See *The Washington Post*, Jan. 27, 1973.

2. H. Edward Sharp, in *The New Republic*, April 21, 1973, pp. 9–10.

3. *Texas Law Review*, 45 (1967), pp. 489–490.

4. Ibid., p. 471. Subquotation is from Paul W. Tappan. Cf. the great differences among over 50 federal judges found in a federal study reported in *The Washington Post*, Sept. 7, 1974. Judge Marvin E. Frankel tells of other flagrant examples in his book *Criminal Sentences: Law Without Order* (New York: Hill & Wang, 1973), e.g., pp. 21–22.

5. See *UCLA Law Review*, 15 (1968), p. 1561.

6. *ABA Journal*, 41 (1955), p. 16.

7. *Federal Rules Decision*, 52 (1971), p. 481.

8. James Steele and Donald Barlett, "Justice in Philadelphia," in *The New Republic*, May 26, 1973, p. 20.

9. Ibid.

10. Ibid., p. 21.

11. *New York University Law Review*, 39 (1964), p. 221.

12. Peter W. Low, in Radzinowicz and Wolfgang, *Crime and Justice*, Vol. II, p. 529. The citation is from the President's Task Force Report: *The Courts*, p. 18.

13. *Texas Law Review*, 45 (1967), p. 471.

14. Cf. *UCLA Law Review*, 15 (1968), p. 1563.

15. *Studies in Jurisprudence and Criminal Theory* (New York: Oceana Publications, 1958), p. 222. Cf. Morris R. Cohen, in Morris R. Cohen and Felix S. Cohen (eds.), *Readings in Jurisprudence and Legal Philosophy* (Boston: Little, Brown & Co., 1951), pp. 300–301. For a shocking detailed account of the actual procedures in many typical criminal cases recently tried in Boston see "Annals of Law in Criminal Court" by Richard Harris in *The New Yorker*, April 14 and April 21, 1973. See also Lois G. Forer, "No One Will Lissen": *How Our Legal System Brutalizes the Youthful Poor* (New York: The John Day Company, 1970).

16. In Cohen and Cohen, op. cit., p. 222.

17. President's Commission Task Force, *Courts*, 1967, p. 9.

18. Cf. ibid., n. 20; also ABA, *Pleas of Guilty*, 1968. See also Edith E. Flynn, in Lloyd E. Ohlin (ed.), *Prisoners in America* (Englewood Cliffs, N.J.: Prentice-Hall, 1973), p. 56.

19. *Machibroda v. U. S.*, 368 U. S. 487 (1962).

20. *Santobello v. New York*, 404 U. S. 257 (1971).

21. Walter E. Hoffman, Chief Judge U. S. District Court for the Eastern District of Virginia, "Plea Bargaining and the Role of the Judge," in *Federal Rules Decisions*, 53 (1972), pp. 503–504.

22. President's Commission Task Force, *Courts*, 1967, p. 9. Cf. ABA, *Providing Defense Services*, 1968; and ABA, *Defense of the Poor*, 1965, especially Tables 5, 10 and 11.

Chapter **6. The Waste of Corrections,** *pages 37–47*

1. President's Commission Task Force: *Corrections*, 1967, p. 1.

2. *Statistical Abstract of the U. S.: 1974*, p. 156.

3. President's Commission Task Force: *Corrections*, 1967, pp. 4–5.

4. Useful figures for computing costs are found in Robert L. Smith's account of recent changes in California, entitled *A Quiet Revolution: Probation Subsidy*, Washington, D. C.: Government Printing Office, 1971.

5. Comments during personal conversation at the Penitentiary Center, Almoloya de Juárez, Nov. 14, 1972. In order to institute far-reaching reforms Mr. Sánchez found it necessary to replace many guards and retrain the rest.

6. Pp. 77–81.

7. *The Washington Post*, Dec. 19, 1971.

8. Pp. 84–85.

9. Philip G. Zimbardo, "The Psychological Power and Pathology of Imprisonment," in Ohmer Milton and Robert G. Wahler (eds.) *Behavior Disorders: Perspectives and Trends*, 3rd Edition (New York: J. B. Lippincott Co., 1973), p. 153.

10. Gresham M. Sykes and Sheldon L. Messinger, in Radzinowicz and Wolfgang, *Crime and Justice*, Vol. III, pp. 77–78.

11. Cf. ibid., p. 83.

12. Op. cit., p. 66.

13. Op. cit., pp. 77–78. Cf. Howard Levy and David Miller, *Going to Jail: The Political Prisoner* (New York: Grove Press, 1971).

14. Op. cit., p. 4.

15. Ibid., p. 11.

16. Ibid., p. 19. Cf. also references to similar observations by Sheldon and Eleanor Glueck, Gerald Robin and Paul Lerman, in Marvin E. Wolfgang, Robert M. Figlio, and Thorsten Sellin, *Delinquency in a Birth Cohort* (Chicago: University of Chicago Press, 1972), pp. 107–108.

17. Wolfgang et al., op. cit., p. 254.

18. 46% plus 35% of the remaining 54%.

19. Ibid., p. 252.

20. Reported by Glaser, op. cit., p. 7.

21. Ibid., p. 10.

22. Wolfgang, Figlio, Sellin, op. cit., p. 88.

23. Ibid., p. 97.

24. Ibid., pp. 166–167.

25. Op. cit., p. 257. Glaser cautions that there are variables reflected here other than the prison contacts themselves.

26. See Robert L. Smith, *A Quiet Revolution: Probation Subsidy*, especially pp. 5, 7, 17, 68, 51, and 48.

27. Ibid., p. 84.

28. Ibid.

Chapter **7. Confusion and Conflict of Purpose,** *pages 47–58*

1. Cf. Frankel, *Criminal Sentences*, p. 7.

2. This comment and the others following are near-verbatim reports of re-

marks made by state judges attending an advanced course on sentencing and probation at the National College of the State Judiciary, Reno, Nevada, 1973, in which it was my privilege to participate.

3. ABA Special Committee on Crime Prevention and Control, *New Perspectives on Urban Crime*, p. i.

4. *What Is Justice? Justice, Law, and Politics in the Mirror of Science* (Berkeley: University of California Press, 1971), pp. 301–302.

5. Ibid., p. 377.

6. Ibid., p. 296.

7. "Punishment," in *Mind*, Vol. 48 (1939), p. 155. For a brief, careful statement and criticism of his view see Jerome Hall, *General Principles of Criminal Law*, 2nd Edition (Indianapolis: The Bobbs-Merrill Co., 1947), pp. 297–302.

8. Jerome Hall, op. cit., p. 298, n. 8.

9. Mabbott, in "Punishment," *Mind*, Vol. 48 (1939), excerpted in Rudolph J. Gerber and Patrick D. McAnany (eds.), *Contemporary Punishment* (Notre Dame: University of Notre Dame Press, 1972), p. 45.

10. See Hall, *Studies in Jurisprudence and Criminal Theory* (New York: Oceana Publications, 1958), p. 40.

11. Cf. Edmond Cahn, *The Sense of Injustice* (Bloomington: Indiana University Press, 1949).

12. Kelsen, *General Theory of Law and the State* (tr. by Anders Wedburg. Cambridge, Mass.: Harvard University Press, 1945), p. 51.

13. Excerpt from ibid., pp. 5–6, in Gerber and McAnany, op. cit., p. 599.

14. "The Educational Role of the Soviet Court," in *The International and Comparative Law Quarterly*, Vol. XXI, No. 1 (1972), p. 82.

15. Ibid., p. 83.

16. *Social Dimensions of Law and Justice*, p. 566, citing an article from Durkheim in *Année Sociologiques*, Vol. 4 (1899), pp. 65–95.

17. Cf. Julius Stone, *Human Law and Human Justice* (Stanford, Calif.: Stanford University Press, 1968), p. 20.

18. Some of the most persuasive statements in support of retribution by Pius XII and C. S. Lewis appear in Gerber and McAnany, op. cit.

19. *De Clementia*, I, xxii, i, from translation by John W. Basore, in *Seneca, Moral Essays* (New York: G. P. Putnam's Sons, 1928), Vol. I, p. 419.

20. *On Crime and Punishment* (tr. by Henry Paolucci. Indianapolis: The Bobbs-Merrill Co., 1963), p. 42.

21. *Federal Rules Decisions*, Vol. 52 (1971), p. 485.

22. *General Principles of Criminal Law*, p. 303, n. 23.

23. *De Clementia*, I, 22, 1–4.

24. Op. cit., XX, pp. 58–59 and XIX, pp. 55–57.

25. See Franklin E. Zimring, *Perspectives on Deterrence* (Rockville, Md.: National Institute of Mental Health, Center for Studies of Crime and Delinquency, 1971), p. 89.

26. For an especially able discussion of general deterrence, see Johannes Andenaes, "General Prevention—Illusion or Reality," *Journal of Criminal Law, Criminology and Police Science*, Vol. 43 (1952), pp. 176 ff.

Chapter **8. Rehabilitation in Many Modes,** *pages 58–67*

1. See Bentham, *An Introduction to the Principles of Morals and Legislation* (1789), Chap. 13.

2. Beccaria, *On Crimes and Punishments,* 1764.

3. Cf. Francis A. Allen, in Gerber and McAnany, *Contemporary Punishment,* p. 215. Allen credits the Italian criminologist Raffaele Garafalo with having made similar statements 70 years earlier.

4. Personal interview July 27, 1972.

5. Ibid.

6. Personal conference July 24, 1972.

7. E.g., see 2.2.

8. Text accompanying Slide 27. The presentation is sold by the Chamber, Washington, D.C. 20006.

9. *The Crime of Punishment.*

10. Cited by Menninger, ibid., p. 139, from Glueck, *Law and Psychiatry: Cold War or Entente Cordiale?* (Baltimore: Johns Hopkins Press, 1962), p. 152.

11. *Struggle for Justice.*

12. P. 146. For a psychiatrist's plea for an end to commitments of people to institutions for treatment of alleged mental illness see Thomas S. Szasz, *Law, Liberty and Psychiatry* (New York: Collier Books, 1972 [orig. 1963]). Another psychiatrist, Samuel Yochelson, promises early publication of a three-volume work "proving" that in dealing with criminal offenders psychiatry has been "a total failure."

13. Ibid., pp. 146–147.

14. Ibid., pp. 152–153.

15. From "The Humanitarian Theory of Punishment," included in Gerber and McAnany, *Contemporary Punishment,* p. 196.

16. *The Washington Post,* Jan. 28, 1973.

17. Certainly we would oppose the Erewhonian view of crime as by definition an illness, to be pitied, humored, and treated! See Samuel Butler's satire *Erewhon* (New York: The Modern Library, 1955 [orig. 1872]).

18. For relevant essays by proponents of "behavior therapy" and similar proposals, with references to other literature, see Milton and Wahler, compilers, *Behavior Disorders.* For an official report of an institution combining more traditional psychotherapy with the behavioral modification methods used in "the Graded Tier System" see *Maryland's Defective Delinquent Statute: A Progress Report: Patuxent Institution* (Jan. 9, 1973), especially pp. 18–20. In the federal Robert F. Kennedy Youth Center results have been so poor that reliance on behavior modification has been abandoned, according to reports I received during a visit there in August 1974.

19. I worked as a volunteer member of her professional staff in the summer of 1954, an unforgettable experience.

20. William Shakespeare, *King Lear,* Act III, Scene 2.

21. I observed an impressive example of such coordination at the Penitentiary Center of the State of Mexico in Almoloya de Juárez, on Nov. 16, 1972. See Chap. 17, n. 45 and n. 48.

22. Remarks at meeting of the Norfolk Fellowship, May 30, 1972, reported in *Norfolk Fellowship Newsletter*, June 28, 1972.

23. Cf. Menninger, *Crime of Punishment*, p. 223, and a historical account of some ways the motifs have conflicted so as to destroy rehabilitative influences, in Lawrence M. Friedman, *A History of American Law* (New York: Simon & Schuster, 1973), pp. 518–522.

24. Cf. ABA, *Standards Relating to Sentencing Alternatives and Procedures* (1968), p. 57.

Chapter **9. Puritanism: a Paradoxical Heritage,** *pages 71–79*

1. Quoted by Michael Kammen, *People of Paradox* (New York: Vintage Books, Random House, 1972), p. 87.

2. Ibid., p. 97, quoted from Erikson, *Childhood and Society* (1950). Cf. Sydney E. Ahlstrom, *A Religious History of the American People* (New Haven: Yale University Press, 1973), p. 635.

3. Cf. Kammen, op. cit., pp. 60 and 162.

4. See especially Chap. 11 below.

5. Ahlstrom, *A Religious History of the American People*, p. 124. Cf. ibid., p. 94 and p. 131, n. 5. On the Puritan origins of the American Baptists see ibid., p. 171. On Virginia Puritanism see H. Shelton Smith, Robert T. Handy, and Lefferts A. Loetscher, *American Christianity: an Historical Interpretation with Representative Documents* (New York: Charles Scribner's Sons, 1960), Vol. I, p. 14. Cf. p. 19, p. 143 and 143n.

6. Cf. Edmund S. Morgan, *Puritan Political Ideas* (Indianapolis: The Bobbs-Merrill Co., 1965), pp. xv–xx. The whole treatment of American religious rootage owes much to discussions with C. C. Goen.

7. *The Spirit of the Common Law* (Francestown, N. H.: Marshall Jones Co., 1921), pp. 14–15.

8. Cf. John Dykstra Eusden, *Puritans, Lawyers, and Politics in Early Seventeenth-Century England* (Hamden, Conn.: Archon Books, Yale University Press, 1968 [orig. 1958]), pp. viii–ix.

9. *Crime, Law and the Scholars* (Seattle: University of Washington Press, 1969), p. 30.

10. Morgan, op. cit., p. 93. Cf. Perry Miller, *Errand into the Wilderness* (New York: Harper & Row, 1964 [orig. 1956]), p. 11.

11. See Eusden, op. cit., p. 122.

12. See e.g., passages from Cotton Mather, in Morgan, op. cit., pp. 248 and 341.

13. P. Miller, op. cit., p. 99. Cf. Ahlstrom, op. cit., p. 190.

14. *Building of the Ship.*

15. Cf. Robert Jewett, *The Captain America Complex: The Dilemma of Zealous Nationalism* (Philadelphia: The Westminster Press, 1973), p. 9.

16. Smith et al., op. cit., I, p. 101. Cf. Morgan, op. cit., p. 48.

17. William Bradford, *History of Plymouth Plantation, 1620–1647* (Boston: Houghton Mifflin Co., 1912), Vol. I, pp. 189–196.

18. See especially "The Liberties of the Massachusetts Colonie in New

England," enacted in 1641, a precursor of the American Bill of Rights. The document appears in Morgan, op. cit., pp. 178–203. Cf. p. 172.

19. Cf. Ahlstrom, op. cit., p. 491. Concerning early common ownership and labor at Plymouth and its failures see William Bradford, op. cit., Vol. I, pp. 299–303.

20. See Mueller, op. cit., p. 10.

21. Reported in Winthrop's Journal. See Morgan, op. cit., p. 106. Cf. Ahlstrom, op. cit., p. 348; P. Miller, op. cit., pp. 131–132.

22. J. F. Stephan, *A History of the Criminal Law of England* (New York: Burt Franklin, n.d. [orig. in London, 1883]), Vol. I, p. 53.

23. Mueller, op. cit., p. 12. Cf. Morgan, op. cit., p. xxiv and pp. 226–233.

24. P. Miller, op. cit., p. 105.

25. See the text of these and other laws in Smith et al., op. cit., Vol. I, pp. 42–44. The full penalties prescribed were rarely imposed.

26. Ibid., Vol. I, p. 237 (emphasis mine). Penn does, however, say that the major part of governmental activities is "more soft and daily necessary." Ibid., p. 238.

27. Cf. John Winthrop's "Declaration in Defense of an Order of Court Made in May, 1637." See Morgan (ed.), *Puritan Political Ideas*, p. 145.

28. See P. Miller, op. cit., pp. 34–35, for citations from the *Connecticut Records*.

29. Smith et al., op. cit., Vol. I, p. 127.

30. Berthoff, *An Unsettled People* (New York: Harper & Row, 1971), p. 100.

31. Cf. Kammen, *People of Paradox*, p. 163.

32. Smith et al., op. cit., Vol. I, p. 218.

33. See Ahlstrom, *Religious History of the American People*, p. 161.

Chapter 10. The Great Awakening and Jeffersonian Humanism, *pages 79–88*

1. Cf. Richard L. Bushman, *From Puritan to Yankee: Character and the Social Order in Connecticut, 1691–1765* (Cambridge, Mass.: Harvard University Press, 1967), p. 187.

2. *Religious History of the American People*, p. 350. Ahlstrom gives an especially clear account of the Great Awakening and its relations with earlier and contemporary conditions and events. See also C. C. Goen, *Revivalism and Separation in New England, 1740–1800: Strict Congregationalists and Separate Baptists in the Great Awakening* (New Haven: Yale University Press, 1962); Alan E. Heimart, *Religion and the American Mind from the Great Awakening to the Revolution* (Cambridge, Mass.: Harvard University Press, 1966); Charles H. Maxson, *The Great Awakening in the Middle Colonies* (Chicago: University of Chicago Press, 1920); Perry Miller, *Jonathan Edwards* (New York: William Sloan Associates, 1949); Douglas J. Elwood, *The Philosophical Theology of Jonathan Edwards* (New York: Columbia University Press, 1960); Stuart C. Henry, *George Whitefield: Wayfaring Witness* (Nashville: Abingdon Press, 1957); and C. C. Goen (ed.), *The Great Awakening*, Vol. 4 of *Works of Jonathan Edwards* (New Haven: Yale University Press, 1972), pp. 1–89.

3. Cf. the appraisal by Heimert, in op. cit.

4. Op. cit., p. 263. Cf. ibid., p. 6.

5. See Douglas Sloan (ed.), *The Great Awakening and American Education: A Documentary History* (New York: Teachers College, 1973).

6. Quotations and basic interpretation are from Perry Miller, *Jonathan Edwards*, pp. 164–166. The sermon, entitled *A Strong Rod Broken*, was published in Boston in 1748.

7. Morgan, op. cit., p. 273. Long excerpts from the letter appear in ibid., pp. 267–304.

8. See ibid., p. 338.

9. This is not to deny Jefferson's use of ideas and even much wording from earlier writers and especially from the Virginia Bill of Rights mainly written by George Mason. See Gilbert Chinard, *Thomas Jefferson, The Apostle of Americanism* (Ann Arbor: The University of Michigan Press, 1966 [orig. 1929]), pp. 69–74.

10. *The Jeffersonian Tradition of American Democracy* (New York: Hill & Wang, 1960 [orig. 1935]), p. 47. Cf. Gilbert Chinard, op. cit., p. 72.

11. Wiltse, op. cit., pp. 56–57. Cf. ibid., pp. 52–55; 11 and 29.

12. Cf. ibid., p. 59. A more personal influence was that of George Wythe, his principal law teacher at William and Mary, collaborator in Virginia politics and trusted friend. See the many references to Wythe indexed in *The Life and Selected Writings of Thomas Jefferson*, edited by Adrienne Koch and William Peden (New York: The Modern Library, Random House, 1944). The congeniality of their ideas and sentiments is evident and Wythe's influence must have been considerable.

13. Cf. Wiltse, op. cit., pp. 70–71.

14. Cf. Jefferson's words commending "a wise and frugal government, which shall restrain men from injuring one another, which shall leave them otherwise free to regulate their own pursuits. . . . " *Inaugural Address*, March 4, 1801.

15. *Autobiography*, Koch and Peden (eds.), op. cit., p. 46.

16. Cf. his *Inaugural Address* of 1801. Cf. also the clear statement of this principle by the liberal American clergyman Joel Barlow in 1792, quoted by Kammen, op. cit., pp. 235–236.

17. Letter to M. Henri Gregoire, Feb. 25, 1809, in the *Life and Selected Writings*, p. 595.

18. Letter to Mann Page, Aug. 30, 1795.

19. Op. cit., p. 40.

20. E.g., see Koch and Peden, *Life and Selected Writings*, pp. 218–219, 277–279, 314–315, and 367–368.

21. Ibid., p. 279, from *Notes on Virginia*.

22. *Life and Selected Writings*, pp. 256–262, from *Notes on Virginia*. Cf. ibid., p. 51, from *Autobiography*.

23. Various historical arguments over this matter appear in Merrill D. Peterson, *The Jefferson Image in the American Mind* (New York: Oxford University Press, 1962). Cf. Kammen, *People of Paradox*, p. 190.

24. For example, note the appeal by Martin Luther King, Jr., in his his-

toric address at the Lincoln Memorial Aug. 28, 1963. There he called the Declaration of Independence "a promissory note" which the Negro people had come to Washington to collect. "I have a dream," he declared, "that one day this nation will rise up, live out the true meaning of its creed: 'We hold these truths to be self-evident, that all men are created equal.'"

25. The other two declare him "Author of the Declaration of Independence" and "Father of the University of Virginia."

26. See Chinard, op. cit., pp. 103–105.

27. Ibid., p. 302.

28. Ibid., p. 301.

29. Address to the California Legislature Oct. 29, 1947. *The Public Papers of Chief Justice Earl Warren*, edited by Henry M. Christman, Revised Edition (New York: Capricorn Books, 1966), p. 7.

30. See Chinard, op. cit., pp. 94–95.

31. Lerone Bennett, Jr., *Before the Mayflower: A History of the Negro in America, 1619–1962* (Chicago: Johnson Publishing Co., 1962), pp. 67–68.

Chapter **11. The Rush for Riches: Its Social Cost,** *pages 88–98*

1. Berthoff, *An Unsettled People*, p. 70.

2. Ibid., p. 58.

3. Quoted by Ahlstrom, op. cit., p. 164 and 164n, from *Magnalia Christi Americana*, 2 vols. (Hartford edition, 1820), 1:59.

4. Quoted by Berthoff, op. cit., p. 55.

5. Ahlstrom, op. cit., pp. 344–345.

6. Berthoff, op. cit., p. 129.

7. Cf. ibid., pp. 65, 125–126, and 170.

8. Cf. Perry Miller, op. cit., p. 207.

9. Cf. Jewett, *Captain America Complex*, pp. 27–56.

10. See Berthoff, op. cit., pp. 148–149.

11. Cf. ibid., p. 173.

12. Cf. ibid., pp. 372, 376. Cf. M. R. Cohen in Cohen and Cohen, *Readings*, p. 302.

13. Cf. Kenneth Lamott, *The Money-Makers* (Boston: Little, Brown & Co., 1969) and Ferdinand Lundberg, *The Rich and Super-Rich* (New York: Bantam Books, 1968).

14. Cf. the many references to such loyalty to "the game plan" as excuse for criminal conduct by members of President Nixon's staff participating in the "Watergate" affairs.

15. *Newsweek*, Sept. 30, 1974.

16. See John G. Fuller, *The Gentlemen Conspirators*.

17. Cf. Kammen, *People of Paradox*, p. 269.

18. Cf. Berthoff, op. cit., p. 203.

19. Ibid., p. 363. Quoted from Angie Debo, *And Still the Waters Run* (Princeton: Princeton University Press, 1940), pp. 21–22. Emphasis Berthoff's. Senator Dawes, like most white Americans, failed to understand the Cherokee law of property, which was not simply communal. See John Phillip Reid, *A Law*

of Blood: The Primitive Law of the Cherokee Nation (New York: New York University Press, 1970), pp. 131–133 and 140–141. Cf. Wilbur R. Jacobs, *Dispossessing the American Indian: Indians and Whites on the Colonial Frontier* (New York: Charles Scribner's Sons, 1972), p. 23.

20. Cohen and Cohen, *Readings*, p. 303, from Walter A. Lunden, *Statistics of Crime and Criminals*, p. 74.

21. *Statistical Abstract of the United States, 1970*, pp. 33–34. Cf. the fantastic data on local moving within American cities and some social effects, in Julius Stone, *Social Dimensions*, pp. 159–160.

22. Cf. Cohen and Cohen, op. cit., p. 303.

23. Other signs are the more than tripled number of illegitimate births per thousand unmarried women since 1940—despite "the pill," other contraceptive means, and abortions; and the increase in cases of gonorrhea at more than four times the rate of population increase. See *Statistical Abstract of the United States, 1970*, p. 50.

24. See the early classic of women's liberation, Betty Friedan, *The Feminine Mystique* (New York: Dell Publishing Co., 1973 [orig. 1963]), and the comprehensive symposium, Louise Kapp Howe (ed.), *The Future of the Family* (New York: Simon & Schuster, 1972).

25. Cf. Paul Deats, "The Youth Revolution?" *Religion in Life* (1971), pp. 557–570.

26. Cf. Leslie T. Wilkins, in *Journal of Criminal Justice*, Vol. I (1973), p. 6.

27. The Effectiveness of a Prison and Parole System, p. 20.

28. Cf. Kammen, op. cit., p. 289.

Chapter 12. Race, National Origin and Violence, *pages 98–109*

1. Harper & Brothers; republished by Harper & Row in 1965.

2. P. 342.

3. See John Winthrop's account in Morgan, *Puritan Political Ideas*, p. 98. Cf. pp. 101 and 208.

4. Thomas F. Gossert, *Race: The History of an Idea in America* (New York: Schocken Books, 1971 [orig. 1963]), p. 229, with citations of earlier sources.

5. "Indian Self-Government," first published in 1949, reprinted in *The Legal Conscience: Selected Papers of Felix S. Cohen* (New Haven: Yale University Press, 1960). John P. Reid, an especially careful scholar in the study of early Indian law, thinks Cohen mistaken about this, contending that Franklin knew little concerning the structure of the Iroquois League while Jefferson knew less. (Reid's letter to me dated Feb. 21, 1974.) Cohen's own respect for the legal structure of the Iroquois League, however, is significant.

6. *Notes on Virginia*; in Koch and Peden, *Life and Selected Writings of Thomas Jefferson*, pp. 210–213.

7. Wilbur R. Jacobs, *Dispossessing the American Indian*, p. 158.

8. See Gossett, *Race*, p. 230.

9. The *Winning of the West* (1889–1896), Vol. I, pp. 334–335, quoted

by Gossett, *Race*, p. 238. Compare the similar statement of General Francis C. Walker, Commissioner of Indian Affairs, in 1871, quoted by Gossett, p. 234.

10. Gossett, *Race*, p. 236.

11. For an able Indian account see **Dee A.** Brown, *Bury My Heart at Wounded Knee: An Indian History of the West* (New York: Henry Holt & Co., 1970). Cf. Vine Deloria, Jr., *Custer Died for Your Sins: An Indian Manifesto* (New York: The Macmillan Co., 1969). For a record of Indian militancy in the 1960s see Alvin M. Josephy, Jr., *Red Power: The American Indians' Fight for Freedom* (New York: American Heritage Press, McGraw-Hill, Inc., 1971).

12. Dale Van Every gives the history of the Cherokees from 1830 to 1848 in *Disinherited: The Lost Birthright of the American Indian* (New York: William Morrow & Co., 1966).

13. *A Law of Blood*, p. 276.

14. *Dispossessing the American Indian*, p. 152.

15. On the deliberate dividing of families and other dehumanizing cruelties of slavery, some recent books offer data and analyses professing to demonstrate a radically revised and ameliorative view. See especially Robert W. Fogel and Stanley L. Engerman, *Time on the Cross: The Economics of American Negro Slavery* (Boston: Little, Brown & Co., 1974). However, I find the arguments advanced unconvincing. Cf. the critical review by Allan J. Lichtman, in *The New Republic*, July 6 and 13, 1974, pp. 22–24. I am grateful to Gerhard O. W. Mueller for photocopies of considerable relevant source material collected by the New York University School of Law. Included are bills of sale of slaves, advertisements, and eyewitness accounts which together expose the absolute prevalence of material interests above any concerns of slaveowners for marriage, filial ties, or the personal happiness of slaves. Exceptions to this selfish ruthlessness were not sufficiently frequent to affect the laws even to the point of acknowledging the existence of marriage among slaves, let alone protecting marriage ties against violation by separate sales or by sexually exploiting masters.

16. Lerone Bennett, Jr., *Before the Mayflower*, p. 38.

17. The Germantown resolution of 1688 appears in Smith et al., *American Christianity*, I, pp. 181–182.

18. Quoted in Gossett, *Race*, p. 31, from Berkeley's *Works* (ed. Fraser, Oxford, 1961), IV, p. 405.

19. Bennett, *Before the Mayflower*, p. 70.

20. Ibid., pp. 70–71.

21. *American Negro Slave Revolts* (New York: International Publishers Co., 1961).

22. *Before the Mayflower*, p. 122.

23. Compare Lawrence M. Friedman, *A History of American Law*, pp. 440–441; Leslie H. Fishel, Jr., and Benjamin Quarles, *The Black American: A Documentary History* (New York: William Morrow & Co., 1970), pp. 258–263; Bennett, *Before the Mayflower*, pp. 183–241, 351–355.

24. Marvin E. Wolfgang, in *Federal Rules Decisions*, Vol. 46 (1969), p. 538.

25. Gossett, op. cit., p. 270.

26. See Friedman, *History*, p. 308.

27. Cf. C. Vann Woodward, *The Strange Career of Jim Crow* (New York: Oxford University Press, 1955).

28. Pp. 416–417.

29. *Report of the National Advisory Commission on Civil Disorders* 1968, p. 161.

30. Ibid., p. 162.

31. *Birth Cohort*, p. 252.

32. In 1972 median black family income was 59.6% of median white (*Statistical Abstract of the U. S. 1974*).

33. Cf. James Baldwin, *Nobody Knows My Name* (New York: The Dial Press, 1962 [orig. 1954]), pp. 65–67.

34. *Birth Cohort*, p. 112.

35. See Gossett, *Race*, pp. 353–404.

36. For a classic account of American nativism and its violent tides see John Higham, *Strangers in the Land: Patterns of American Nativism 1860–1925* (New Brunswick, N. J.: Rutgers University Press, 1955).

37. *Crime of Punishment*, pp. 162–163.

38. *Federal Rules Decisions* 46 (1969), p. 535.

39. Ibid., p. 539.

40. Richard Hofstadter and Michael Wallace (eds.), *American Violence: A Documentary History* (New York: Vintage Books, 1971 [orig. 1970]), p. 7.

41. Ibid.

42. Hofstadter and Wallace give documentary accounts of more than 100 such violent episodes, with thoughtful commentary. Op. cit.

43. See also the Final Report of The National Commission on the Causes and Prevention of Violence, entitled *To Establish Justice, to Insure Domestic Tranquility* (Government Printing Office, 1969). Relevant also are much of Jewett, *The Captain America Complex*, and many passages of Kammen, *People of Paradox*.

Chapter **13. Minority Religions,** *pages 109–116*

1. Smith et al., *American Christianity*, Vol. I, p. 37.

2. Ibid.

3. Cf. the defense of "vindictive punishment" by Pope Pius XII in the address included in Gerber and McAnany, *Contemporary Punishment*, pp. 59–72. The mood of Vatican Council II was less self-righteous and more humane, but retributive justice was not specifically discussed in the documents of the Council.

4. Ahlstrom, *Religious History*, p. 111.

5. Ibid., p. 209.

6. See Elmer Hubert Johnson, *Crime, Correction, and Society*, pp. 482–484.

7. See American Friends Service Committee, *Struggle for Justice*, pp. v and 35–36. See also Menninger, *Crime of Punishment*, p. 71.

8. Cf. Johnson, op. cit., p. 486. Johnson says "the solitary system in the United States" was ended by 1866. Ibid., p. 487.

9. *Struggle for Justice*, p. 91.
10. Ibid., pp. 97–98, 146.
11. Ibid., p. 36.
12. Ibid., p. 146.
13. *Religious History*, p. 573.

Chapter **14. Time and Space in American Culture,** *pages 116–122*

1. Sidney E. Mead, *The Lively Experiment* (New York: Harper & Row, 1963), p. 6.
2. Ibid., p. 6.
3. Berthoff, *An Unsettled People*, p. 25.
4. Ibid., p. 37.
5. Ahlstrom, *Religious History*, p. 737.
6. Mead, op. cit., p. 20.
7. Kammen, *People of Paradox*, p. 58.
8. Smith et al., *American Christianity*, I, pp. 119, 121, 122.
9. *The Simple Cobbler of Aggawam*, quoted in Mead, op. cit., p. 13.
10. Mead, op. cit., p. 13.
11. Smith et al., op. cit., I, pp. 50–51.
12. Mead, op. cit., p. 12.
13. Ibid., p. 7.
14. Cf. ibid., p. 15.
15. Tr. by Marjorie Kerr Wilson (New York: Bantam Books, 1967 [orig. German 1963]).
16. Lorenz does hold out hope that in the future, new ethical tradition may save man from himself.

Chapter **15. Two Americas,** *pages 122–130*

1. *De la démocratie en Amérique,* quoted in English translation in many writings. See the translation by Henry Reeve, *Democracy in America* (London: Oxford University Press, 1946).
2. *People of Paradox*, p. 292.
3. Mississippi alone, of all the states, does not require school attendance. Its legislature may soon correct this deficiency. Meanwhile, schooling is offered to all children.
4. Cf. Gunnar Myrdal, *An American Dilemma* (New York: Harper & Row, 20th Anniversary Edition, 1962; Postscript by Arnold Rose). Despite his invaluable analysis, Myrdal failed to see that the characteristic kinds of base prejudice and aggressively selfish behavior he observed in the United States were not mere failures to live up to American ideals. Rather they are rooted in a system of counterideals deliberately cultivated and consciously institutionalized throughout American history. We cannot deal with them effectively without recognizing this, their true character.
5. See Gus Tyler, *Organized Crime in America* (Ann Arbor: University of

Michigan Press, 1962), especially Part II, "The Matrix of Organized Crime." Tyler cites many other authors in support of this thesis.

6. See Paul R. Ehrlich, *The Population Bomb* (New York: Ballantine Books, 1968), and Philip Wogaman (ed.), *The Population Crisis and Moral Responsibility* (Washington, D. C.: Public Affairs Press, 1973).

7. See report of the National Commission on Technology, Automation, and Economic Progress: Howard R. Bowen and Garth L. Mangum (eds.), *Automation and Economic Progress* (Englewood Cliffs, N. J.: Prentice-Hall, 1966), pp. 10–21.

8. See Vance Packard, *The Waste Makers* (New York: Pocket Books, Inc., 1965 [orig. 1960]). Cf. Daniel Bell, *The Coming of Post-Industrial Society* (New York: Basic Books, 1973), pp. 126–133. Bell shows, however, an increasing proportion of employment in services. He does not analyze the proportions of the GNP in things and services.

9. Tables I and II, drawn from "Recent Congressional Publications on Foreign and Military Assistance and Defense Appropriations: the FY 1973 Budget," *Sane World Quarterly*, December 1973, pp. 59, 60.

10. See Stewart L. Udall, *The Quiet Crisis* (New York: Avon Books, 1963); John H. Storer, *Man in the Web of Life* (New York: New American Library, 1968); Garrett DeBell (ed.), *The Environmental Handbook* (New York: Ballantine Books, 1970); Donella H. Meadows et al., *The Limits of Growth* (New York: Universe Books, 1972); and Frederick Elder, *Crisis in Eden* (Nashville: Abingdon Press, 1970).

11. Cf. Herbert Marcuse, *One-Dimensional Man* (Boston: Beacon Press, 1970 [orig. 1964]), pp. 241–242. Cf. also Eugene C. Bianchi, "Help Kill the Individualism Myth," *National Catholic Reporter*, July 1973.

12. Cf. Berthoff, *An Unsettled People*, p. ix, and Richard Hofstadter, *The American Political Tradition and the Men Who Made It* (New York: Random House, 1948), p. x.

Chapter **16. An Emerging Ethical Consensus,** *pages 133–156*

1. Arthur A. Cohen, *The Myth of the Judeo-Christian Tradition* (New York: Harper & Row, 1970 [orig. 1957]), pp. xxi and 223.

2. *Challenge of Crime*, p. 6B.

3. *Courts on Trial* (New York: Atheneum, 1971), p. 371.

4. Testimony to Subcommittee No. 3 of the Committee on the Judiciary of the House of Representatives, Ninety-Second Congress, published under title, *Corrections*, Serial No. 15 (Washington: Government Printing Office, 1972), p. 113.

5. Cf. H. L. A. Hart, *Law, Liberty and Morality* (Stanford, Calif.: Stanford University Press, 1963), p. 17.

6. Quoted with approval by Milton R. Konvitz, in Konvitz (ed.), *Judaism and Human Rights* (New York: W. W. Norton & Co., 1972), p. 87.

7. See Julius Stone, *Human Law, Human Justice*, p. 24. Cf. pp. 25, 27–28; also the Mishnah, *Jerusalem Megillah*, IV, 74d.

8. Stone, ibid., p. 26, citing Deut. 18:15; Ps. 119:126; *Yevanoth* 90b, *Bracht* 63a, *Avodah Zarah* 40a, *Gloss of Tosefoth Mabboth* 23b.

9. See Nelson Glueck, *Hesed in the Bible* (tr. by Alfred Gottschalk. Cincinnati: Hebrew Union College Press, 1967), for a careful exposition of this principle.

10. See Milton R. Konvitz, *Judaism and Human Rights*, pp. 123–124.

11. Stone, op. cit., p. 29.

12. Article "Justice" in *Encyclopedia Judaica* (Jerusalem: Keter Publishing House, 1971).

13. Stone, op. cit., p. 21.

14. Cf. the citations given by Stone, ibid., p. 22; also cf. Haim H. Cohn, *Jewish Law in Ancient and Modern Israel* (New York: KTAV Publishing House, 1971), pp. 75–78.

15. Stone, op. cit., p. 20. Cf. Louis Finkelstein, in Konvitz, op. cit., pp. 140–141.

16. Ben Zion Bokser, in Konvitz, ibid., p. 146. Bokser cites the Mishnah, *Makkot* 1:10.

17. Ibid.

18. Konvitz, op. cit., p. 243.

19. "Problematics of Jewish Ethics," in Daniel Jeremy Silver (ed.), *Judaism and Ethics* (New York: KTAV Publishing House, 1970), p. 128.

20. Cf. Konvitz, op. cit., p. 119.

21. Cf. Nelson Glueck, *Hesed*, pp. 37–38.

22. Richard G. Hirsch, in Konvitz, op. cit., pp. 245–246.

23. Cf. Konvitz, in op. cit., p. 250, and the essays which follow, by Samuel Belkin and Samson Raphael Hirsch.

24. E.g., see Deut. 22:23–29.

25. See Stone, op. cit., p. 30.

26. Cf. Konvitz, op. cit., pp. 159–176.

27. Stone, op. cit., p. 343.

28. Cohn, *Jewish Law in Ancient and Modern Israel*, p. xvii.

29. Ibid. Cf. *Babylonian Talmud.* Sanhedrin: Baba Batra, 60B; Menhot, 37B–38D; and Moses Maimonides, *Laws of Apostasy*, Chap. 2, Sec. 5.

30. See, e.g., Sanhedrin 4:1.

31. Sanhedrin 3:3; notes by Eugene J. Lipman on *Gittin* 2:5, in *The Mishnah* (New York: W. W. Norton & Co., 1970), p. 188.

32. See the discussion, with references, by Julius Kravetz, in Silver, *Judaism and Ethics*, pp. 278–281.

33. Cf. Cohn, op. cit., pp. 109n, 139.

34. Bava Matzi'a 4:10.

35. Bava Kama, 5:4.

36. For a current Roman Catholic criticism of this solution see Charles E. Curran, *Contemporary Problems in Moral Theology* (Notre Dame, Ind.: Fides Publishers, 1970), pp. 225–226.

37. Cf. Emil Brunner's defense of capital punishment as an especially pure "expression of God's holy wrath," in *Justice and the Social Order* (New York: Harper & Brothers, 1945), p. 223.

38. The views of Pius XII (in a 1954 speech to Italian lawyers) and C. S. Lewis are included with many different ones in the useful book *Contemporary Punishment: Views, Explanations and Justifications*, edited by Rudolph J. Gerber and Patrick D. McAnany. Cf. my review-article, "From Retribution to Prevention and Social Restoration," in *The Jurist*, Vol. 33, No. 1 (Winter 1973), pp. 25–48.

39. Tr. by Marguerite Wieser (Garden City, N.Y.: Doubleday & Co., 1960).

40. See especially ibid., pp. 68–70.

41. See ibid., p. 139.

42. Tr. by Cecelia G. Kings (New York: Seabury Press, 1969).

43. Ibid., p. 174.

44. By Heinz-Horst Schrey, Hans Hermann Walz, and W. A. Waterhouse (London: SCM Press, 1955).

45. Ibid., p. 190.

46. Ibid., p. 195.

47. *Consultation on Penal Policies 18–25 June, 1970* (Chateau de Bossey, 1298 Celigny, Switzerland: Ecumenical Institute, 1970), pp. 24, 46, 47. Unfortunately published only in mimeographed form with limited circulation.

48. Ibid., p. 23. Cf. pp. 24, 22, 38, 40.

49. Ibid., p. 22.

50. Ibid., pp. 25, 40, 42.

51. *Deeds and Rules in Christian Ethics* (New York: Charles Scribner's Sons, 1967), p. 2.

52. *Moral Responsibility: Situation Ethics at Work* (Philadelphia: The Westminster Press, 1967), p. 15. Cf. Paul L. Lehmann, *Ethics in Christian Context* (New York: Harper & Row, 1963), p. 54.

53. *Contemporary Problems in Moral Theology*, pp. 228–229.

54. *An Interpretation of Christian Ethics* (New York: Harper & Brothers, 1935), p. 140.

55. New York: Harper & Brothers, 1958. See also his book of sermons entitled *Strength to Love* (New York: Harper & Row, 1963) and all his other books.

56. Cf. my treatment of koinonia love in *Responsible Freedom* (New York: Harper & Row, 1971), pp. 106–110; also Lehmann, op. cit., p. 54, and James M. Gustafson, *Theology and Christian Ethics* (Philadelphia: United Church Press, 1974), p. 175.

57. *Theological Ethics* (New York: The Macmillan Co., 1966), pp. 133–134. Cf. the official statement on "World Community" in *The Book of Discipline of The United Methodist Church 1972* (Nashville: The United Methodist Publishing House, 1973), p. 95.

58. Cf. Mt. 6:1–6.

59. E.g., see Luke 5:29–32; 7:34.

60. See, e.g., Mk. 10:21; 10:46–52; Luke 19:8–10; 23:39–43; Mt. 25:31–46.

61. *United Methodist Discipline 1972*, pp. 95–96.

62. New York: The Macmillan Co., 1961.

63. Ibid., p. 311. Cf. pp. 411–416.

64. Dewey and James H. Tufts, *Ethics* (New York: Henry Holt & Co., 1910), p. 414.

65. Frankena, *Ethics* (Englewood Cliffs, N. J.: Prentice-Hall, 1963), pp. 3–5, and 7–8.

66. Bertocci and Millard, *Personality and the Good* (New York: David McKay, 1963), p. 316.

67. E.g., see George Trumbull Ladd, *What Ought I To Do?* (New York: Longmans, Green and Co., 1915).

68. *Anthropology and Ethics* (Cleveland: The Press of Case Western Reserve University, 1968), p. 225.

69. *The Reconstruction of Humanity* (Boston: Beacon Press, 1948), pp. 101 and 61.

70. In Richard B. Brandt (ed.), *Social Justice* (Englewood Cliffs, N. J.: Prentice-Hall, 1962), pp. 125–126.

71. *Ethics* (New York: Henry Holt & Co., 1910), p. 417.

72. In Brandt, *Social Justice*, p. 53.

73. Frankena, *Ethics*, p. 44. Cf. his support of similar teachings by Josiah Royce and William James, ibid., p. 52. Cf. also Paul Weiss' commendation of the Golden Rule and similar injunctions to benevolent respect for others, from the writings of Thomas Hobbes, Immanuel Kant, John Stuart Mill, Thomas Aquinas, Hillel, and the teachings of Confucianism, Buddhism, Taoism, Hinduism, Zoroastrianism, and other religions. Weiss, *Man's Freedom* (Carbondale and Edwardsville, Ill.: Southern Illinois Press, 1950), pp. 138, 298–308, and 314.

74. Op. cit., p. 98.

75. *Human Nature and Its Remaking* (New Haven: Yale University Press, 1923), pp. 374, 376–377.

76. In Brandt, *Social Justice*, p. 124.

77. Frankena, *Ethics*, p. 76.

78. In Brandt, *Social Justice*, p. 99.

79. In personal conversation with me in Warsaw, in September 1973. The Polish government does restrict the freedom of all citizens and foreign visitors more than Americans would tolerate, though less than various other governments.

80. In Brandt, *Social Justice*, p. 48. Cf. Frankena, in same symposium, p. 23.

81. Ibid., p. 51.

82. *Ethics*, p. 98.

83. Cf. the declared purpose, in the Preamble to the Constitution, to "secure the Blessings of Liberty to ourselves and our Posterity."

84. *Personality and the Good*, p. 403.

85. *Reason and Goodness*, p. 311.

86. *Reconstruction of Humanity*, pp. 184–185.

87. Ibid., p. 226.

88. New Haven: Yale University Press, 1934, p. 87.

89. *Anthropology and Ethics*, p. 224.

90. In Brandt, *Social Justice*, p. 102.

Chapter **17. A Basic Philosophy of Criminal Justice,** *pages 156–173*

1. The National Advisory Commission on Criminal Justice Standards and Goals, *Corrections* (Washington, D.C.: Government Printing Office, 1973), p. 601. Cf. the brief Edited Version prepared by the National Council on Crime and Delinquency (1973), p. 57. Hawaii had already adopted a single new penal code in April 1972. Several other states have new codes under consideration.

2. Cambridge, Mass.: Harvard University Press, 1971.

3. Ibid., p. 8.

4. Ibid., p. 11.

5. Ibid., pp. 136–142.

6. Cf. Rawls' own comparisons, pp. 11, 140–141, and 252.

7. P. 302.

8. P. 287.

9. P. 302.

10. Pp. 544–547.

11. P. 576.

12. P. 577.

13. Cf. ibid., pp. 314–315 and 576.

14. *The City of God*, Book IV, Chap. 4.

15. Cf. Jerome Hall's words, "Dean Pound has largely determined even the conception of jurisprudence as a discipline, in this country" (*Studies in Jurisprudence and Criminal Theory*, p. 134). Cf. also Gerhard O. W. Mueller's characterization of Pound as "the most eminent of all law professors" (*Crime, Law and the Scholars*, p. 95) and again as the American who was first able to "spark a modern criminal law scholarship" (ibid., p. 111).

16. *The Spirit of the Common Law*, p. 91. Cf. Jurisprudence (St. Paul, Minn.: West Publishing Co., 1959), Vol. 3, pp. 7 and 16.

17. Ibid., Vol. 3, p. 16.

18. See ibid., pp. 23–24; illustrated in pp. 25–324.

19. Cf. *Introduction to Philosophy of Law* (New Haven: Yale University Press, 1971 [orig. 1922]), pp. 42–43.

20. Stone, *Social Dimensions*, p. 180.

21. Ibid., p. 179.

22. The work of Ralph Nader and his associates must be mentioned here.

23. *Social Dimensions*, p. 172. Phillip Heck appears to speak only of private and public interests, the public embracing all which are here called social. See especially Heck, "The Formation of Concepts," in *The Jurisprudence of Interests* by Max Rümelin, Heck et al. (Cambridge, Mass.: Harvard University Press, 1948), pp. 132–133.

24. *Jurisprudence*, Vol. 3, p. 236.

25. On interests and rights see ibid., p. 25.

26. For Pound's classification see ibid., Vol. 3, pp. 25–324.

27. Cf. Pound's references, ibid., Vol. 3, p. 277, n. 34.

28. Ibid., pp. 277–278.

29. Some recent examples of such reasoning are to be found in my book, *Responsible Freedom*, pp. 144–178, and Bertocci and Millard, *Personality and*

the Good, pp. 315–360. Cf. also references to Brand Blanshard, John Dewey, and William K. Frankena above, Chap. 16, C.

30. *Jurisprudence*, Vol. 3, p. 334. Cf. pp. 330–331 and 45–46.

31. "Method of Interest Jurisprudence," in Rümelin et al., *The Jurisprudence of Interests*, p. 317.

32. *Jurisprudence*, Vol. 3, pp. 342–343. Cf. p. 264.

33. P. 343.

34. Ibid., p. 352. Cf. pp. 344–345.

35. P. 353.

36. Pp. 363–365 and 66–67.

37. P. 324.

38. Pp. 307–308.

39. E.g., see John Kleineg, *Punishment and Desert* (The Hague: Martinus Nijhoff, 1973); a favorite antinomy in various writings of Reinhold Niebuhr; and C. S. Lewis, "The Humanitarian Theory of Punishment," in Gerber and McAnany (eds.), *Contemporary Punishment*, pp. 194–199.

40. See Ancel, *Social Defense: A Modern Approach to Criminal Problems* (tr. by J. Wilson. London: Routledge & Kegan Paul, 1965).

41. Ibid., p. 116.

42. Ibid., p. 174.

43. Ibid., p. 175. Cf. p. 197.

44. See Augustine, *City of God*, Book 19, Chap. 16; Pope Pius XII, "Crime and Punishment," from a 1954 discourse to the Italian Association of Jurists, in Rudolph J. Gerber and Patrick D. McAnany, *Contemporary Punishment*, pp. 61, 68; Leviticus 20; G. W. F. Hegel, *The Philosophy of Right*, Section 101.

45. For an account of the reforms, their basic philosophy, and a prime example see Antonio Sánchez Galindo, "El Penado, Escencio del Derecho Penitenciario," in *Revista Mexicana de Prevención y Readaptación Social*, Vol. 1 (1972), No. 1, pp. 21 ff.

46. Sánchez has written an impressive 216-page manual for the training of prison personnel which gives many insights into his spirit and purpose. See *Manual de conocimientos básicos de personal penitenciario* (Toluca: Editiones Gobierno del Estade de México Dirección de Gobernación, 1974).

47. See ibid., 52–55, for further regulations, their rationale, and some consequences.

48. I observed this process for a full half-day staff meeting on Nov. 16, 1972, with the valued assistance of instant interpretation by Dr. John L. Groves, a long-time personal friend, now Dean and Professor of Christian Ethics in Union Theological Seminary of Mexico City. It was an unforgettable experience of concerned but crisp, efficient professional cooperation with strong benevolent purpose.

49. *Revista Mexicana de Prevención y Readaptación Social*, Vol. 1 (1972), No. 1, p. 21. Translation from the Spanish mine. For a legal scholar's appreciative article on the Penitentiary Center of the State of Mexico and its director see H. H. A. Cooper, "Comparative Penology—Some Salutary Lessons from Mexico," in *Chitty's Law Journal*, Vol. 22 (1974), No. 1, pp. 34–36.

Chapter **18. Fortifying the Community,** *pages 177–184*

1. *Challenge of Crime 1967*, p. 15.

2. Ibid.

3. *Community Crime Prevention* (Washington: Government Printing Office, 1973), p. 3. This volume will be cited hereafter as *SG Community*. The other four volumes, all published in the same year, will be cited as *SG System* (for *Criminal Justice System*), *SG Police*, *SG Courts* and *SG Corrections*. Cf. also the statement in the short (75-page) edited version of *A National Strategy to Reduce Crime* prepared and published by the National Council on Crime and Delinquency in December 1973, p. 1. This Edited Version will be cited hereafter as *SG-NCCD*.

4. See annual *Statistical Abstract of the United States* tables of income distribution.

5. See *SG-NCCD*, pp. 12–14.

6. Nashville: Abingdon Press, 1968.

7. See *SG Community*, pp. 197–198.

8. Ibid., pp. 198–202.

9. See John F. Decker's report in *Criminology*, August 1972, pp. 127–142. For account of a change of design ending a nearly worldwide fad of delinquent conduct see Mueller, *Delinquency and Puberty: Examination of a Juvenile Delinquency Fad*, New York University CLEAR Center Monograph Series, Vol. 5 (South Hackensack, N. J.: Fred B. Rothman & Co., 1971).

10. *SG Community*, pp. 200, 194–202. Cf. C. Ray Jeffrey, *Crime Prevention Through Environmental Design* (Beverly Hills: Sage Publications, 1971).

11. Teen Challenge, a theologically conservative Protestant organization, frequently works with courts in this way, especially in the care of offenders against narcotics laws.

12. See especially *SG Community*, Chap. 4.

13. See summary on this subject in *SG-NCCD*, p. 5.

14. *To Establish Justice, to Insure Domestic Tranquility*, p. 195.

15. Ibid., p. 197.

16. Ibid., pp. 199–200.

Chapter **19. The Victim: Forgotten Person of American Criminal Justice,** *pages 184–195*

1. Montreal: Les Presses de l'Université de Montréal, 1970.

2. U. S. Bureau of the Census, *Statistical Abstract of the United States: 1970*, p. 146.

3. *The Challenge of Crime*, p. 39.

4. *The Criminal and His Victim*, pp. 121–125.

5. Stephen Schafer, *The Victim and His Criminal* (New York: Random House, 1968), p. 78.

6. Fattah, op. cit., p. 15.

7. Cf. Schafer, op. cit., pp. 3–4, etc.

8. Quoted by J. F. Stephen, *A History of the Criminal Law of England*, Vol. I, p. 56.

9. Cf. Pound, *Jurisprudence*, Vol. 3, p. 281, n. 41.

10. Alan Miller (ed.), *African Penal Systems* (London: Routledge & Kegan Paul, 1969). In a stricter usage which Stephen Schafer recommends, these arrangements are for restitution, rather than for compensation. Restitution, as he defines it, is made by the offender and is an integral part of the process of criminal law and corrections. Compensation is civil in character and represents assistance to the victim by society, although sometimes related to a criminal case in court and sometimes providing for recovery from the criminal by the state. However, this usage is not universal and even Schafer does not strictly conform to it. See Schafer, op. cit., p. 112 and cf. p. 11. In this book I am usually employing the term "compensation" in its broad sense, to include restitution by the criminal as well as compensation by society.

11. "Traditional African Criminal Law and Punishment Pertaining to Assault, Murder, and Theft." A course paper presented at The American University in 1972, p. 3.

12. See especially his book, *A Humanist in Africa* (Nashville: Abingdon Press, 1966), pp. 34–35.

13. "Victim Compensation in Crimes of Personal Violence," in *Minn. Law Review*, 50 (December 1965).

14. Op. cit., pp. 11–14.

15. Ibid., pp. 18–19.

16. Ibid., p. 21, quoting from William Tallack, *Reparation to the Injured, and the Rights of the Victim of Crime to Compensation* (London: 1900), pp. 6–7.

17. See Schafer, op. cit., pp. 121–126.

18. Cf. ibid., pp. 116–121 and 131.

19. Learned during my visit there.

20. Restitution is sometimes encouraged or required in the United States as an alternative to formal prosecution. See, e.g., the account of such a practice in Iowa, as mentioned by Elizabeth W. and James Vorenberg, in Ohlin, *Prisoners in America*, p. 159.

21. "Equality and Governmental Action," New York University Law Review, 39 (1964), pp. 205 and 224. Cf. Schaffer, op. cit., pp. 122 and 129, and for contrary rationale in law elsewhere, ibid., pp. 118 and 121.

22. Cf. Schafer, *Victim and Criminal*, p. 125.

23. Gerhard O. W. Mueller in *Minn. Law Review*, 50 (December 1965), pp. 249–250.

24. Op. cit., p. 82. Cf. Henri Ellenberger, "Relation psychologiques entre le criminal et la victime," in *Revue Internationale de criminologie et de Police Technique*, 1954, pp. 103–121.

25. *Minn. Law Review*, 50 (Dec. 1965), pp. 249–250.

26. *Trial*, May-June 1972, p. 14.

27. These comparative facts are from Floyd, ibid., p. 16.

28. *Minn. Law Review*, 50 (December 1965), p. 237.

Chapter **20. Criminal Law: Its Scope and Penalties,** *pages 195–205*

1. Cf. statements of need for a consistent basic philosophy and some problems resulting from a lack of it in the report of the National Advisory Commission on Criminal Justice Standards and Goals, *SG-System*, pp. 1–2, 182–183.

2. *SG-NCCD*, p. 61; *SG System*, pp. 173–178. Cf. Frankel, *Criminal Sentences*, p. 9.

3. See especially *SG System*, pp. 5–36, 50–51, and 68–69; also *SG-NCCD*, p. 70. Cf. David A. Ward, "Evaluative Research for Corrections," in Ohlin, *Prisoners in America*, pp. 184–206.

4. Cf. Pound, *Jurisprudence*, Vol. 3, pp. 362, 370; Lawrence M. Friedman, *History*, pp. 510–513; Lewis R. Katz, Lawrence B. Litwin, and Richard H. Bamberger, *Justice is the Crime: Pretrial Delay in Felony Cases* (Cleveland: The Press of Western Case University, 1972), p. 4. See also Karl Menninger, *Whatever Became of Sin?* (New York: Hawthorn Books, 1973), especially pp. 65–73.

5. See *SG-NCCD*, p. 4; *SG Courts*, pp. 293–294.

6. In personal consultation, July 26, 1972. Cf. *Rutgers Camden Law Journal*, 3 (Fall 1971), p. 361.

7. Cf. *SG-NCCD*, p. 60. Cf. Norval Morris and Gordon Hawkins, *The Honest Politician's Guide*, pp. 12–13.

8. *SG-NCCD*, p. 58. The National Advisory Commission reports 1,804,900 for the same year. See *SG System*, p. 903.

9. *SG-NCCD*, p. 60.

10. *SG Police*, pp. 90–91.

11. See above Chap. 4, A.

12. Cf. Morris and Hawkins, *Honest Politician's Guide*, pp. 8–10; *SG-NCCD*, pp. 58–59.

13. *SG-NCCD*, p. 59.

14. Cf. Harold J. Berman's main thesis on the dialectical but mutually supportive relations of religion and government in his book, *The Interaction of Law and Religion* (Nashville: Abingdon Press, 1974).

15. See *SG-NCCD*, pp. 58–59.

16. Cf. *SG-NCCD*, p. 60; *SG Courts*, pp. 168–170.

17. Morris and Hawkins, op. cit., p. 57.

18. *SG-NCCD*, p. 63.

19. Morris and Hawkins, op. cit., p. 66.

20. See Morris and Hawkins, op. cit., pp. 56–57, 68–69; Schafer, *Victim and His Criminal*, pp. 93 and 97. Cf. *SG-NCCD*, p. 64. See also National Commission on the Causes and Prevention of Violence, *To Establish Justice, To Insure Domestic Tranquility*, pp. 174–175.

21. *SG-NCCD*, p. 65.

22. *SG-NCCD*, p. 62.

23. Morris and Hawkins, op. cit., p. 65.

24. The whole discussion of this subject by Morris and Hawkins is especially informative and useful. See ibid., pp. 57 and 63–71.

25. Ibid., p. 62.

26. Ibid., p. 64.

27. "The Death Penalty, Deterrence and Police Safety," in Norman Johnston, Leonard Savitz, and Marvin E. Wolfgang (eds.) in *The Sociology of Punishment and Correction* (New York: John Wiley & Sons, 1970), pp. 372–374.

28. Ramsey Clark, *Crime in America*, p. 309. Cf. Morris and Hawkins, op. cit., pp. 75–76.

29. See Progress Report of the Secretary-General to the United Nations Economic and Social Council, 27 February 1973 (Document E/AC. 57/12).

30. California State Assembly *Report of Subcommittee of Judiciary Committee on Capital Punishment*, 1957, pp. 12 ff.

31. Cf. *SG System*, p. 180. Cf. the similar conclusions, explicitly and emphatically stated in Bruce L. Pearson et al., *The Death Penalty in South Carolina, A Report Prepared for the South Carolina House of Representatives*, January 1974, especially pp. 79–83.

32. For an especially thoughtful and well-informed treatment of the subject from the perspective of Christian ethics see Robert W. Moon, "Life Instead of Death," in *Engage/Social Action*, October 1974, pp. 14–19.

Chapter 21. The Police, *pages 205–209*

1. Cf. James Q. Wilson, *Varieties of Police Behavior* (New York: Atheneum, 1971), pp. 292–293; also *SG-NCCD*, pp. 19–21; *SG Police*, pp. 29–46.

2. *SG Police*, p. 71. Cf. pp. 80–82. Cf. also *SG-NCCD*, p. 19.

3. For an account of such a program, the Vera Institute's Manhattan Bowery Project, see Elizabeth W. and James Vorenberg, in Ohlin, *Prisoners in America*, p. 175.

4. *SG Police*, p. 352.

5. James Q. Wilson, op. cit., pp. 151–152.

6. *SG Police*, p. 357.

7. See *SG Police*, pp. 356–357.

8. Ibid., p. 357.

9. *SG Police*, p. 329; *SG-NCCD*, p. 22.

10. *SG Police*, p. 343.

11. Ibid., pp. 342–345. Cf. *SG-NCCD*, pp. 26–27. For some figures see *The Washington Post*, Sept. 24, 1974, p. C5. The Police Foundation, 1909 K St. NW, Washington, D. C. 20036, has published "Policewomen on Patrol: Major Findings: First Report, Vol. I."

12. Cf. *SG Police*, pp. 433–435 and 29–37.

13. *SG Police*, p. 83; *SG-NCCD*, p. 28.

14. For some relevant facts and further discussion see *SG Police*, pp. 83–85. Other sources of information and of helpful insights on police policies and problems include Albert J. Reiss, Jr., *The Police and the Public* (New Haven: Yale University Press, 1971); Leonard Ruchelman, *Police Politics: A Comparative Study* (Cambridge, Mass.: Ballinger Publishing Co., 1974); and Elizabeth W. Vorenberg and James Vorenberg, in Ohlin, *Prisoners in America*, pp. 156–159.

Chapter **22. The Courts,** *pages 209–216*

1. ABA Special Committee on the Administration of Criminal Justice, "Criminal Justice: The Vital Problem of the Future," *ABA Journal,* Vol. 39 (1953), p. 743.

2. Katz, Litwin, and Bamberger, *Justice is the Crime,* pp. 1–2.

3. Address to the American Bar Association Aug. 10, 1970, included in Howard James, *Crisis in the Courts* (New York: David McKay Co., 1971), p. iv.

4. Ibid., p. v.

5. Cf. *SG Courts,* pp. 171–191.

6. *SG-NCCD,* p. 34. Cf. *SG Courts,* pp. 74–76.

7. Katz et al., op. cit., p. 37.

8. ABA speech of Aug. 10, 1970, in James, op. cit., pp. viii and ix.

9. *SG Courts,* p. 68. Cf. *SG-NCCD,* p. 33.

10. *SG Courts,* p. 46. Cf. *SG-NCCD,* pp. 32–33.

11. *SG Courts,* p. 46.

12. Frankel, *Criminal Sentences,* p. 77. Cf. *SG Courts,* p. 113. There are rare exceptions. See Frankel, op. cit., pp. 75–85.

13. ABA *Standards Relating to Appellate Review of Sentences.*

14. See *SG Courts,* pp. 112–143.

15. See Frankel, op. cit., especially Chap. 3, for elaboration of this and other proposals to improve sentencing.

16. *SG-NCCD,* p. 42.

17. *SG Courts,* p. 293. Cf. pp. 289–307.

18. Ibid., p. 294.

19. See the useful handbook, *State Rules Permitting the Student Practice of Law: Comparisons and Comments (Including Federal Rules),* 2nd Edition, prepared by The Institute of Judicial Administration and published by the Council on Legal Education for Professional Responsibility, Inc., 1973.

20. *SG-NCCD,* p. 40.

21. *SG Courts,* pp. 145–159.

22. *Harvard Law Review,* 26 (1912–1913), p. 327. For an able judge's recent argument for such training see Frankel, *Criminal Sentences,* Chap. 6.

Chapter **23. Corrections,** *pages 216–227*

1. See *SG Corrections,* pp. 107–109.

2. Cf. Benedict S. Alper, *Prisons Inside-Out: Alternatives in Correctional Reform,* (Cambridge, Mass.: Ballinger Publishing Co., 1974), pp. 28, 36–37. Cf. Edith E. Flynn, in Ohlin, *Prisoners in America,* pp. 49–85; Daniel Glaser, in ibid., pp. 101–102; and Elizabeth W. Vorenberg and James Vorenberg, in ibid., pp. 158–159.

3. *SG Corrections,* pp. 237–238. Cf. *SG-NCCD,* pp. 44, 45.

4. See Alper, *Prisons Inside-Out,* pp. 53–60, 101–125; cf. Hawaii Penal Code of 1972, Sections 620–623.

5. *SG-NCCD*, p. 44.

6. *SG Corrections*, pp. 357–359; *SG-NCCD*, p. 51.

7. See Alper, *Prisons Inside-Out*, p. 69, n. 1. Cf. *SG-NCCD*, pp. 48–49.

8. See *Detention at the Government's Pleasure*, published in 1971 by the Central Recruitment and Training Institute of the Prison Service and the Care of Criminal Psychopaths Service, Pompstationsweg 34, The Hague.

9. *SG Corrections*, pp. 234–235.

10. Alper, op. cit., p. 75.

11. *The Netherlands Prison System* (published in The Hague by the Central Recruitment and Training Institute of the Prison Service and the Care of Criminal Psychopaths Service, 1971), pp. 7–8.

12. *SG Corrections*, p. 235.

13. *SG Corrections*, p. 287.

14. *Effectiveness of Prison and Parole*, p. 19.

15. E.g., see Sheldon Glueck and Eleanor Glueck, *Criminal Careers in Retrospect* (New York: Commonwealth Fund, 1943); and Paul Lerman, "Evaluative Studies of Institutions for Delinquents: Implications for Research and Social Policy," in *Social Work*, July 1968, pp. 55–64.

16. Lloyd E. Ohlin et al., "Radical Correctional Reform: A Case Study of the Massachusetts Youth Correctional System," in *Harvard Educational Review*, Winter 1974.

17. See data in ibid.

18. See ibid.

19. All three kinds of service are being given on an impressive scale by students of West Virginia Wesleyan College, with guidance by Professor John Warner. The New Dawn Youth Center, founded and initially financed by two students and a recent graduate, in the summer of 1974, receives juvenile offenders sent there by the cooperating judges of two counties. An unexpected benefit reported in March 1975 is the remarkable outpouring of community support for this new mode of juvenile care, in response to the youthful proprietors.

20. *SG Corrections*, p. 387.

21. *SG-NCCD*, p. 56.

22. *SG Corrections*, p. 66.

23. *SG Corrections*, p. 68.

24. Baton Rouge: Louisiana State University Press, 1969.

25. See ibid., pp. 3–12. Cf. my report on the Penitentiary Center in the State of Mexico, above, Chap. 17, D.

26. Op. cit., pp. 103–109.

27. A useful book is Michele G. Herman and Marilyn G. Haft (eds.), *Prisoners' Rights Source Book* (New York: Clark Boardman Co., Ltd., 1973). Note Foreword by Robert B. McKay. Cf. *SG Corrections*, pp. 17–72.

28. See *The New York Times*, Nov. 12, 1974.

29. See *The Kingdom of The Netherlands: Facts and Figures*, 13 (1970–71) and other official bulletins. More details were learned during my personal visit in Holland in September 1973.

30. Alper, *Prisons Inside-Out*, p. 74. Cf. report of The Provo Experiment in Utah by LaMar T. Empey and Jerome Rabow, in Radzinowicz and Wolf-

gang (eds.), *Crime and Justice*, Vol. III, pp. 266–283; also by Empey, in Lloyd Ohlin (ed.), *Prisoners in America*, pp. 41–43. Cf. ibid., p. 48.

31. *SG Corrections*, p. 3.

32. Indeed they are so named in *SG Corrections*, p. 570.

33. See Alper, op. cit., pp. 103–116 and other passages. On the rapidly developing "CRC's" in Canada see *Report of the Task Force on Community-Based Residential Centres*, published under authority of The Solicitor General of Canada in 1973.

34. *SG Corrections*, pp. 463–495.

35. Cf. *SG Corrections*, pp. 417–421.

36. See *SG Corrections*, pp. 422–424.

37. Cf. similar and more detailed recommendations by the National Advisory Commission. *SG Corrections*, pp. 587–590.

Chapter **24. Citizen Responsibilities in Criminal Justice,** *pages 227–234*

1. *Newsweek*, Sept. 16, 1974, p. 53. Cf. *SG Community*, pp. 317–318.

2. *SG Community*, pp. 315–318.

3. See *Parade*, May 26, 1974, p. 19.

4. Cf. above, Chap. 19, C, 4.

5. *SG Community*, p. 15.

6. Ibid., p. 305.

7. Attica-BRIDGE, Inc. is assisted by a grant ($117,000) from the federal Law Enforcement Assistance Administration and $40,000 from private contributions.

8. Cf. Herbert S. Miller, *The Closed Door* (Washington, D. C.: Georgetown University Law Center, 1972).

9. See documentation by Glaser in *Effectiveness of Prison and Parole*, p. 221.

10. From the script of a 20-minute audio-visual presentation, "Modernizing Corrections," sold by the Chamber. Cf. the Chamber's freely distributed booklet, "Marshaling Citizen Power to Modernize Corrections," 1971.

11. *SG Community*, pp. 129–134.

12. Information from my visit to Langley House in September 1973. Cf. the very different but also useful crisis center for street people in Amsterdam of which a brief account was given above, Chap. 18, E.

13. *SG Community*, p. 15. Cf. ibid., p. 305.

Index of Topics

(*See also Contents*)

Abortion, 135
Advocacy, public, 163, 179
Africa, 72, 101, 188
Aggressiveness and violence idealized, 22, 72, 88, 89–90, 91–94, 97–109, 121, 124, 234
Alcohol, 5, 12, 126, 182–183, 186, 198, 202–203, 209, 230, 232
Alcoholics Anonymous, 170, 183, 198, 206, 230, 232
Alienation, 11, 66, 97, 101, 155, 156, 167–169, 177–178, 195, 217, 222, 224, 226–227, 229, 234
American Bar Association, 25, 49, 60, 266n, 210, 213, 233

Bail, 26, 34–35, 217
Baptists, 73, 76, 80n
Behavior modification, 62–63
Benevolence. *See* Lovingkindness
Bible, The, 54, 73, 74, 76–77, 82, 102, 125, 140, 143–145, 147–149, 167
Bill of Rights, 76, 86–87
Blacks, 4, 19–20, 34, 72, 84, 85–86, 94, 101–106, 161, 185–186
Boston University, ix

California, 24, 39n, 44, 45–46, 109, 113, 194, 220, 224
Calvinists, 72, 73, 81
Canada, 4, 224, 226
Capital punishment, 21, 47–48, 97, 111, 125, 140, 141n, 203–205
Chamber of Commerce of the U.S., 60, 231, 233
Christian ethics, 133, 141–149, 166, 190, 200, 205
Christian Scientists, 116
Cities, 11, 22, 94, 120–121, 234

Codes, new penal, 196
Common law, 74, 101
Community-based corrections, 38, 225–226
Community, inclusive, 98, 138, 145–146, 153–154, 177–180
Community responsibility, 75–76, 138, 153–154, 190–191, 227–234
Compensation to victims, 184–185, 187–195. *See also* Restitution
Conjugal visiting, 171–172, 223–224
Consistency and coherence, 149–150, 155, 164, 166, 179, 196–197, 227, 230, 232
Constitution of the U.S., 7–10, 135, 152n, 155, 211, 213
Correctional Officers, 39–41, 155, 157, 226, 229, 233
Corrections, 37–47, 184, 216–227, 230
Corruption, 3, 11–13, 20–21, 22, 127, 177, 181, 199–200, 212, 222, 223
Courts, 8–9, 21, 26–27, 30, 31–37, 43, 45, 134, 164, 184, 206, 209–216, 221, 230, 233
Crime statistics, 4–6, 11–13, 18, 20

Death penalty. *See* Capital punishment
Declaration of Independence, 82, 83, 84, 85–86, 88, 123, 152
Decriminalization, 197–201
Defense counsel, 26–27, 36, 37n, 214–215
Democracy, 1–3, 6, 7–10, 75–76, 81–82
Design, preventive, 180–181
Deterrence, 48, 55–56, 58–59, 160, 195, 211–212
Disablement. *See* Incapacitation
Diversion, 181–183, 205, 206, 230, 232–233
Dred Scott Decision, 103

Drugs, 126, 182–183, 187, 199, 209, 222, 230, 232–233
Drunken driving, 5, 201, 202–203
Drunkenness. *See* Alcohol

Ecology, 128–130, 158
Education as purpose of law, 52–53
Education in prevention and rehabilitation, 62, 178, 179, 180, 220–221
Egalitarianism, 84–86, 88, 151–152, 155, 158, 178–179, 190n, 205, 208, 213, 227
Embezzlement, 5, 231
Employment, 11–12, 180, 221–222, 230, 231–232, 233
England, x, 4, 73–77, 79, 83, 87, 117, 179, 188, 232
Enlightenment, The, 79, 81, 83, 87, 88
Ethics, ix, 14, 17, 73–74, 78–79, 133–173
Europe, x, 88–89, 91, 106–107, 117–118, 123, 124, 166, 188–189, 202–203

Fairness, justice as, 157–161
Family, 12–13, 94–95, 101, 156, 208, 214, 222–224, 229
Federal Bureau of Investigation, 5, 6, 7, 8, 18, 30–31
Fines, 34, 218–219
Fraud, 5, 11–12, 92, 125, 126, 179, 186
Friends, American, 61, 76, 77, 110, 111–114

Gambling, 22, 31, 181, 199–200
Gault, Re, 214
Generosity, 75–76
Germany, 7
Gideon v. Wainwright, 214, 218
Grand jury, 211
Great Awakening, The, 79–82, 87, 88
Great Britain, 117, 179, 219, 232
Guaranteed income, 179–180
Guards, prison. *See* Correctional officers
Guns, 18, 201–202

Halfway houses, 225–226, 231
Hawaii, 24–25, 157n, 192, 193–194, 219
Homicide, criminal, 4, 5, 24, 47, 48, 99, 104, 109, 156, 186, 203–205
Homosexuality, 23, 224
Humanism, 79, 88, 96, 123, 133, 142, 165, 171

Illinois, 23, 30, 220
Immigration, 72, 91, 106–107, 124
Incapacitation, 47, 48, 57–58, 59, 195–196
Independence, national, 3, 73, 79–81, 122
Index crimes, 5–7, 11, 18, 19, 106, 177, 179

Indians, American, 72, 98–101, 124, 125, 152–153, 161
Individualism, 11–13, 22, 66–67, 78–79, 81, 88–95, 97, 124–125, 164, 234
Interests, Theory of, 162–166, 167
Intolerance, 76–79, 110–111, 119

Jackson State University, 18, 155
Jails, local, 34–35, 37, 59, 198, 211, 217, 218
Japan, 4, 124, 224
Jewish ethics, 114–116, 135–141, 149, 166, 190, 200
Jews, 110, 114–116, 133–134
Judges, 31–37, 47–51, 53, 61, 127, 140, 155, 157, 162, 164, 165–166, 182, 192–193, 198, 203, 209–211, 213–214, 215–216, 219–220, 226
Junior Chamber of Commerce, 230
Juries, 35–37, 127, 155, 203, 211, 228
Justice, its meaning and purpose, 33, 38–39, 46–67, 134–173, 233
Justice, social, 11, 146–147, 151, 153–154, 156, 160–161, 178–180
Juvenile delinquency, 43–44, 53, 56, 165, 180n, 181, 191, 197–198, 206, 208, 214, 220–221, 229, 230, 232–233

Kent State University, 18, 155
Kentucky, 32

Latter Day Saints, 76, 116
Lawyers, 26–27, 231, 233. *See also* American Bar Association; Defense counsel
Legislators, 162, 164, 166, 195–205, 209
Lovingkindness or benevolence, 64, 75–76, 77–78, 111–112, 136–137, 142, 143–145, 148–149, 150–151, 153, 154–155, 166, 178, 179, 183, 184, 190, 191, 206, 217, 222, 229, 230, 232, 234

Machibroda v. U.S., 36
Malcontent colonists, 72, 118, 124
Mandatory sentences, 25
Marijuana, 23–24, 47, 199
Maryland, 110, 119, 194
Massachusetts, x, 35n, 44, 63–64, 73, 78, 79, 93, 165–166, 193–194, 220–221, 225
Massachusetts Bay Colony, 74–77, 82, 99, 104, 119
Mayflower Compact, 76, 123
Media, news, 3, 7–8
Medical care, 11, 13, 178–179, 199
Mexico, x, 39, 64, 170–172, 189, 225
Minorities, 4, 19–20, 66, 98–116, 152–153, 155, 161, 185–186, 189–190, 207–208, 226

Miranda v. Arizona, 8
Mississippi, 223–224
Mobility, 22, 94, 119–121
Moral awakening, 63–64
Morality, 3–4, 11–12, 17, 41–42, 80, 82, 94–97, 100, 123–124, 129, 234. *See also* Ethics
Mormons. *See* Latter Day Saints
Movies, 183–184
Murder, 41, 47, 109, 126, 203–205

National Advisory Commission on Criminal Justice Standards and Goals, 178, 180, 182–183, 195n, 196–233
National College of the State Judiciary, 47n, 216
National Council on Crime and Delinquency, 178n, 196, 233
National Endowment for the Humanities, ix, xi
Nativism, 106–107, 125
Natural law ethics, 49, 51, 141, 190
Nebraska, 24–25
Netherlands, the, x, 4, 182, 189, 202–203, 218, 219, 225
New York City, 27, 31, 117, 180, 191, 228
New York State, 23, 43, 44–45, 192, 193–194, 230
New Zealand, 189
Norms, ethical, for criminal justice, 133–135, 154–156
Norway, x, 189, 202

Organized crime, 20–21, 22, 24–25, 35, 126, 181, 199–200

Paradox of American culture, 71–72, 77–79, 87–88, 110–116
Parole, 26, 38, 41, 192, 225, 231
Parole boards, 26, 127, 155, 157, 164, 226–227
Parole officers, 229, 230
Pennsylvania, 77, 109, 111–112
Pentecostals, 116
Philadelphia, 6, 26n, 34, 106, 112, 211
Philippines, 4, 7
Philosophical ethics, 133–134, 135, 149–154, 166
Plea bargaining, 21, 26, 27, 35–37, 212–213
Plessy v. Ferguson, 104
Pluralism, 134, 154
Plymouth, 74, 76, 98, 117, 123
Poland, x, 152, 189
Police, 6–7, 8–9, 18–20, 26, 27–31, 155, 156–157, 164, 184, 203–204, 205–209, 220, 226, 227–228, 233

Poor, protecting the, 138, 146–147, 155, 178–180, 189–190, 215, 229, 230, 232
Population, 128
Positivism, legal, 47, 48, 49–51
Poverty and crime, 11, 12, 13, 22, 186, 229, 234
Poverty occasioning injustice, 34–35, 36, 37n, 155, 165, 205
Presbyterians, 73
Pretrial release, 34–35, 217
Prevention, 165, 170–171, 177–184, 206, 207, 234
Prisons, 37–47, 67, 112–114, 121–122, 142, 169–172, 189, 192, 195–196, 216–220, 221–227, 229–230, 233
Probation, 38, 41, 45–46, 59, 182, 183, 192, 229, 230
Prostitution, 22, 24–25, 171, 223
Protestants, 109–110, 141–143, 144–147
Psychiatry, 60–62, 172, 220
Public distrust, 7–9, 17–22
Puritanism, 71–80, 82, 89, 99, 109–110, 114, 119, 125, 143

Quakers. *See* Friends, American

Racism, 13, 22, 34, 98–108, 205
Rape, 5, 23, 186–187, 228–229
Recidivism, 25, 43–46, 137, 220, 227, 229–230, 231
Rehabilitation, 47–48, 58–66, 170–171, 195, 214, 216, 231
Religious conversion, 63
Reprobation, 160. *See also* Vindication
Resources, natural, 118, 128, 157–158, 163, 164
Restitution, 140–141, 159, 165, 167, 170, 172, 181–182, 187–189, 191–193, 218, 219, 222, 228. *See also* Compensation to victims
Retribution, 38–39, 47–48, 52, 53–55, 65–66, 76–77, 80, 84, 111, 115, 125, 136–137, 145, 151, 160, 165, 166, 167–169, 170–171, 172–173, 191
Riches, rush for, 88–98
Roman Catholics, 110–111, 141, 143, 144

Santobello v. New York, 36n
Scandinavia, 3, 179, 202
Scope of criminal law, 75, 76–77, 80, 82, 83–84, 138–139, 142, 148–149, 152, 161, 195–205
Selfishness, 89–93, 199, 224, 234
Self-righteousness, 76–77, 79, 125, 146, 234
Sentencing, 1, 23–25, 35–36, 47–59, 51–59,

Sentencing (*cont.*)
    61–62, 66–67, 76–78, 84, 97, 127, 157, 165–167, 188–189, 192, 195–196, 198–199, 202–203, 204, 211–212, 213–214, 216, 217–220
Seventh Step program, 170, 230
Sexual offenses, 23, 200, 208
Slavery, 85–86, 87–88, 101–103, 108–109, 152
Social defense, 160, 166–167, 172–173, 177–234
Social readaptation, 64–65, 142, 170–171, 172, 221–224
Social restoration, 140, 156, 167–173, 177–234
Soviet Union, 52–53, 189, 224
Space as problem solver, 116–122
Students in criminal justice, 18, 215, 221
Supreme Court, U.S., 7–9, 21, 36, 48, 101, 103, 104, 135, 155, 213, 214

Teen Challenge, 63, 182n, 183, 232–233
Television, 183–184
Texas, 24, 199
Therapy, 60–62, 170–171, 206, 221
Time as problem solver, 116–117
Tolerance, 86–87, 110–111, 119, 234
Traffic laws, 4–5, 201, 202–203, 210

Unemployment, 11, 178, 180
Uniform Crime Reports. *See* Crime statistics
Unitarian Church, 230
United Kingdom, 4, 194, 201
United Methodist Church, 146–147, 230
Utility, justice as social, 51, 58–59, 82, 190

Value, criterion of, 149–150, 151, 153, 164
Vera Institute, 217
Victimless crimes. *See* Scope of criminal law
Victims of crime, 6, 20, 140–141, 166, 167, 170, 172, 184–195, 227, 228–229, 230
Vietnam War, 18, 32, 119, 128–129
Vindication of law, 51–52. *See also* Reprobation
Violence, 4, 7, 18, 45, 57, 97, 98–109, 118, 121–122, 124, 126, 141, 150, 168, 171, 182, 183–184, 193, 201–202, 204–205, 218, 234
Virginia, 73, 75, 77, 82, 85, 86, 103, 119, 125
Volunteers, 182–183, 221, 222, 226, 228–234

War, 128–129
Washington, D.C., 6, 19, 29–30, 32, 35, 181, 193
Watergate, x, 3, 12, 31, 92, 97, 116, 125–126, 177, 181
"Weekender" incarceration, 219–220
Wesley Theological Seminary, ix
White collar crime, 5, 11–12, 13, 92, 97–98, 106, 177, 179, 202–203
Winship, In Re, 155
Witchcraft, 78
Women, 207–208, 226, 227, 228
Work release, 192, 219, 222, 225, 231

Youth, 18–19, 34, 43–44, 45, 63, 95–97, 183–184, 199, 214, 219, 221

Index of Personal Names

Adams, Larry E., x
Agnew, Spiro, 7, 12, 155
Ahlstrom, Sydney E., 71n, 73, 75n, 76n, 77n, 78n, 80, 81, 89n, 111n, 114, 118n
Akiba, Rabbi, 137
Alexander, Shana, 92
Alfred, 77, 83, 187–188
Allen, Francis A., 59n
Alper, Benedict S., 217n, 218, 219n, 225n, 226n
Ancel, Marc, 166–167
Andenaes, Johannes, x, 56n
Andrejew, Igor, x
Aptheker, Herbert, 102
Aquinas, Thomas, 150n
Augustine, 160–161, 167, 168n

Baab, George William, 32
Baldwin, James, 106n
Ballinger, Graham, x
Baltimore, Lord, 110
Bamberger, Richard H., 197n, 209n, 211n
Banneker, Benjamin, 88
Barlett, Donald, 34n
Barlow, Joel, 84n
Barth, Karl, 146
Basore, John W., 55n
Beccaria, Cesare, 55, 56, 58–59, 83, 112
Beisel, Albert, ix
Belkin, Samuel, 138n
Bell, Daniel, 11n, 128n
Bennett, James V., x, 59
Bennett, Lerone, Jr., 88n, 101n, 102n, 103n
Bentham, Jeremy, 58, 84, 112
Berkeley, George, 102
Berman, Harold J., x, 52, 200
Berthoff, Rowland, 78, 89n, 90n, 91n, 93n, 117n, 130n

Bertocci, Peter A., x, 149, 153, 164n
Bianchi, Eugene C., 129n
Black, Edward J., x
Black, Sherrie, x
Blanshard, Brand, 149, 153, 164n
Bohlinger, George, III, 65
Bokser, Ben Zion, 137
Boone, John O., x
Bordenkircher, Donald, x
Bowen, Howard R., 128n
Boyle, Tony, 109
Bradford, William, 75–76
Brandeis, Louis D., 115
Brandt, Richard B., 150n, 151n, 152n, 154n
Brennan, William J., 203
Brown, Dee A., 100n
Brunner, Emil, 141n
Buckminster, Joseph Stevens, 118
Burger, Warren E., 210, 211, 212
Bushman, Richard L., 80n
Butler, Samuel, 62n

Cahn, Edmond, 51, 116
Calvin, John, 73
Campbell, James S., 26n
Canasatego, 99
Capone, Ralph, 56
Cardozo, Benjamin N., 115
Carlson, Norman A., x, 59–60
Carlyle, Thomas, 117
Carnegie, Andrew, 92
Chavez, César E., 109
Chinard, Gilbert, 82n, 87n, 88n
Christman, Henry M., 87n
Cicero, 83
Clark, Ramsey, 11, 204n
Clay, Charles, 86–87
Clifford, William, 188

Coates, Robert B., x
Cohen, Arthur A., 133n
Cohen, Felix S., 35n, 91n, 94n, 99, 116
Cohen, Morris R., 35n, 91n, 94n, 116
Cohn, Haim H., 136n, 139, 140n
Coke, Sir Edward, 83
Columbus, Christopher, 114
Combs, Edward, x
Comte, Auguste, 49
Cooper, H. H. A., 172n
Cooper, J. Fenimore, 90, 100
Cotton, John, 78, 119
Curran, Charles E., x, 141n, 144

Dash, Samuel, x, 30–31, 116
Dawes, Henry L., 93, 124
Dawson, Robert O., 26n
Deats, Paul K., x, 96n
Debell, Garrett, 129n
Debo, Angie, 93n
Decker, John F., 180n
Defoe, Daniel, 185
Deloria, Vine, Jr., 100n
Dewey, John, 149, 150, 153, 164n
DeWolf, Edward M., 188
DeWolf, Madeleine M., x
Dodd, John, 232
Downie, Leonard, Jr., 26n, 27
Durkheim, Emile, 53
Dutton, Robert L., x

Echeverría Álvarez, Luis, 170
Edel, Abraham, 150, 153
Edel, May, 150, 153
Edwards, Jonathan, 79, 80n, 81
Ehrlich, Paul R., 128n
Elder, Frederick, 129
Ellenberger, Henri, 193n
Ellul, Jacques, 141
Elwood, Douglas J., 80n
Empey, LaMar, 225n
Engerman, Stanley L., 101n
Erikson, Erik H., 71
Eusden, John Dykstra, 74n

Fairbanks, Philip M., x
Fattah, Ezzat A., 185, 186, 187
Figlio, Robert M., 43n, 44n, 45n, 104,
    106, 185, 186–187
Finkelstein, Louis, 137n
Fishel, Leslie H., Jr., 103n
Fletcher, Joseph, 144
Floyd, Glenn E., 194
Flynn, Edith E., 35n, 217n
Fogel, Robert W., 101n
Ford, Henry, 92
Forer, Lois G., 35n
Fortas, Abe, 115

Frank, Jerome, 116, 134
Frankel, Marvin E., 32n, 47n, 196n, 213,
    214n, 216n
Frankena, William K., 149, 150n, 151,
    152, 164n
Frankfurter, Felix, 115
Franklin, Benjamin, 83, 99
Frenkel, F. E., x
Freund, Paul A., 116, 151, 153
Frieden, Betty, 95n
Friedman, Lawrence M., 65n, 103n, 104n,
    116, 197
Friedman, Milton, 179–180
Friedmann, W., 116
Fuller, John G., 12n, 92n
Furgeson, William Royal, Jr., 32

Garofalo, Raffaele, 59n
Gerber, Rudolph J., 50n, 51n, 54n, 59n,
    62n, 111n, 141n, 166n, 168n
Gewirth, Alan, 150, 151
Glaser, Daniel, 11n, 40, 42, 43, 44, 45,
    96, 220, 231n
Glueck, Eleanor, 12, 13n, 43n, 116, 220n
Glueck, Nelson, 136n, 138n
Glueck, Sheldon, 12, 13n, 43n, 61, 116,
    220n
Goen, C. C., x, 74n, 80n
Goldberg, Arthur, 34, 115, 190
Goldwater, Barry, 179–180
Gossett, Thomas F., 99n, 100n, 102n,
    104n, 107n
Gottschalk, Alfred, 136n
Grant, Madison, 107
Grasty, Kyle D., x
Gray, William J., x, 232
Gregoire, M. Henri, 84n
Gribben, Robert, x
Grotius, Hugo, 83
Groves, John L., x, 172
Gubiński, Arnold, x
Gustafson, James M., 145n
Guza, Kenneth, x

Haft, Marilyn G., 224n
Hall, Jerome, 35, 50, 56, 161n
Hammurabi, 188
Handy, Robert T., 73n, 75n, 77n, 78n,
    102n, 110n, 119n
Harris, Richard, 35n
Hart, H. L. A., 134n
Hawkins, Gordon, 23n, 198n, 199n, 201n,
    202n, 203n
Hayes, Rutherford B., 104
Heck, Phillip, 163n
Hegel, G. W. F., 54, 167, 168n, 173
Heimert, Alan E., 80n
Henry, Stuart C., 80n

Hentig, von, Hans, 29n, 104, 185, 186
Herman, Michele G., 224n
Higham, John, 107n
Hillel, 150n
Hirsch, Richard G., 137, 138n
Hirsch, Samson Raphael, 138n
Hobes, Thomas, 150n
Hocking, William Ernest, 151
Hoffman, Walter E., 37n
Hofstadter, Richard, 108, 109n, 130n
Holmes, Oliver Wendell (Justice), 135
Homer, 188
Hooker, Thomas, 78, 119
Hopper, Columbus B., 224
Horn, Ragnar, x
Hosken, Dean, ix
Howe, Louise Kapp, 94n
Hoyles, J. Arthur, x
Hulsman, L. H. C., x
Hutchinson, Anne, 78, 119
Hyde, Laurence M., Jr., x

Ihering, von, Rudolf. *See* Jhering
Irey, Elmer L., 56
Isay, Hermann, 164

Jackson, Andrew, 101
Jackson, Helen Hunt, 98
Jackson, Robert, 209
Jacobs, Wilbur R., 93n, 99n, 101
James, Howard, 210n, 212n
James, William, 150n
Jasiński, Jerzy, x
Jefferson, Thomas, 82–88, 99, 123, 125, 190
Jeffery, C. Ray, 181n
Jesus of Nazareth, 115, 125, 136, 144–149
Jewett, Robert, 75n, 90n, 109n
Jhering, von, Rudolf, 163
John XXIII, Pope, 144
Johnson, Elmer Hubert, 12n, 13n, 112n, 113n
Johnston, Norman, 11n, 12n, 204n
Jones, Major J., x
Josephy, Alvin M., 100n

Kames, Lord, 83
Kammen, Michael, 71, 78n, 84n, 86n, 92n, 97n, 109n, 119n, 123
Kant, Immanuel, 54, 150n, 152, 158, 173
Katz, Lewis R., 197n, 209, 211n
Kaunda, Kenneth, 188
Kelsen, Hans, 49–51
Kempsky, Nelson F., x
Kennedy, John F., 107–108
Kennedy, Robert F., 108

Keyserling, Leon, 180
King, Martin Luther, Jr., vi, 86n, 107–108, 142, 144–145
Kings, Cecelia G., 141n
Kittrie, Nicholas N., x, 24n
Kleinig, John, 166n
Knowlton, Robert E., 31
Koch, Adrienne, 83n, 84n, 85n, 99n
Konvitz, Milton R., 116, 135n, 136n, 137n, 138n, 139n
Kravetz, Julius, 140n

Ladd, George Trumbull, 149n
Lamott, Kenneth, 92n
Lawes, Lewis, 29
Leavy, Joseph, 220
Leenhouts, Keith, 229
Lehmann, Paul L., 144n, 145n
Leo XIII, Pope, 111
Lerman, Paul, 43n, 220n
Levy, Howard, 42n
Lewis, C. S., 54, 61–62, 141, 166n
Lichtman, Allan J., 101n
Lincoln, Abraham, 3n, 75, 123
Lipman, Eugene J., 140n
Litwin, Lawrence B., 197n, 209n, 211n
Locke, John, 81, 82, 190
Loetscher, Lafferts A., 73n, 75n, 77n, 78n, 102n, 110n, 119n
Lombroso, César, 172
Longfellow, Henry W., 75
Lorenz, Konrad, 121
Low, Peter W., 34n
Lowell, James Russell, 71
Lundberg, Ferdinand, 92n
Lunden, Walter A., 94n

Mabbott, J. D., 50
Madison, James, 83, 87
Maimonides, Moses, 139n
Mangum, Garth L., 128n
Marcuse, Herbert, 129n
Marshall, Thurgood, 203
Mason, George, 82n, 83
Mather, Cotton, 75n, 89
Maxson, Charles H., 80n
McAnany, Patrick D., 50n, 51n, 54n, 59n, 62n, 111n, 141n, 166n, 168n
McDaniel, Kenneth, x
McGee, Richard A., x
McGeehee, Lloyd, x
McKay, Robert B., 224n
McKinley, William, 90
McLaughlin, Virginia W., x
Mead, Sidney E., 116, 117, 118n, 119n, 120
Meadows, Donella H., 129n
Menéndez de Avilés, Pedro, 110

Menninger, Karl, 21, 39, 60, 61, 65n, 108, 112n, 197n
Messinger, Sheldon L., 42
Meyer, Michael A., 137
Mezyński, Ruth Lawrence, x
Mezyński, Z. Antoni, x
Mill, John Stuart, 150n
Millard, Richard M., 149, 153, 164n
Miller, Allan, 188n
Miller, David, 42n
Miller, Herbert S., 231n
Miller, Jerome G., x, 134, 220
Miller, Perry, 74n, 75n, 77n, 78n, 80n, 82n, 90n
Milton, Ohmer, 40n, 63n
Miranda, Ernest, 8
Montaigne, de, Michel E., 84–85
Montilla, M. Robert, x
Moon, Robert W., x, 205n
Moore, Winston E., x, 59
Moors, William R., 230
Morgan, Edmund S., 74n, 75n, 76n, 77n, 78n, 82n, 99n
Morris, Albert, ix, x
Morris, Norval, 23n, 198n, 199n, 201n, 202n, 203n, 204n
Moss, Larry J., x
Muelder, Walter G., x
Mueller, Gerhard O. W., x, 74, 77, 101n, 161n, 180n, 192n
Myrdal, Gunnar, 124n

Nader, Ralph, 163n
Newton, Isaac, 81, 84
Niebuhr, Reinhold, 144, 146, 166n
Nixon, Richard M., 6, 12, 30, 92, 125, 126, 155, 180

Ohlin, Lloyd E., x, 35n, 189n, 197n, 206n, 209n, 217n, 220n, 225n

Packard, Vance, 129n
Page, Mann, 85n
Paine, Thomas, 99–100
Paolucci, Henry, 55n
Paul, the Apostle, 144, 148
Pearson, Bruce L., 205n
Peden, William, 83n, 84n, 85n, 86n, 99n
Penn, William, 77, 99, 111–112
Perkins, Robert F., x
Peterson, Merrill D., 86n
Pius XII, Pope, 54, 111n, 141, 167, 168n
Pound, Roscoe, ix, 74, 162–165, 188n, 197n, 210, 215–216
Prosser, Gabriel, 102

Qua, Stanley E., ix–x, 165–166
Quarles, Benjamin, 103n

Rabow, Jerome, 225n
Radzinowicz, Leon, 4n, 19n, 20n, 34n, 41n, 42n, 225n
Ramsey, Paul, 144
Rawls, John, 157–161, 164
Rees, Leslie Lloyd, x
Reeve, Henry, 123n
Reid, John Phillip, 93n, 99n, 101
Reiss, Albert J., Jr., 209n
Rizzo, Frank L., 26n
Robin, Gerald, 43n
Rochefoucauld, François, Duc de la, 84–85
Rockefeller, John D., 92
Roosevelt, Franklin D., 93
Roosevelt, Theodore, 90, 100, 124
Rosen, Lawrence, 12n
Royce, Josiah, 150n
Ruchelman, Leonard, 209n
Rümelin, Max, 163n, 164n, 165n

Sánchez Galindo, Antonio, x, 39, 65n, 170–172
Savitz, Leonard, 11n, 12n, 204n
Schafer, Stephen, 186n, 187n, 188, 189n, 190n, 191n, 193, 201n
Scheier, Ivan, 230
Schrag, Clarence, 20
Schrey, Heinz-Horst, 142n
Schwartz, Richard F., 30–31
Sellers, James, 145
Sellin, Thorsten, 43n, 44n, 45n, 104, 106, 185, 204
Seneca, 55, 56
Sewall, Samuel, 78
Shakespeare, William, 64
Sharf, Andrew, 136
Sharp, H. Edward, 32n
Shinn, Roger L., x
Silver, Daniel Jeremy, 137n, 140n
Simons, John F., 23n
Skinner, B. F., 62, 63
Skupiński, Jan, x
Slagter, S., x
Sloan, Douglas (ed.), 81n
Smith, H. Shelton, 73n, 75n, 77n, 78n, 102n, 110n, 119n
Smith, John, 76
Smith, Robert L., x, 39n, 46n
Sobeloff, Simon E., 33
Solomon, Gus J., 33, 56
Sorokin, Pitirim A., 150, 153
Steele, James, 34n
Stephen, James F., 54, 77n, 188n
Stern, Gerald, 23, 24
Stoddard, John, 81
Stoddard, Solomon, 79

Stone, Julius, x, 13n, 53, 54n, 94n, 115–116, 136, 139n, 162–163
Storer, John H., 129n
Sutherland, Edwin H., 12
Sykes, Gresham M., 42
Szasz, Thomas S., 61n

Tallack, William, 188n
Tappan, Paul W., ix–x, 32n
Tennent, Gilbert, 79
Theobald, Robert, 179–180
Thornberry, Terence P., 185, 186–187
Tocqueville, de, Alexis, 123
Toynbee, Arnold, 145
Tufts, James H., 149n, 150
Turner, Nat, 103
Tyler, Gus, 126n

Udall, Stewart L., 129n

van der Grient, J., x
van der Linden, x
Van Every, Dale, 100n
Van Halm, W., x
Van Waters, Miriam, ix–x, 63–64
Verberne, Paul, x
Vesey, Denmark, 102–103
Vlastos, Gregory, 150, 152
Voltaire, François M. A., 111–112
Vorenberg, Elizabeth W., 189n, 206n, 209n, 217n
Vorenberg, James, 189n, 206n, 209n, 217n

Wahler, Robert G., 40n, 63n
Walczak, Stanislaw, x
Walker, Francis C., 100n
Wallace, Michael, 108n, 109n

Walz, Hans Hermann, 142n
Ward, David A., 197n
Ward, Nathaniel, 78, 119
Warner, John R., x, 221n
Warren, Earl, x, 87, 135
Waterhouse, W. A., 142n
Wedburg, Anders, 51n
Weiss, Paul, 150n
Wertham, F., 185
Wheelwright, John, 119
Whitefield, George, 79, 80n
Wieser, Marguerite, 141n
Wilkins, Leslie T., ii, x, 96n
Willard, Samuel, 78
Williams, Abraham, 82
Williams, Elisha, 82
Williams, Roger, 78, 99, 119
Wilson, James Q., 206n, 207
Wilson, Jerry V., 29–30
Wilson, Marjorie Kerr, 121n
Wilson, Woodrow, 75
Wiltse, Charles M., 82–83, 85
Winthrop, John, 74, 75, 77, 78n, 89, 99n
Wogaman, Philip, x, 128n, 180
Wolfgang, Marvin E., x, 4n, 11n, 12n, 13n, 19n, 20n, 34n, 41n, 42n, 43n, 44–45, 104, 106, 108, 185, 188, 194–195, 197–198, 204n, 225n
Woodward, C. Vann, 104n
Wythe, George, 83n

Yablonski, Joseph A., 109
Yochelson, Samuel, 61n
Young, Brigham, 119
Youngdahl, Luther E., x

Zimbardo, Philip G., 40n
Zimring, Franklin E., 56n